Forensic Scriptures

Forensic Scriptures

Critical Analysis of Scripture and What the Qur'an Reveals about the Bible

BRIAN ARTHUR BROWN

Foreword by
Joy Abdul-Mohan, St. Andrews Theological College,

with

Rabbi Justus Baird, Auburn Multi-faith Center,
Walter Brueggemann, Columbia Theological Seminary,
and Amir Hussain, Loyola Marymount University

CASCADE *Books* · Eugene, Oregon

FORENSIC SCRIPTURES
Critical Analysis of Scripture and What the Qur'an Reveals about the Bible

Cascade Books
A Division of Wipf and Stock Publishers
199 W. 8th Ave., Suite 3
Eugene, OR 97401

www.wipfandstock.com

ISBN 13: 978-1-60608-289-8

Cataloging-in-publication data:

Brown, Brian A., 1942–

Forensic scriptures : critical analysis of scripture and what the Qur'an reveals about the Bible / Brian Arthur Brown ; foreword by Joy Abdul-Mohan.

xxxii + 204 p. ; 23 cm. Includes bibliographical references.

ISBN 13: 978-1-60608-289-8

1. Bible. O.T. Pentateuch—Criticism, redaction. 2. Documentary hypothesis (Pentateuchal criticism). 3. Bible. N.T. Gospels—Criticism, redaction. 4. Q hypothesis (Synoptics criticism). 5. Koran—Relation to the Bible. I. Abdul-Mohan, Joy. II. Title.

Manufactured in the U.S.A.

Scriptures quoted under the publishers' guidelines are from:

Hebrew Bible. London, UK: British and Foreign Bible Society, 1960
Tanakh, The Holy Scriptures. Philadelphia, PA: The Jewish Publication Society, 1985.
Greek New Testament. London: British and Foreign Bible Society, 1966.
The Holy Bible, King James Version. Nashville, TN: Thomas Nelson Publishers, 1611 ed.
The Holy Quran, A. Yusuf Ali Translation. Beirut, Lebanon: Dar Al Arabia, 1968.
The Sublime Quran, Laleh Bakhtiar Translation. Chicago, IL: Kazi Publications, 2007.

"A Diagram of Synoptic Relationships" by Allan Barr © 2005 by T. & T. Clark is reproduced in facsimile by permission of The Continuum Group, New York, NY. Used by permission.

Computerized graphics for the cover art and other downloadable illustrations have been produced by *Karen Arbour* of Toronto.

*To the Riverside Church in the city of New York,
which has provided me with singular opportunities for
preaching, consulting, and programming over the years,
including the hosting of the three-day conference for
the launching of this book, organized by Eugene Melino
and a magnificent team of Riverside colleagues; and to
St. Andrew's Theological College in Trinidad and Tobago,
to principal Joy Abdul-Mohan, and to faculty colleagues
who tested these materials in Old and New Testament
courses and in Interfaith Studies; and to my class of sixty-
four fine students who are called by God and being trained
in disciplines required for ministry.*

Contents

Contents

Illustrations

Exhibits

Computerized graphics for the cover art and other downloadable illustrations have been produced by Karen Arbour of Toronto. These diagrams are also available at BrianArthurBrown.com for viewing and downloading.

Acknowledgments

Arraignment

M Y FIRST DEBT IN connection with this book is to my teachers in related subjects at Dalhousie and McGill universities: John Corston, Wilfred Cantwell Smith, Stanley Frost, Willard Oxtoby, George Johnston, John Kirby, John T. Hatfield—luminaries whom many readers would recognize, all of whom are dead now except for the last named. Their minds live on in their students. Dr. Hatfield taught me comparative religion at McGill University in Montreal, and I was delighted when he became president of the Western Region of the American Academy of Religion a few years ago.

Writing a book is like giving birth, and during my labor Walter Brueggemann, Phyllis Trible, Kurt Richardson, Joy Abdul-Mohan, Whitney Bodman, and an adult class at Stoney Creek United Church in Hamilton were among the many in the Christian community who favored me with conversations, visits, e-mails, and writings of their own.

Sometimes in only a phone call or an e-mail, Justus Baird, Ellen Frankel, and Carol Meyers did the same, with suggestions and questions from the Jewish academic community. Laleh Bakhtiar, Raheel Raza, and Amir Hussain were especially generous in discussions on the Muslim side of the family, but none more helpful than Mahmoud Ayoub.

K. C. Hanson, my editor at Cascade Books, is himself a scholar of high repute in the very fields investigated in *Forensic Scriptures*, and my publishers have been especially creative in the format including the diagrams and Web site. Eugene Melino is recognized in the dedication, for organizing what must be one of the best book-launch conferences ever, with the assistance of many friends and colleagues at Riverside Church, including Susan Switzer, Arnold Thomas, Robert Coleman, Jeff Slade, Desirée Baxter, and senior minister Brad Braxton, a veteran of interfaith endeavors, as well as those in finance, administration, and communications departments.

Good friend and institutional administrator at churches, hospitals, and elsewhere, Karen Arbour has the skills for the intricate computer work that turned my hand-drawn diagrams into the effective "forensic" tools for scholarship you find in the book and on the Web site that supports it. Dr. Ray Ordinario, creative photographer, produced the facsimile of the "Diagram of Synoptic Relationships" on the back cover, used with the permission of my friends at T. & T. Clark / The Continuum International Publishing Group. He also produced the photo facsimiles of the pages of Scripture in Hebrew, Greek, Arabic, and English that separate the three parts of the book.

Any writer fortunate enough to have a supportive family is blessed. I am triply blessed in the daily sifting and sorting of views on all these matters with my wife, Jenny Brown, who is my research associate and primary editor, in the fact checking and grammatical precision of my son, Arthur Gosine-Brown, and in the literary skills and theology of my daughter, Indira Sinton, author of the poetic work that forms the epilogue of this book. I thank them all, especially Jenny, both for the creative home life we share in "retirement" and for accompanying me on the lecture circuit and to teaching assignments and preaching opportunities on these themes in Canada, the United States, and the West Indies.

I am also grateful for any responses to *Noah's Other Son* or *Forensic Scriptures* that may be addressed to me at <bbrown17@cogeco.ca>, and I am always available to participate in events or to make presentations in support of the commitments shared with my readers.

Foreword

An Advocate

A s THE NEW TESTAMENT cannot be read without reference to the Old Testament, it appears that the Qur'an presumes an adequate knowledge of both, direct or filtered through the Hadith. This realization came to me during a conversation on the college verandah over coffee with Brian Arthur Brown; with his wife Jenny, who is his support system in things theological and otherwise; and with his mother-in-law, Lily Gosine, the matriarch of a family with Christian, Hindu, and Muslim branches here on the Island of Trinidad. Trinidad is also where Judaism first took root in the Americas, among Jewish crewmembers who settled here when prohibited from returning to Spain after the third voyage of Christopher Columbus. It is in the context of this family and this society that Dr. Brown serves St. Andrew's Theological College as Professor Emeritus of Holy Scripture in our spring semester and grounds himself annually in World Religions.

It would now appear that in our Abrahamic family of scriptural resources, Islam has treasures to offer Jews and Christians in the twenty-first century that may be compared to the impact of the Dead Sea Scrolls in the twentieth century, with an added value in that these resources relate to a living community with whom we must now engage. These are new thoughts since my own seminary days at Princeton, over a decade ago. As such ideas came flooding my way, I realized the truth of Walter Brueggemann's comment that "Brown is a responsible, reliable teacher who can help us find access to these texts." Brian Arthur Brown is an advocate for understanding among the members of what he sometimes calls "the dysfunctional family of Abraham, Sarah and Hagar."

As a vigilant womanist in the Presbyterian Church in my part of the world, I especially appreciate the rigorous investigation of the role of women in the production and dissemination of Scriptures in all three traditions as described in *Forensic Scriptures*, another illustration of some genuine new thinking by Brian Arthur Brown. To recognize the leadership role of Muslim women in Asian politics (as documented in Brown's earlier book), or their role in Scripture production, both historically and in the present (as in this text), is not to deny the challenges women face in Islam, as elsewhere, but to provide a deepening context, as we are attempting to do in the Forensic Scriptures Conference as well. Notes from that conference brochure are included in this book as an appendix for those unable to attend.

As the principal of a seminary, I recommend that *Forensic Scriptures* be used jointly by three departments, in introductions to Hebrew Scriptures, Christian Scriptures, and Interfaith Studies. I have every confidence that this book will find its way to both libraries and classrooms of theological institutions everywhere, and contribute to the growing scholarship of the laity in many of our congregations: Jewish, Christian and Muslim.

As a participant in the conference launching Professor Brown's latest book, *Forensic Scriptures*, at Riverside Church in New York City in May of 2009, I took opportunities in months preceding the conference to solicit thoughts from other academics who would be participating or had an interest. Rabbi Justus Baird is the director of the Center for Multifaith Education at the Auburn Theological Seminary in New York, a Presbyterian institution like my own, so in the interfaith context it seemed appropriate to ask him how these things are being received by Christians. Walter Brueggemann, Professor of Old Testament emeritus at Columbia Theological Seminary in Atlanta, a frequent contributor at Princeton while I was there, has offered an articulate anticipation of the Muslim connection to biblical studies. So it seemed only fitting to ask Professor Amir Hussain to comment on the situation as it relates to Jews, especially the Jewish students of this Muslim professor at the Loyola Marymount (Roman Catholic) University.

We dare do these things in the spirit of this book, and under the New Golden Rule for Religions presented by Brian Arthur Brown in his recent book, *Noah's Other Son: Bridging the Gap between the Bible and the Qur'an*, and in presentations to students here at St. Andrew's Theological College last year and elsewhere since then: "Understand others in the most generous spirit possible without doing violence to your own beliefs, as you would wish they might understand and support your position as generously as possible."

—Principal Joy Adbul-Mohan
St. Andrews Theological College

Foreword

DISCOVERING A PREVIOUSLY UNKNOWN source of holy words is a rare, but certainly not new, event in Jewish tradition. In biblical times, the priest Hilkiah found a new scroll in the house of the Lord—probably the book of Deuteronomy, scholars tell us (2 Kgs 22:8ff). In the thriteenth century Moses de Leon found a foundational work of Jewish mysticism, the Zohar. And in our time, Mohammed Ahmed el-Hamed, a Bedouin goatherd, found caches of parchment in Qumran that became known as the Dead Sea Scrolls. Leaving aside the questions of authorship that each of these events stirred up, we can focus on the results of each "discovery." For some, this newly discovered material was new information, and for others it was new inspiration.

Brian Arthur Brown challenges non-Muslims to see in the Qur'an a similar opportunity to discover a new source of information, if not inspiration. He challenges us with the question: what can we learn about our own religious tradition by studying the Qur'an? Because the Qur'an is the holy book of over a billion people, and because its style is quite different from most of the Hebrew Bible and the New Testament, taking on Brown's challenge demands of us three things: curiosity, humility, and sensitivity. Investigating another religious tradition without being threatening or feeling threatened is not so easy.

Auburn Theological Seminary, a Presbyterian institution that strives to engage deeply in responsible interfaith education, is proud to have hosted the launch of Brown's previous book, Noah's Other Son in 2007. Two years afterwards, we are proud to once again launch this new work, Forensic Scriptures, with our friends at the Riverside Church in Manhattan. It is my hope that curious readers will find in this book a humble and sensitive guide as they begin to learn from the Qur'an, and perhaps by doing so, discover new things about their own religious tradition and their own relationship with God.

—Rabbi Justus Baird
Center for Multifaith Education
Auburn Theological Seminary

I HAVE BEEN GLAD to be introduced to Brown's work. I am only at the beginning of my attention to the Qur'an, and I suspect it is the same for many people whom Brown addresses. I have no doubt that a greater critical familiarity with the Qur'an is an urgent enterprise among us.

I have the glad impression that Brown is a responsible, reliable teacher who can help us find access to these texts. It will be important in time to come to be engaged with Muslim colleagues; and in order to do that, some understanding in the subject is important. Brown's work will be an important resource for that coming task.

I thank Brown for sharing his work with us and wish him and his readers well in moving the discussion forward to a new space where Jews, Christians and Muslims may begin to share the fruits of the their separate scholarships.

—Professor Walter Brueggemann
Columbia Theological Seminary

I AM A CANADIAN Muslim who teaches theology at a Catholic university in America. As such, I have experience with interfaith dialogue across the various religious cultures of North America. It is my distinct privilege to endorse and complement the work of my countryman, Dr. Brian Arthur Brown, a minister of the United Church of Canada, a body with which I have had a long and fruitful association in the interfaith work that is engaging a wider and wider circle in Canada, America, and much of the world in these challenging times of such great potential. Although separated by a few decades, Brian and I shared the same teachers in Wilfred Cantwell Smith and Willard Gurdon Oxtoby, both senior scholars in comparative religion and interfaith dialogue. For me, Brian captures the heart of interfaith dialogue that we both learned from our teachers: not that we seek to convert each other, but that we help each other to find what is meaningful in our own traditions of faith.

After reading Noah's Other Son: Bridging the Gap between the Bible and the Qur'an, I was among many who realized the potential for further developments in this direction, and I am pleased to contribute what I can to Forensic Scriptures, both the book and the historic conference which launches it at the Riverside Church in New York City.

By addressing the Qur'an as material that God may have earlier addressed to Jews, Christians, Sabeans, and Zoroastrians and preserved in their Scriptures "either faithfully or in garbled form," Brian Arthur Brown has brilliantly opened up the possibility of reviewing Islamic holy writ from a critical perspective without doing violence to traditional Islamic teaching concerning the uniqueness and completeness of the Qur'an. On this basis we can make comparisons, learn from each other, and see what we hold in common without suggesting that the Qur'an is necessarily a compilation of "sources" rather than the fresh corrective and final revelation Muslims believe it to be. New levels of shared scholarship between the three branches of Abraham, Sarah, and Hagar's family may now be based on mutual respect for the scriptural traditions of each, with considerable benefits to all concerned. Forensic Scriptures represents part of the trend towards Muslim participation in the theological mainstream of North America and consequently the rest of the world.

As I have come to expect from a United Church of Canada source, Brian Brown's theology is both deep and generous. My Muslim sisters and brothers will find no trace of the old negative polemics in his writings. I recommend Forensic Scriptures to all my students, especially to Jewish and Muslim ones, who can learn so much from each other. Of course, the book should be available in the libraries of all Christian educational institutions.

—Professor Amir Hussain
Loyola Marymount University

Prologue

THE LAST FORTY YEARS (a strikingly convenient biblical measurement of an era) of the twentieth century saw a focus on black and white race relations in the United States and the threat of Communism, a cold war in which an iron curtain divided Europe in that era. Race relations and the threat of Communism were partly defined by spiritual, theological, and faith perspectives—by faith perspectives in facing down "godless communism" and by spiritual and theological perspectives in a civil rights movement largely led by churches. Communism has now collapsed and at least on Christmas and Easter, churches are full in Moscow, Beijing, and even Havana. The election of an African American president has possibly signaled the turning of a page in American race relations. These issues are still important but no longer evoke quite the same passion or intensity.

In contrast, beginning with September 11, 2001, the first forty years of the twenty-first century (again measuring an era with this biblical number) may well be defined by faith relations rather than race relations, and by the threat of terrorism rather than the threat of Communism. Muslim-Christian-Jewish relations may not be more intrinsically important than relations with Hindus, Buddhists, and Sikhs, for example; but from New York through Madrid, London, Bali, and Mumbai to Iraq, Iran, southern Russia, Pakistan, Afghanistan, Israel-Palestine, and even western China the hot-button issues seem to emanate from the dysfunctional family of Abraham, Sarah, and Hagar, which now makes up some 55 percent of the world's population.

Much depends on a mature engagement of these tense relationships, and once again religion is specifically and overtly fundamental to a successful outcome. This is even more basically true than in the issues of race relations and the threat of Communism, since, while religion per se is rarely the root cause of such conflicts, it is religious identities that frame the issues of justice, freedom, governance, and military power.

Prologue

The book *Noah's Other Son: Bridging the Gap between the Bible and the Qur'an* was one of many preliminary attempts to grasp these issues from a faith perspective. Because the world's agenda in the twenty-first century has such a looming religious component ("the elephant in the room"), *Forensic Scriptures* goes even further in looking to the Scriptures of the Abrahamic traditions as potentially a fruitful avenue in the pursuit of understanding. The seemingly arcane has become acute, and matters sometimes regarded as a musty preserve of religious scholars have become quintessentially meaningful.

The conferences in various parts of the world launching this book, and study groups in many communities, are also part of the effort to establish a theological underpinning beneath the mix of political, military, media, and academic attempts at understanding this crisis of our new time. Jewish, Muslim, and Christian seminaries, congregations, and individual believers have rarely had a more urgent agenda. At the very heart of their efforts we find the disciplines of scriptural criticism and analysis, in which there exists a solid professional orientation that may be the resource the world is seeking. A summary of this potential for new understandings is the essence of the text that follows: *Forensic Scriptures: A Critical Analysis of Scripture and What the Qur'an Reveals about the Bible.*

Preface

Documentary Evidence

HAVE YOU HEARD THE joke about the minister, the rabbi, and the imam? I suspect not, because we have not reached the level of community relationships that enable us to comfortably include imams in our humor. Jokes often have a dynamic that comes from three directions, so we are content with "the rabbi, the minister, and the priest," even though two are Christian. They are usually on the golf course together, out in a boat, or arriving at the pearly gates, and some humorous angle of their shared Scriptures makes for convivial merriment. The relationships between Muslims, Christians, and Jews are not funny, at least not yet. But the relationships are beginning to get more comfortable, starting with clerics and those more active in spiritual matters; and it is the shared Scriptures that are the main bases of an increasing bond that may soon have wider manifestations.

The Bible is always news, both for scholars and people at large, and this is as true in the twenty-first century as ever. We will begin at the beginning with the Jewish Torah, often called the Pentateuch (five scrolls) by Christians and others. Over the last 150 years the Documentary Hypothesis about its composition has shown the Jewish Torah to be a rich spiritual tapestry woven together from various source documents, known as J, E, D, and P, by a final editor known as R, the "redactor." This hypothesis, in some version, held almost absolute sway for well over a century, went through a brief period of question and doubt near the end of the last century, and has been revived and reinforced in the new century. Such is the weight of evidence at this point that in *Forensic Scriptures* I propose to revise the description of the "hypothesis" to have it called simply the "documentary evidence" of the sources of the Pentateuch. We will review the hard evidence, consider circumstantial evidence in passing, and float a few possibilities for future investigations of the Torah, the Gospels, and the Qur'an.

This inquiry, intended as much for seminary students as for intelligent lay readers, is therefore an overview of the argument as presented in both the academic classroom and the congregational study group in recent years. New resources are now showing Christians, who always regard the Hebrew Scriptures as foundational, how recent Jewish studies illustrate the ways in which the writings of the Torah/Pentateuch helped shape messianic theology. Stunning new paradigms from Muslim sources about the roles of women in producing the Scriptures of Qur'an and the Hadith, and how these may be applied to Hebrew and Christian Scriptures, are also detailed in this book, which presents the Bible with the help of the kind of forensic evidence made available by professional investigators in court cases carried by the popular media. We begin with what we know and what we might reasonably assume. To briefly illustrate, let me paraphrase the legend on the cover, which also hints at future possibilities. The order is changed for reasons that will become apparent.

THE PENTATEUCHAL SOURCES

The Yahwist: J

The J document, named for its use of the divine name, Yahweh (Jehovah), was written in Jerusalem soon after the kingdom that David bequeathed to his son was split by Solomon's own lackluster sons into Israel in the north and Judah in the south. In his 1990 bestseller, *The Book of J*, American literary critic Harold Bloom popularized the notion that the material known as the J source was most likely written by a woman, whom he tentatively identified as a daughter of David. One of the women who produced such Scripture might well have been not merely an author, but also the compiler and editor who left her own stamp and the marks of educated sisters and foreign sisters-in-law on materials in the archives of the royal house of David.

This possibility was first raised by Richard Elliott Friedman in the first edition to his *Who Wrote the Bible?* published three years prior to Bloom's work, in 1987, and cited by Bloom, but who failed to acknowledge this particular debt. Sadly, the questionable scholarship in the rest of Bloom's book earned the scorn of much of the academic establishment, which accounts for the widespread dismissal of the notion of female authorship for J highlighted by Bloom, perhaps the single most intriguing notion of his career. But a persuasive new paradigm from the Muslim world makes it seem increasingly possible that Friedman's conjecture and Bloom's instincts may have been correct about women as household scribes in ancient palaces where their role may have been somewhat analogous to the religious role of women in peasant households, though on a more sophisticated level.

The Elohist: E

In the north, God was respectfully identified by the more ancient and generic word, *El* or *Eloh* (or *Allah* in Arabic) until the story records God's revelation of his name, Yahweh, to Moses. The memory of Moses plays a role among the Levitical priests in the old northern capital, Shiloh, akin to the dominance of Abraham in the south among the Aaronide priests in the Jerusalem temple. J had been written in Jerusalem about 900 BCE and shows how both theology and temple worship from the days of the kingdom's founding in the desert pointed toward the Davidic throne and the temple—both at Jerusalem. The document known as E appeared as a response to J some fifty years later to validate the northern kingdom, its Mosaic theology and the Levitical priesthood at Shiloh, the first capital of the Hebrew nation during the conquest era and a site they were possibly promoting as a central shrine for the new northern kingdom.

The Deuteronomist: D

The Deuteronomic source is from that same Levitical school after they moved south to Judah following the collapse of Israel in the north, decimated by Assyria in 721 BCE. To establish their place in the southern kingdom, this circle brilliantly amalgamated J and E into one document with political instinct and skill modern people rarely associate with the ancients. They were apparently as keen about their newly developed literacy as the first computer generations have been about similar cut-and-paste features of their new technology. Old King Hezekiah and later young King Josiah welcomed the Levites as a counterbalance to the Aaronide priesthood, then powerful in national politics. The Levites annotated an ancient Mosaic law book in their possession, "found" it in the Jerusalem temple during renovations, and promoted it along with JE as a "second law" or "deutero-norm," and got a popular response. Their circle included Jeremiah and his secretary, Baruch, who may have also produced the books of Joshua, Judges, First and Second Samuel (about the prophet-priest at Shiloh) and 1 and

2 Kings (about monarchs north and south, good and bad). Deuteronomy was updated after Judah also fell, after its temple was desecrated, and its king tortured and marched away in chains. This concluding book of the Pentateuch then reflected God's promises about the temple and the messianic assurances about leadership (regarded then as coming from David's line) as an eternal hope, and universally applicable. The people of Judah understood these prophecies in the way such prophecies were later received by Christians, both orthodox and gnostic, as well as by Muslims, whose image of the messiah is surprisingly close to the Christian gnostic tradition in certain particulars.

The Priestly Source: P

For some time, the priestly source was thought to consist of documents compiled in exile in Babylon, connecting temple worship with desert experiences of the tabernacle, and perhaps blended immediately with J and E, and with Deuteronomy appended as an anchor. The jury is now out on the date of P, with recent examination of the evidence pointing to preexilic dating of material that originally formed just a single document, paralleling J and E in content, but with a more sacramental emphasis by the Aaronide priestly establishment. Their spiritual agenda, as they understood it, was to protect their prerogatives in Jerusalem against the more populist religious trends represented by the Levites, whose influence was growing at court and among the people. Believers recognize that each of these authors or schools contributed material that is inadequate or incomplete in and of itself, but which reflects facets of the divine intention for the Torah or Pentateuch.

The Redactor: R

The redactor, or final editor of all this material, must now be seen as a literary genius. Increasingly presumed to be Ezra, and so regarded in antiquity, the redactor wrote almost nothing himself. He evidently knew the history of J and E's having been successfully combined in what is a very intricate fashion politically and religiously acceptable to all parts of the earlier community. Ezra faced a similar situation when the Judean aristocracy, priesthood, and civil service returned from the Babylonian exile to Jerusalem to rebuild the city, the temple, and the state in concert with the local Judean peasants, Levites, and others. To meld these broad, diverse and mutually suspicious groups, Ezra even more skillfully blended the P parallels into J and E and then added the beloved D material as a conclusion to the compendium because it was the last to be revised, possibly by a Levite who was still on the scene.

Ezra's work, possibly the most intricate masterpiece ever produced in world literature, earned him the appellation "The Second Moses" in the Talmud. It was accepted so completely that for over two thousand years people all over the world took the Torah compendium to be by one author. This author was presumed to be Moses himself, who was perhaps rightly regarded as the originator of these traditions, though he lived almost five hundred years before there was a written form of Hebrew. The Torah, as the foundation of Jewish culture, and of at least a hundred national cultures since, now stands as a cornerstone of an emerging world culture and a subject of fascination by student and scholar alike.

The critical techniques developed for the study of the Torah/Pentateuch occupy approximately a third of this book. They have also been applied to the study of Christian Scriptures over the last century, though not in a format accessible to the laity until recently, and amplified here. Our focus in Christian Scriptures will be on the first three books of the New Testament, the so-called Synoptic Gospels. My work in this section depends on Allan Barr's *A* "Diagram of Synoptic Relationships," a resource that inspired my own diagram described below. This section will also extend some findings about possible female influence in the writing of the gospels to other parts of the New Testament.

Out of this expanded analysis of the text something new is emerging as a result of a determined critique seeking to understand the role of women in Scripture, certainly "behind the scenes" and "between the lines" but also as divinely inspired authors of primary materials in the Old and New Testaments. The basis for application of these same techniques to the study of the Qur'an represents a breakthrough that is welcomed by Muslims in particular, as well as by Jews and Christians now becoming aware of how much the Qur'an reveals about the Bible, including the stunning conclusion of this investigation presented as a Muslim template which can be applied to other Scriptures.

A generation ago, Christians went through a phase of regarding their faith as more Greek than Jewish, thanks to then-current assessments of Paul's contribution or dominance. This was followed in the 1990s and the first decade of the twenty-first century by scholarship that resulted in the recovery and renewed appreciation of Jewish influence in both the New Testament and in the church. Now Jews and Christians together are moving forward in a new quest to uncover the ancient and long interplay between themselves and their Muslim cousins, with seemingly dramatic results so far, as described by this book and its launch conference.

The book is in three parts. Part 1, *Opening the Hebrew Scriptures*; part 2, *Opening the Christian Scriptures*; and part 3, *Opening the Muslim Scriptures*, are designed so that they can be read separately, after the common introductory material, by students of the various departments. Enough material is repeated in summary in order for students in each department to grasp the whole. The frequent recapitulation may also serve general readers in reviewing concepts that may be new to them. Students studying only part 1 or part 2, however, should also visit the exercises described at the beginning of chapter 19 in part 3.

I do not intend to introduce very much here that is new, but rather to report a consensus of critical opinion at the beginning of the twenty-first century that is strong enough to be presented as "documentary evidence," as opposed to "hypotheses," and to point toward the sources of that evidence. At the same time, and at a more modest level, there are three or four elements here that are rather new and of a critical nature.

From the Hebrew Scriptures I offer the "Diagram of Sources of the Pentateuch," long overdue as an aid to students Jewish, Christian and, increasingly, Muslim. For Christians, I offer a tentative opinion about the authorship of a gospel document called Q, which points toward potential answers to some longstanding questions. For Muslims, there are two things, perhaps because in these times the place of Islamic tradition in world culture looms large. In the first instance, this book and its launch conference offer Muslims an entrée into the disciplines of scriptural analysis, as practiced by Jews and Christians, that does no violence to the traditional Islamic understanding of the origins of the Qur'an. In the second place, there is a recognition that from the Muslim community comes, unexpectedly to many, what we might call the *pièce de résistance* of this book, in the quest to identify the substantial role women must have played in scriptural production as authors, and in certain circumstances, behind the scenes and between the lines.

Yet let us not be overly sanguine about the impact of such studies. The denomination to which I belong, the United Church of Canada, launched a "New Curriculum" for Sunday school and adult Christian education classes back in the 1960s, in which critical techniques were introduced to the laity. The fallout from negative reactions to the curriculum coincided with a 50-percent drop in the number of children attending Sunday school and, after a temporary increase, practically decimated the adult study program. Perhaps we are more ready now, but fifty years after that breakthrough/debacle, in an attempt to measure any benefits, I asked all the board chairs, women's-group presidents, chairs of trustees, Sunday school superintendents, and other local church leaders I could find, who wrote the first five books of the Bible? A few guessed it might be David, some said God, nobody said it was Moses (so let's not be nervous about challenging that pious legend), but most said they had no idea and did not much care.

After hearing the summary of critical opinion in this book, these current leaders of congregations large and small, urban and rural, trained in the New Curriculum, told me that they were more interested in the stories and their meaning than in questions of authorship. When pressed, they insisted that these days they are less concerned about confrontations between liberals and conservatives in these debates than about Moses's confrontation of Pharaoh; and less anxious about theories constructed by critics than about the golden calf constructed by Aaron, in terms of challenges and parallels in their own lives. Yet they seemed to know that Adam and Eve are corporate and symbolic names for humanity, and none of them was disturbed in the least that the Bible opens with two creation stories that are often in conflict. People in the religious mainstream know more about some things and care less about others than I could possibly have guessed. They are almost certainly correct in their priorities.

However, as Islam, another branch of Abraham's family, moves into the Western world in force and grows faster than the other two branches, there is a new urgency to the task of critical analysis as a tool to increase popular understanding. The upshot of such criticism in the twenty-first century is to illustrate that God's people have been through this before: the migrations, the foreign populations, the refugees, the new beginnings, even the terrorisms, and most especially the discoveries about each others' Scriptures. As we move together and with others toward a new world culture in a global village, scriptural criticism may indeed help us understand each other and our own origins in faith, even if these techniques never do affect the value of the stories themselves, as laypeople in my own church and elsewhere may appreciate more than scholars realize.

We open with a review of the documentary evidence concerning the Torah or Pentateuch; we move through the Gospels to see how critical techniques apply to the New Testament; and finally we apply these same scriptural principles in the study of the Qur'an and other revered documents of Islam. Since this is all about Scripture, one important element of understanding about the discussion of Scripture in this family must be put in place first.

I have otherwise well-informed Christian and Jewish friends who have almost a surfeit of goodwill toward Muslims, but who remain ignorant of the essential character of a basic Islamic tenet concerning the Qur'an. Some of these people are respected colleagues with years of experience in interfaith activity, but whose Muslim friends are hesitant to confront them on this hurtful matter, out of respect.

Many non-Muslims know that Muslims love the Qur'an and regard it as containing the very words of God. We who are non-Muslims often fail to recognize the importance of this essential aspect of Islam when we casually refer to the influences on Muhammad as his "sources" for the material in the Qur'an. Muslims view these influences in a reverse manner, regarding items and stories revealed clearly in the Qur'an and recorded accurately there as having been partially revealed previously and recorded in a frequently garbled fashion. We can perhaps accept this as their view, but the Islamic doctrine of the Qur'an refreshing previous Scriptures requires a sensitivity that many other matters under discussion do not require, at least not in the same measure.

When Jews dialogue with Christians, they may not accept that Jesus is the Son of God, but they recognize that most Christians hold that doctrine of the doctrine of the incarnation as the sine qua non, that without which there would be no Christianity; and so they do not constantly belabor the point or belittle the notion. Likewise not many Christians subscribe to ethnic identity as the cornerstone of their faith experience, though some denominations are colored in this way. Yet down through the ages the Jewish identity has been communal and ethnic in an essential way, unlike anything to which Christians subscribe. The sine qua non for Jews is the covenant community, without which there would be no Judaism, religious or secular.

To be in dialogue even while constantly implying that Jews should get over this, or that they should assimilate into the societies around them, would be offensive to the point of outrage. Current Jewish-Christian dialogues have been built on understandings of these parameters that have taken centuries to work out.

Since the similar sine qua non in the Muslim community involves Scripture, Christians and Jews simply must proffer a similar status of unique respect to their doctrine of the Qur'an, even while Muslims in dialogue must concede an acceptance of the Jewish communal identity and at least a recognition of the Christian doctrine of the incarnation.

For Muslims, the practice of Jewish and Christian scholars casually attributing the Qur'an to "sources" is similar to constantly reminding Christians that sensible people cannot possibly relate to their belief that Jesus of Nazareth was God in the flesh, or to be continually insisting to Jews that if they would assimilate like other ethnic groups their troubles would go away. Even at the risk of belaboring the point, a new sensitivity to the Muslim understanding of the nature of their Scripture, a designation they use in reference only to the Qur'an, is essential. In spite of Muslim attempts at tolerant goodwill, I believe without some greater accommodation on this point, the conversations can go no further than the present impasse, where we are limited to polite discourse but little progress.

Of course there will be critics—Jewish, Christian and others, including dissident Muslims—who may continue to insist that the Qur'an is a compilation from other sources, some hundreds of years before Muhammad and many a hundred years later. But for the family discussion to proceed on a basis of mutual respect, it is not necessary to challenge the traditional Muslim understanding of their Scripture in order to experience the full benefit of critical analysis on the basis outlined in this book. If the academic discussion ever moves beyond that point, Christian and Jewish scholars should be prepared to simply follow or respond to Muslim colleagues with respect to any developments, just as they have learned to do with each other in large part.

The resolution to this question provided in the present work has been attempted by others elsewhere, but not quite developed in the manner extolled in the foreword by one of America's foremost Muslim communicators who described my resolution as having "brilliantly opened up the possibility of reviewing Islamic holy writ from a critical perspective without doing violence to traditional Islamic teaching concerning the uniqueness and completeness of the Qur'an." While I am humbled and incredibly honored by this description, I repeat it here only to underline and clarify the point that what non-Muslims are inclined to regard as "sources," Muslims simply regard as previous revelations of the same material.

In Muslim belief, with a certainty equal to the centrality of Christ to the church and of the covenant community to Jews, these revelations were given freshly to Muhammad, with an awesome, holy cadence and with clarification from God. Muslims would hold to this even if it could be illustrated that Muhammad might have heard such stories earlier in their previous corrupt or accurate, garbled or inspired versions. He may have brought an awareness of some of the previously revealed material to the cave where he received it afresh in the same manner that he brought his ability to understand the Arabic language in which the revelations were presented.

Once their understanding of the freshness and uniqueness of the Qur'an is acknowledged, Muslim scholars are free to work with their Jewish and Christian counterparts in the analyzing and critiquing of the material, as it appears both in the Qur'an and in the Bible. No critical compromise is required, and the analysis can proceed on the basis of the evidence, in much the same manner as atheists like Sigmund Freud and Isaac Asimov have contributed positive insights to Jewish and Christian understandings of certain biblical texts, without necessarily adopting the belief context of those with whom they discussed these matters. Indeed, we can do even better as respectful fellow believers within the great family of Abraham, Sarah, and Hagar, but before proceeding to the treasures this approach may reveal, our scholars need to check their attitudes as rigorously as some of the more prejudiced commentators in the media and people in the streets. This is a prerequisite for reading this book and for the conference that launches it.

I am still sometimes asked how is it possible to be fully appreciative of one another's Scripture and completely comfortable in one's own scriptural skin at the same time. Believers who are confident in their own tradition should be able to practice the Golden Rule of Religion described by Joy Abdul-Mohan in the foreword to this book with benefit to themselves. Just as learning a second language does not require forgetting or foreswearing one's mother tongue but actually enriching it, there is a delight in being open to spiritual experiences that ring true for others as a means of growth within one's own tradition. We may all be surprised at how much we learn.

For that matter, Hindus, Buddhists, and others elsewhere in the world have their own Scriptures, which represent the other side of the equation.

While the Scriptures of Abraham's family of Jews, Christians, and Muslims are revelations of the Divinity reaching toward humanity, the other major Scriptures reflect the aspirations of humanity reaching toward Divinity: a worthy subject, but beyond the scope of the present inquiry.

Material often covered in footnotes is integrated into this text because in many cases my book is about the material referenced. Readers will find a full amplification of such resources in the bibliography.

Meanwhile, there was this rabbi, this priest, and this imam. They had just come from the golf course and were in a boat, soon to arrive at the pearly gates, when a funny thing happened . . .

Introduction

DNA

FIFTY YEARS AGO, IN 1959, I entered a Canadian university in Halifax, Nova Scotia, as an undergraduate student in Arts and Science. My pretheology degree at Dalhousie University would include some sciences and broad programs in understanding how the world works, as well as Greek, Latin, English literature, philosophy, history, and psychology: a four-year honors program in the Faculty of Arts and Science. This was intended to prepare one for the rigors of theological study, which was still then referred to as "the queen of the sciences," offered only in colleges, seminaries, and faculties of theology or divinity, quite separate from the rest of the academic community.

There was then no Department of Religious Studies at Dalhousie, or at any other university that I knew of, and there were certainly none of the courses on Islam that are attracting so much attention now. That trend to religious studies is now a reality in the faculty of arts and science of practically every respected university of the twenty-first century, but back then at Dalhousie, there was a lone half course called "Introduction to the English Bible" in the English department, and so I signed up.

On the first day, Professor Corston introduced the notion that we do not know who wrote the opening books of the Bible. But I drew to his attention that my copy of the King James Authorized Version of the Bible opened with the title of "The First Book of Moses, called Genesis." He wanted the class to use the Revised Standard Version (RSV), which was then practically hot off the press as the first of a generation of new versions; but he was distressed to note that the RSV too began with "The First Book of Moses, commonly called Genesis." He insisted that this addition of one word was significant and predicted (correctly, it turned out in the New Revised Standard Version of 1989) that future translations would be simply called Genesis.

1

He seemed rattled by my presumptuous and impertinent interjection, and he did not do as well as he might have in explaining the multiple authorship of this communal document and the several that followed. He proceeded to wade through the rest of the Old Testament text without calling the authorship much into question. The good professor fared ever so much better when we reached the New Testament, with the aid of a four-color chart, about a square meter or square yard in size, depicting the four main sources of materials in what are called the Synoptic Gospels, or gospels that may be viewed together: Matthew, Mark, and Luke. We could see clearly how one copied from another, which one had to be the first to be written, and how Luke probably spoke for the others in acknowledging that his material was obtained from various sources and eyewitness interviews, which he then edited together.

I was beginning to learn, and by this time John Corston and I had become quite friendly. So I said to him, "Don't you wish you had that kind of chart to illustrate the opening books of the Old Testament?" His reply was a direct challenge. "You are going into theology after you leave here. You should construct such a chart and eventually submit it as your thesis project." I thought I might just do that, so while the idea was fresh, and to prepare for the coming exam, I produced my first draft of the diagram over the Christmas break at my grandparents' home in 1959 with a pen and a ruler, an Underwood typewriter and some children's crayons.

In 1963 I enrolled in theological studies in the Faculty of Divinity at McGill University in Montreal to study for the Master of Divinity degree in preparation for ordination for ministry in the United Church of Canada. Naturally, both Old Testament and New Testament courses were on the curriculum for every year, and in the first year we also took Hebrew and Greek language studies, church history, and an introduction to systematic theology. Comparative religion was an optional extra in the final year for those who might be interested.

The study of Hebrew Scriptures, as the Old Testament is now called in many places, included an introduction to the various techniques used for critical analysis of the texts of Scripture. We were taught form criticism, historical criticism, textual criticism, source criticism, redaction criticism, and literary criticism—all the investigative techniques that would give the students information and insights we were expected to digest and to later reproduce in the context of congregational life through preaching and Bible study that would engage the wider church in helpful ways.

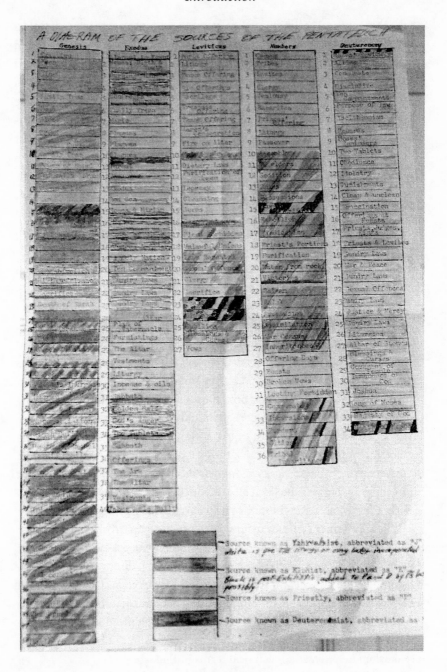

1959 STUDENT SKETCH, ORIGINALLY IN 4-COLORS

These critical techniques were roughly split into categories known as "higher criticism," which is the study of sources, historical contexts, and literary methods used by biblical writers, and "lower criticism," which includes the critical examinations of the actual wording of the finished product, the Bible as we have it. In future years we would learn of narrative criticism, psychological criticism, social-science criticism, feminist criticism, rhetorical criticism, and postmodernist criticism. These disciplines gave us perspectives of the Bible from behind the scenes, between the lines and from the *Sitz im Leben.*

The terms of biblical study were mostly in German from the Protestant scholars who developed these techniques in the hundred years previous at theological schools in Tübingen, Strasburg, and elsewhere. The *Sitz im Leben*, for example, was the sociological situation or "life setting" of the biblical writers, in which we could see the Holy Spirit operating in a way that would help us someday better communicate that spirit to congregations.

The first thing to get over was the fact that this subject is called biblical criticism. It turns out that we were not to criticize the Bible, but to critique it—that is, to analyze it: appreciating the difference between parables and history, or identifying the parts of the New Testament that are quotations from the Old Testament and appreciating the significance of that fact. I never understood why the subject was not called biblical analysis, but the word *critique* seems to have that sense, perhaps based on German usage. Once again, the greatest challenge for most of us as students was to grasp the multiple authorship or the several sources of the Pentateuch, the first five books of the Old Testament, in any coherent, comfortable, and spiritually significant way, or in any way that was intellectually convincing and responsive to what was clearly a respectable and important field of scientific research.

New Testament studies seemed easier to grasp, partly because fluency in Greek was then a normative entrance requirement at McGill's Faculty of Divinity, and because much of the research had been done by British scholars in English using technical terms we could understand like *manuscript, pedigree,* and *transmission,* or Greek words that have found their way into English, like *parable, evangelist,* and *synagogue.* The professor, Dr. George Johnston, was in the habit of speaking to the class in Greek, but we got a break when he referred to technical terms in English.

The best break, however, occurred when out came the four-colored chart, "A Diagram of Synoptic Relationships." I breathed a sigh of relief, as did a few others who were already familiar with what we regarded as a kind

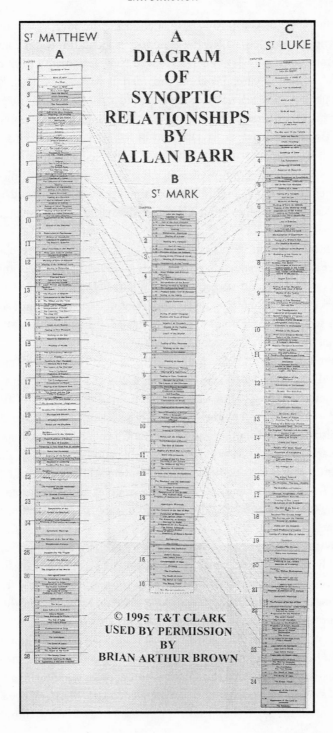

of Cliffs Notes or Coles Notes explanation for the sources and origins of the Synoptic Gospels, called the Synoptic Problem. Professor John Kirby, Johnston's assistant, who taught advanced New Testament Greek and who ran the student research program, provided us with Barr's chart. Kirby assured us that the chart was 100 percent valid as an authentic research tool.

This chart produced by Allan Barr of Edinburgh and published by T. & T. Clark in 1938 as "A Diagram of Synoptic Relationships" enables students to grasp and at least discuss the Synoptic Problem intelligently. It reduces an overwhelming welter of information to a colorful model that intelligent twelve-year-olds in confirmation class can understand, as I have since learned, and does so in a manner that is intriguing, engaging, and spiritually fruitful.

In one column, Barr's chart shows the material by Mark chapter by chapter and story by story, in pink. Beside it are two longer columns for the gospels of Mathew and Luke, both of whom had obviously copied almost all of Mark's material but, judging by important omissions, had not seen each other's work. Material unique to Matthew's gospel is shown in white, and material unique to Luke's account in yellow.

From the chart it is also immediately clear that a significant amount of material, shown in blue, is copied sometimes word for word from another document possessed by the authors of both Matthew and Luke. They both had Mark's gospel, and neither had each other's work, so it is clear that they both also possessed another early document, a collection of sayings of Jesus that Mark had not possessed during his publication of the gospel that bears his name. This is the document known among scholars around the world as "Q," from the German *Quelle*, meaning "source," and it is one of the more exciting treasures uncovered by this kind of forensic investigation of New Testament materials.

With the help of the chart, we can clearly see Mark's presentation, probably produced in Rome, apparently Peter's collection of stories of Jesus, produced very soon after the martyrdom of that saint. We can see Matthew's agenda in aiming his unique material at readers in the Jewish Diaspora, Luke's material intended for Gentile readers in the non-Jewish world, and the Q activities and stories of Jesus, cherished by the very early church, possibly originating in Jerusalem or Antioch, at the other end of the Mediterranean, since the Q collection appears unknown to Mark at Rome. Perhaps Q was written as a supplement to Mark, or even a rival collection of the sayings of Jesus from Jerusalem as an early church headquarters rivaling or surpassing Rome at that time. Or perhaps Q was the first gospel.

This classic "A Diagram of Synoptic Relationships" has been republished more than twenty times, and while some theological schools decline to use it now because of advances in scholarship since then, many still find it helpful as a landmark in the history of critical analysis and a watershed tool in mastering the techniques required in the discipline of New Testament studies. This engaging resource has an enduring place in theological education, lay and professional, and remains easily available from the publishers, T. & T. Clark, through Amazon.com, or any theological bookstore.

Meanwhile, back at McGill University, Professor Stanley Frost in the classroom and Dr. Willard Oxtoby in the research lab were trying to get through to the students regarding the authorship and communal folk sources of the Pentateuch. Strands of materials, oral campfire stories written down at various times, songs and poems, prayers and hymns, sources as diverse as authors working alone and committees of editors . . . Who could grasp all this confusion . . . and who would want to try? It was easier to keep insisting that Moses wrote the whole thing, as some students attempted to do, only to be forced to deal with internal textual evidence to the contrary.

This branch of biblical scholarship, as presented to the first-year students, was encompassed by the Four Document Hypothesis, produced in Germany in 1884 by Julius Wellhausen, and often simply called the Documentary Hypothesis. His thesis presented the Pentateuch as a carefully edited compilation of writings based on campfire stories from the northern tribes of Israel about Moses and the exodus from Egypt; based on folk memories of Abraham, Isaac, and Jacob from the southern tribes of Judah; combined with urban legends of David from Jerusalem; with a later summary of the law presented as speeches by Moses; and with a final layer of material by the priestly editors, who, according to Wellhausen, pulled the whole thing together and gave it the theological meaning and significance intrinsic to the experience of humanity in that ancient time and place.

With insights from Professor Frost, the students developed an understanding of this material as the Word of God in which the whole people of God had a role in the inspiration that lay behind the material, a role in its transmission, and a function in its application. But sorting the material in the lab with Dr. Oxtoby meant going over it again and again, with our faltering Hebrew, using scissors and paste to reconstruct the sources or "documents" known as J (southern), E (northern), D (deuteronomic), and P (priestly).

The research lab was established when the original Dead Sea Scroll manuscripts were paid for by McGill, Manchester, and Heidelberg universities; by the McCormick Theological Seminary in Chicago; and by the Vatican Library, all of whom only finally acquired early second-generation copies, but these were enough to enable students at McGill to appreciate the latest scientific research into the origins of our Bible. (McGill University also owns a fragment of a Chester Beatty papyrus, the earliest fragment of John's gospel found in the Egyptian desert, and other treasures—the kind of true "relics" of early Christianity that deeply move even Protestant students.)

But our experiences in the lab left all of us dreading the final examination in Old Testament. If only there were a four-color chart like the one that made everything plain in New Testament Studies. I was not cut out to be a scholar of the Old Testament or the New, but I determined there and then to complete the chart I had begun years earlier at my grandparents' home, for my own use at least. My classmates were delighted, and Dr. Frost, on the eve of his retirement, smacked his head in feigned frustration that he had never thought of producing such a tool. Aware of my limitations, Frost offered permission for me to use any or all of his written source list, a table that formed the appendix of a textbook he had just written on the subject. I sketched out the more detailed diagram for myself and others in preparation for the exams and planned to flesh it out further for possible publication as soon as I had time.

Then forty-five years of congregational ministry intervened. Every time I taught an introductory Bible class in a community college or congregation, I wished a better version of that chart was available. Half a dozen seminarians have come to me over the years in utter frustration over learning the techniques of critical analysis. I showed them the Barr chart for the opening books of the New Testament, if they had not seen it, and my own rough sketch of a similar tool for the first five books of the Old Testament, and they understood it.

Having recently retired from the pulpit vocation to focus on writing, an "avocation" all these years, my first task has been promotional tours of my 2007 book, *Noah's Other Son: Bridging the Gap between the Bible and the Qur'an*. That book takes the Qur'anic story of Noah's youngest son, Canaan, who drowns as a consequence of ignoring the warnings of his father, as a parable for our times when important warnings about the environment, pandemics, conflict, and poverty are ignored.

Introduction

In response to a challenge from Salman Rushdie, contained in the fore-word to that book, several chapters of *Noah's Other Son* are partly dedicated to the task of illustrating the techniques of critical analysis of Scripture for the benefit of Muslim readers—so that we can begin bridging the gap from both sides. On the lecture circuit these chapters on biblical criticism have proven to be of immense interest, not least to Muslim audiences. I illus-trated the points with the help of the New Testament "Diagram of Synoptic Relationships"; but, again, no fully adequate Old Testament diagram was available, far less one that might help chart the component parts of the Qur'an, as called for by some of the Muslim readers of *Noah's Other Son*.

Both *Noah's Other Son* and this sequel, with its completed diagrams, were designed for general Jewish, Christian, and Muslim readers in these new times, as well as for use in the new discipline of Interfaith Studies in undergraduate departments of religion, and in seminaries by those pre-paring for professional ministries. The hope is that the application of the techniques of critical analysis to the cherished Muslim Scripture, the Holy Qur'an, might also assist in the exciting developments currently underway in the Islamic world. This is a sensitive matter that I attempt to address appropriately in both *Noah's Other Son* and *Forensic Scriptures*.

These two books also attempt to show that Islam has significant of-ferings to contribute to the Judeo-Christian community as part of what we might call the dysfunctional family of Abraham, Sarah and Hagar. The Muslim contribution might include some recovery of personal modesty in a sex-obsessed society, and possibly a renewal of a sense of sheer holiness in certain religious communities which are currently focused on social justice—a focus that, in Islamic opinion, may only bring the desired re-sults if it is in response to an encounter with the Divine, an area of some possible agreement.

By far the greatest contribution of Islam to the Christian and Jewish communities, however, may come from insights in the field of biblical stud-ies derived from the Qur'an, as lore from the ancient Middle East pours forth to shed light on biblical mysteries. Jews and Christians have only just recently "discovered" the Qur'an, hidden from them all these years because of their own prejudices, and its value in the next fifty years should exceed the importance of the Dead Sea Scrolls and the Nag Hammadi library in the last fifty. High-level conferences and seminars are being proposed on the very topic of "What the Qur'an Reveals about the Bible." I was recently privileged to be invited to moderate an initial such conference sponsored by the Riverside Church in New York City with the support of the surrounding seminary communities and scholars from all over North America and abroad.

This specific field requires a common technical language, provided to Muslims by adoption of Jewish and Christian critical techniques, a process to which studies such as this book can contribute at an elemental level. The inclusion of the charts of the Old and New Testaments, and a prototype of the third for the Qur'an, is another attempt at developing common tools. Documentation of these scholarly trends among Muslims is provided in the concluding chapters of this work: part 3. There we also acknowledge the long centuries of intense academic endeavor in Islam where scholars employ techniques of their own and of a different order, methods of scriptural study and analysis that may prove to be an exciting boon to the rest of Abraham's family in the current climate of mutual respect among academics. This sharing is a two-way street. For example, the very latest discipline among Jews and Christians is what is called rhetorical criticism, a subject to which we shall return, but which has been well established among Muslim scholars for centuries. For their part, Muslims are increasingly adding to their repertoire what they choose to call "forensic" critical techniques adapted from Christians and Jews.

Such conversations within this family represent a major enterprise in the theological community these days. As has been mentioned, when I was in seminary, comparative religion was an optional elective subject for those who were interested. Now we call it interfaith studies, and it is a necessity for students as well as ministers and laypeople in every community. The objectives include making a significant contribution to world peace through increased religious tolerance and spiritual unity, and individual growth in understanding of each person's own faith in a larger context. In seminary days I could never have imagined how comparative religion or interfaith studies could provide me an impetus to complete my lifelong ambition to produce my chart of the Pentateuch.

In book launches for *Noah's Other Son* in several countries, and on the lecture circuit through the United States and Canada, discussions of the chapters on biblical criticism produced frequent acknowledgment that critical analysis of the sacred texts by Christians and Jews has not resulted in a diminution of the status of their Scriptures, as more timid believers initially feared. Rather, the discovery of the Dead Sea Scrolls and the analysis of their contents, and the unearthing of the Nag Hammadi library, with its *Sitz im Leben* of the early church, have actually enhanced the status of Scripture as an authentication of the integrity of the texts. There are parallels in the Muslim world that we will examine. As has been noted, the learning a second or third language does not diminish one's ability in or love for one's mother tongue; and Jews, Christians, and Muslims in many quarters are becoming more adventurous and courageous in interfaith studies, appreciating each other's offerings without the necessity of defensively making points at every turn.

Written to accompany the publication of my Old Testament diagram at last, this book is a spin-off sequel of *Noah's Other Son* in many ways, and a few sections of the material are lifted directly from the text of that book. I described Allan Barr's New Testament diagram in that book, and I tried to help people imagine the material now depicted on my Old Testament diagram, just to make the explanations clear. In lectures and media events, I have used the Barr diagram, and I have tentatively shown my rough prototype of the Old Testament diagram. This project, begun so long ago, is now complete, even as it hints at more to come and invites the participation of Muslims and others of goodwill in regard to a prototype of a similar diagram of the Qur'an produced within these covers and on the related Web site, BrianArthurBrown.com. If you noticed instinctively that the "Diagram of Sources of the Pentateuch" is truncated on the front cover, you are a scholar. May I suggest humorously that if you did not realize that the last fifteen chapters of both Genesis and Exodus have been cut off, perhaps you are still a student.

Having completed this fifty-year project, I offered it with this text to several of my previous publishers, requesting a format large enough to put a square-meter chart on a double-folded dust jacket, or the cover of a coffee–table-style publication. T. & T. Clark offered permission for Allan Barr's "A Diagram of Synoptic Relationships" to go with it as a centerfold, but few could imagine successful sales prospects for my oversized dream.

I finally found a publisher in New York who agreed to use what we called the *Rand McNally Road Atlas* format, just when my current West Coast publisher came up with a better proposal that combined a traditional publishing format with images available on the Internet. We decided on small facsimiles of the forensic diagrams of the New Testament and Qur'an for the back cover to give the idea, and a shortened, even tiny, but readable facsimile of the "Diagram of Sources of the Pentateuch" on the front cover. We combine this with permission for every purchaser to download the full chart in whatever size suits for reading, study, or lecturing.

Genesis

	21-22 The sin of Reuben
36	1-30 Descendants of Esau
	31-43 Kings of Edom
37	1-2a Jacob becomes a nation
	2b, 3b, 5-11, 19-20, 23 Joseph's dream
	3a, 4, 12-18, 21-22, 24 Colorful coat
	25b-27, 28b, 31-35 Saved by Midianites
	25a, 28a, 29, 30, 36 Sold to Ishmaelites
38	1-30 Tamar's vindication
39	1-23 Joseph falsely imprisoned
40	1-23 Interprets dreams there
41	1-45a, 46b-57 Favor with Pharaoh
	45b-46a Rises to rule
42	1-4, 8-20, 26-34, 38 Interrogation
	5-7, 21-25, 35-37 Gift of grain
43	1-13, 15-17, 24-34 Benjamin
	14, 18-23 Reconnected with brothers
44	1-34 Entrapment of brothers
45	1-2, 4-28 Joseph reveals his identity
	3 Terror and reconciliation
46	1-5a Jacob goes to Egypt
	5b, 28-34 Family settles in Egypt
	6-27 Descendants of Jacob
47	1-6, 11-27a, 29-31 Hebrews flourish
	7-10 Jacob blesses Pharaoh
	27b-28 Joseph's promise to Jacob
48	1-2, 8-22 Ephraim and Manasseh
	3-6 Covenant extended
	7 Rachel's tomb at Bethlehem
49	1-27 Jacob blesses his sons
	28 The twelve tribes of Israel
	29-33 The death of Jacob
50	1-11, 14, 22 Burial of Jacob
	12-13 at Machpelah near Mamre
	15-21, 23-26 Joseph is embalmed

The minute they picked up this book, scholars realized that both Genesis and Exodus were missing fifteen chapters on the front cover. While not color coded here, the final portions of these biblical books are shown in proportions available for downloading at BrianArthurBrown.com by anyone who owns a copy of this book.

Exodus

26	1-37 Tabernacle plans
27	1-27 Altar laws
28	1-43 Priestly vestments
29	1-46 Ordination
30	1-38 Anointing and incense
31	1-18 Sabbath observance
32	1-35 The Golden Calf
33	1-23 Covenant renewal
34	1a, 2-4a, 4c-28 Stone tablets
	1b, 4b like the former ones
	29-35 Moses' face radiant
35	1-35 Building supplies
36	1-38 Framing the tabernacle
37	1-29 Construction of furnishings
38	1-31 Altar and court
39	1-43 Bejeweling the vestments
40	1-38 Consecrating the tabernacle

The Remnants of Genesis and Exodus

For those who are interested and have the ability, possibly every reader these days, a very useful chart size is 11 inches by 17 inches. This can be printed off in color by many home computers or downloaded and redirected to one's neighborhood copy shop. Legal paper, 8½ inches by 14 inches also works quite well but is harder to read. The image is available to whomever acquires a copy of the book. One presumes that clergy, theological students, and congregational members are unlikely to steal my intellectual property without buying or obtaining a book. Please visit me at BrianArthurBrown. com to obtain a free downloadable copy of the "Diagram of Sources of the Pentateuch" and related matter.

In certain respects, Christians and Jews in the twenty-first century are now in a postcritical phase of biblical studies. Having accepted and digested the critical contribution, they are moving on in a deeper appreciation of the meaning of the scriptural message and applying it. But critical analysis is still important. Just as the Protestant Reformation was followed by the Catholic Counter-Reformation, biblical study in the current postcritical era will always be influenced by biblical criticism, a development of such magnitude and such significance that theological students, and now also laypeople, will need and desire to master it, along with our Muslim colleagues in relation critical analysis within their own context.

This book, with its diagrams, should therefore be of value to Christian and Jewish laypeople and to students who need a simplified tool to master this discipline before moving on in the postcritical quest for meaning. It may be of special value in illustrating critical techniques within the Muslim community that, in certain respects, is just now entering another critical era of its own. Non-Muslim readers will find the inclusion of the Qur'an in this study of interest from the interfaith perspective. The Qur'anic material also provides Christians and Jews with an independent nonbiblical illustration of forensic criticism, validating the techniques from an objective viewpoint for the rest of us—techniques that may facilitate the outpouring of new information and new understanding from this source.

It is the Turkish use of the term "forensic" to describe their use of critical techniques that gave me the title for this book. If such a title seems overly scientific, perhaps this discipline should adopt that cachet once again to illustrate its importance in an age that still nurses a scientific hangover from the more secular, technological, and scientific twentieth century when religion, spirituality, and global ethics were not the front-page news they are today. Muslims have little difficulty taking their religion that seriously. The "Queen of the Sciences" may be back!

We have come to the realization that if the Scriptures do indeed hold truth, and their message is valid, then we have nothing to lose and possibly much to gain from critical analysis. That has been the experience of Christians and Jews over the last hundred years, as I argued first in my recent book, *Noah's Other Son*. This is a cause of excited amazement by Muslim scholars and students today. But to me the most unexpected response to those chapters on the techniques of critical analysis is the response from Christian laypeople, seminary students, and even ministers. "I took that in seminary, but I never really understood it until now," was the comment of more than one ministerial colleague.

I believe my success in communicating the essence of the critical approach to biblical analysis has been due to the constant vision of the chart, "A Diagram of the Sources of the Pentateuch," in my mind's eye, produced now and included on the cover of this publication and its associated Web site, after careful vetting by well-known and respected experts acknowledged elsewhere. It presents material from the Hebrew Torah in a format that illustrates techniques that can be grasped and employed now by Jews, Christians, and Muslims alike.

For example, as developed in *Noah's Other Son*, Jews say, "The Messiah is coming," and Christians assert, "Here he is," and Muslims believe, "Yes, that was him, and he is coming again." The three phases of critical analysis in this book confirm and make plain the core elements of messianic theology as held in the three branches of the family. That is not the subject of this book, but it is expected that readers will be able to go further in such investigations and comparisons of their own.

After I made some initial presentations of *Noah's Other Son* on the lecture circuit, Muslim student associations have invited me back to various American universities for dialogues on stage with their favorite imams, going right to the heart of these matters. And having initially done a Muslim book launch in the midst of the large Islamic community in the West Indies, I was asked to return to do programming on the Islamic Television Network based in Trinidad, illustrating the whole idea of deepening the common understanding of the Old and New Testament texts with the aid of the two diagrams. The Barr diagram of the opening chapters of the New Testament and a full-color presentation of my own diagram of the opening chapters of the Old Testament now make excellent visual aids for my presentation on TV. My prayer is that such resources may also enhance the Muslim understanding of their beloved Qur'an, as Jewish and Christian critical techniques become accepted in Islam, resulting in a similar diagram of benefit to us all.

In the future, with the assistance of Muslim scholars, I anticipate the completion of just such a diagram illustrating the different emphases of those chapters in the Qur'an that were produced in Mecca, as compared with those produced in Medina. In an analysis of the divinely inspired poem or psalm recitations given by God to Muhammad in the Cave of Hera and over the years, it is clear that many relate to his earlier caravan experiences. If indeed just as God used Muhammad's knowledge of the Arabic language, Allah was also addressing material not totally foreign to Muhammad. So the new Muslim diagram might compare the revelations relating to Muhammad's divinely inspired understanding of gnostic material with the material of Nestorian Christians in Syria; to Persian encounters among the Zoroastrians and again, further down the Arabian peninsula, with experiences of the desert monotheists known as the Hanifs. In addition, one color would identify those passages in the Qur'an that have parallels with the Hebrew Scriptures and another would delineate those clearly paralleling (or correcting, in the Muslim view) passages in the Christian New Testament.

There is nothing for orthodox Muslims to fear from such an enhanced appreciation of the text of the Qur'an, and nothing per se that challenges the belief that the inspiration for this material came to Muhammad with every detail straight from God through the angel Gabriel. We all have much to learn in these connections in an era of respectful interfaith studies. Muslims may grow in appreciation of the way God used the gifts he had already given to the Prophet—his mother tongue and his caravan experiences for example. Other members of Abraham's family may at last appreciate the miracle of revelation that the Qur'an represents to Muslims, to whom it seems clear that much of what Allah revealed perfectly in the Qur'an may have been revealed earlier to Jews, Christians, and even to Zoroastrians and others, and preserved by them in faithful or even in garbled form in their own Scriptures.

Meanwhile, theological education has changed in more ways than merely universities switching from anemic faculties of theology to robust departments of religious studies. Students preparing for ministry are not now required to be fluent in biblical languages, since half or more now enter theology in a midlife switch from another career, or in retirement, in the case of Muslims in North America. Many of them have undergraduate degrees or previous careers in disciplines like education, engineering, and commerce rather than in specific pretheology subjects, all of which may benefit the congregations they serve in our new times. This does not mean that there is no place for a scientific approach in theology, and it does not mean that such candidates for ministry need not be as well prepared as previously. They may be better suited for ministry in many respects, though they will always require the basics as represented by this introduction to the critical analysis of Scripture.

For example, St. Andrew's Theological College in Trinidad, a small seminary where I teach in the spring semester at present, has sixty-four students in training for ministry, four Anglican, two Methodist, and fifty-eight Presbyterian. Of these students, seventeen are in full-time degree programs leading to ordination, the majority coming into theology from other professions. Forty-seven others are in part-time diploma courses, during which they maintain positions in other jobs and professions. They all need a thorough grounding, and I hope the publication of this chart illustrating the sources of the Pentateuch may be welcomed with this explanatory text by them and by professors and by students in seminaries and colleges around the world. It is of value in both undergraduate and professional theological studies, as a short course summary of the techniques of biblical criticism suited to the variety of ministerial training tracks now available.

In dedicating this book to a class of seminary students and also to a congregational study group, I hope to make another point. The life of the whole church has changed in a similar way, as have biblical studies. In North America at least, through the twentieth century, church life in Christian denominations of the Protestant Reformation was centralized, or "centripetal" in momentum, with energies and money flowing toward a head office and institutions associated with centralized agendas. Roman Catholics and Orthodox Christians have always had that centralized perspective. Synagogue and mosque have never shared it, having national offices that act more as clearinghouses for dynamic local organizations. However, to the consternation of some, leadership of the North American Christian mainstream is shifting from a head-office mentality to a grassroots style in mission, money, and personnel, as well as in other activities, including theological training, in a decentralized centrifugal way of operating across the denominations. For those who survive this massive shift, congregations now need at least a semiprofessional level of resources available to members becoming lay workers, and I hope this book can provide something significant in that direction.

Anticipating this trend throughout my ministry, while teaming with a number of sterling ordained colleagues, I shared in the training of over a dozen lay workers for full time lay ministry. Our congregations benefited enormously from the gifts of those whose lay ministries are becoming part of a new norm in the twenty-first century. Most Christian denominations are acknowledging this with new semiprofessional designations recognizing the roles of such workers. Islamic schools and seminaries abound throughout the world, but formal training for Muslim clergy also resembles this twenty-first-century variety of approaches, in which recognition of gifts for ministry is at least as important as the formal and less-formal training. Many Sunni imams in North America have retired from engineering, medicine, teaching, and other professions and get their training for local ministries on the job.

Half of my locally trained lay workers eventually went on to formal training in traditional seminaries, but the point is that theological education is increasingly undertaken in a variety of settings, and resources need to be designed with this in mind. The apprenticeship model for training clergy has a long and honored history, which may now be integrated with the programs in the new robust departments of religion frequently housed in the beautiful old seminary buildings on campus. Indeed the seminary style of special training may function as a graduate school of these same departments, offering what is required for ordination in the denominations, specifically in those historically associated with particular universities, but not limited to them. These facts are important enough to call for resources to be available in the style and in the format of this book.

This study, *Forensic Scriptures*, and its "A Diagram of Sources of the Pentateuch" are thus well suited to clergy and laity in churches, synagogues, and mosques (or masjids, as many prefer), as well as by erstwhile professional scholars in the seminaries of Judaism, Christianity, and Islam. They have been incubating in that context for nearly half a century, and they appear now as aids for the growing masses of amateur (for-the-love-of-it) theologians who are increasingly leading church, synagogue, and masjid in the study of God's Word. This is not *Biblical Criticism for Dummies*, because this study presumes a thorough and intimate knowledge of the Scriptures on the part of students and readers, even those who did not notice the truncation of Genesis and Exodus on the front cover.

Like the "Diagram of Synoptic Relationships," the "Diagram of Sources of the Pentateuch" is basically a snapshot of a watershed turning point in research, a historical point from which so much more insight was derived in a field that is still developing. In itself, Wellhausen's Documentary

Hypothesis does not represent every twist and turn of contemporary scholarship, which continues to evolve. For purposes of this investigation, however, we will overlay the diagram with some of the very latest insights at the beginning of the twenty-first century, as explained in the chapters that follow, and apply the same to the embryonic "A Diagram of Revelations of Allah in the Holy Qur'an."

PART 1

Opening the Hebrew Scriptures

בְּרֵאשִׁית

א בְּרֵאשִׁית בָּרָא אֱלֹהִים אֵת הַשָּׁמַיִם וְאֵת הָאָרֶץ: וְהָאָרֶץ הָיְתָה תֹהוּ וָבֹהוּ וְחֹשֶׁךְ עַל־פְּנֵי תְהוֹם וְרוּחַ אֱלֹהִים מְרַחֶפֶת עַל־פְּנֵי הַמָּיִם: וַיֹּאמֶר אֱלֹהִים יְהִי אוֹר וַיְהִי־אוֹר: וַיַּרְא אֱלֹהִים אֶת־הָאוֹר כִּי־טוֹב וַיַּבְדֵּל אֱלֹהִים בֵּין הָאוֹר וּבֵין הַחֹשֶׁךְ: וַיִּקְרָא אֱלֹהִים לָאוֹר יוֹם וְלַחֹשֶׁךְ קָרָא לָיְלָה וַיְהִי־ ה עֶרֶב וַיְהִי־בֹקֶר יוֹם אֶחָד:

פ

וַיֹּאמֶר אֱלֹהִים יְהִי רָקִיעַ בְּתוֹךְ הַמָּיִם וִיהִי מַבְדִּיל בֵּין מַיִם לָמָיִם: וַיַּעַשׂ אֱלֹהִים אֶת־הָרָקִיעַ וַיַּבְדֵּל בֵּין הַמַּיִם אֲשֶׁר מִתַּחַת לָרָקִיעַ וּבֵין הַמַּיִם אֲשֶׁר מֵעַל לָרָקִיעַ וַיְהִי־כֵן: וַיִּקְרָא אֱלֹהִים לָרָקִיעַ שָׁמָיִם וַיְהִי־עֶרֶב וַיְהִי־בֹקֶר יוֹם שֵׁנִי:

פ

וַיֹּאמֶר אֱלֹהִים יִקָּווּ הַמַּיִם מִתַּחַת הַשָּׁמַיִם אֶל־מָקוֹם אֶחָד י וְתֵרָאֶה הַיַּבָּשָׁה וַיְהִי־כֵן: וַיִּקְרָא אֱלֹהִים ׀ לַיַּבָּשָׁה אֶרֶץ וּלְמִקְוֵה הַמַּיִם קָרָא יַמִּים וַיַּרְא אֱלֹהִים כִּי־טוֹב: וַיֹּאמֶר אֱלֹהִים תַּדְשֵׁא הָאָרֶץ דֶּשֶׁא עֵשֶׂב מַזְרִיעַ זֶרַע עֵץ פְּרִי עֹשֶׂה פְּרִי לְמִינוֹ אֲשֶׁר זַרְעוֹ־בוֹ עַל־הָאָרֶץ וַיְהִי־כֵן: וַתּוֹצֵא הָאָרֶץ דֶּשֶׁא עֵשֶׂב מַזְרִיעַ זֶרַע לְמִינֵהוּ וְעֵץ עֹשֶׂה־פְּרִי אֲשֶׁר זַרְעוֹ־בוֹ לְמִינֵהוּ וַיַּרְא אֱלֹהִים כִּי־טוֹב: וַיְהִי־עֶרֶב וַיְהִי־ בֹקֶר יוֹם שְׁלִישִׁי:

פ

וַיֹּאמֶר אֱלֹהִים יְהִי מְאֹרֹת בִּרְקִיעַ הַשָּׁמַיִם לְהַבְדִּיל בֵּין הַיּוֹם וּבֵין הַלָּיְלָה וְהָיוּ לְאֹתֹת וּלְמוֹעֲדִים וּלְיָמִים וְשָׁנִים: וְהָיוּ טו לִמְאוֹרֹת בִּרְקִיעַ הַשָּׁמַיִם לְהָאִיר עַל־הָאָרֶץ וַיְהִי־כֵן: וַיַּעַשׂ אלהים

GENESIS

1 When God began to create[a] heaven and earth—[2]the earth being unformed and void, with darkness over the surface of the deep and a wind from[b] God sweeping over the water—[3] God said, "Let there be light"; and there was light. [4]God saw that the light was good, and God separated the light from the darkness. [5]God called the light Day, and the darkness He called Night. And there was evening and there was morning, a first day.[c]

[6]God said, "Let there be an expanse in the midst of the water, that it may separate water from water." [7]God made the expanse, and it separated the water which was below the expanse from the water which was above the expanse. And it was so. [8]God called the expanse Sky. And there was evening and there was morning, a second day.

[9]God said, "Let the water below the sky be gathered into one area, that the dry land may appear." And it was so. [10]God called the dry land Earth, and the gathering of waters He called Seas. And God saw that this was good. [11]And God said, "Let the earth sprout vegetation: seed-bearing plants, fruit trees of every kind on earth that bear fruit with the seed in it." And it was so. [12]The earth brought forth vegetation: seed-bearing plants of every kind, and trees of every kind bearing fruit with the seed in it. And God saw that this was good. [13]And there was evening and there was morning, a third day.

[14]God said, "Let there be lights in the expanse of the sky to separate day from night; they shall serve as signs for the set times—the days and the years; [15]and they shall serve as lights in the expanse of the sky to shine upon the earth." And it was so. [16]God made the two great lights, the greater light to dominate the day and the lesser light to dominate the night, and the stars. [17]And God set them in the expanse of the sky to shine upon the earth, [18]to dominate the day and the night, and to separate light from darkness. And God saw that this was good. [19]And there was evening and there was morning, a fourth day.

[a] Others "In the beginning God created."
[b] Others "the spirit of."
[c] Others "one day."

1

Forensics

THE WORD "FORENSIC," FROM the Latin *forensis*, is derived from *forum*, referring to the place in ancient Rome where the court of public opinion, as well as the legal courts, heard evidence. The term requires the translation of "forensics" as "before the forum" or "before the courts." In our time, the most popular usage is perhaps when DNA evidence is brought forward. Medicine, engineering, and other scientific fields may contribute evidence to identify the body or to prove something to the jury or to the public. Ultimately the "grand jury" is the public who should feel themselves involved in the system of justice and the rule of law.

This is the case in the matter of what I have called scriptural DNA, "identifying the bodies of Scripture," in which we present evidence of the Bible's origins and purpose in the search for deeper understanding. I employ the forensic terminology in respect for the seriousness with which many in the Muslim community are taking the critical techniques of this science, and, for interest, I extend that terminology to the chapter headings as if scholarship itself and the scholars of Scripture were on trial.

The whole community of believers has always had a role in experiencing God's revelation in the Holy Bible, preserving it and transmitting it in a way that made it live in each generation. This happened through the long processes of inspiration, reciting, writing, and editing, through selecting books for inclusion in the sacred collection of the community, and even through groups of monks mass-producing copies by hand. God's spirit moved through the technology of human innovation when the Gutenberg printing press was invented to speed up the process. Its first product was the Bible. This led to even wider dissemination through the Bible Societies, and the demand grew for more meaningful translations, versions, and editions.

This exponential growth in demand led to the production of more translations and versions of the Bible during my lifetime than in all the years of history prior to my own birth and the birth of others of my generation. As the bestseller every year since Gutenberg, the Bible remains before the court of public opinion in our time, and we now have evidence of its origins that offer proof of its meaning and purpose.

Professors and students, rabbinical scholars and Sunday school teachers, all have roles to play with this "work in progress," an understanding of the nature of the Bible that I hope to elucidate. But it is finally in the heart and mind of each believer that God speaks through the Holy Spirit as these words are read or heard, and God's Word is given. The reader or hearer is as much a part of God's work in progress as the original writers, whether priests of old in Jerusalem or women who were the writers among the "people of the house" in Muhammad's time. Connecting the two is the task before us in this research. The diagrams depict the evidence in a way not unlike the graphic charts produced for famous trials like that of O. J. Simpson, which made certain aspects of evidence clear to the jury and even to the television audience. I hope to make things just that clear. I depend on the expert work of scriptural professionals, but for reasons given, it is equally important today to express these findings in street language for the readers who are the jury.

The chart depicting the sources of the Pentateuch is produced to investigate its origins and to illustrate its contents. It may equip those with less technical training than the professional scholar to understand and appreciate their own roles in this unfolding drama, much as a jury might consider itself part of the justice system that participates in the outcome of a trial. Every person, from writer to reader in the scriptural continuum, has an important God-given role to play.

Some may take these two charts of the opening books of the Old and New Testaments as the starting point in what may become a professional career in biblical scholarship. Others may take very seriously the challenge of producing a Qur'anic diagram based on the prototype that appears as a two-page spread in this publication. Most readers Jewish, Christian, and Muslim, may simply use these tools to become more comfortable and at home with the technical concepts of critical analysis of Scripture. This will hopefully undergird their faith, which may be already meaningful beyond any need of proof, but in a way which becomes especially delightful, even thrilling, with the benefit of a more complete understanding.

With the encouragement of my friend, Professor Reuven Firestone of the Hebrew Union College in Los Angeles, I continue to make occasional use of the term "Old Testament" to describe the "Hebrew Scriptures," the phrase deemed more politically correct in many circles. Professor Firestone frequently insists that the collection of Hebrew texts from Genesis to Malachi is also an Old Testament for modern Jews. Judaism as we know it, or "rabbinical Judaism" as it is sometimes called, is a new religion, separate from, and developed on the base of the Old Testament, making Jews, Christians, and Muslims all "supersessionist" in respect to the charge sometimes leveled against those believing that one religious movement supersedes another.

Rabbinical Judaism became the new religion of a majority of the Jewish people after the destruction of the Second Temple in 70 CE by the Romans. For centuries before this, the Judaism that produced the Old Testament Scriptures had centered on religious practice and sacrifices at the temple in Jerusalem, as prescribed in detail by the God of Israel in the *Tanakh* (the name by which this "Old Testament" is best known to-day among Jews). Without the temple as a center of worship and religious life, the Jews were unable to honor the temple practices described in the Hebrew Scriptures. Once they were in "diaspora" around the world, the Jews evolved their religion into an entirely new format and organization. This happened between the second and sixth centuries of the Common Era, producing a religion as new as Christianity itself. So the term "Old Testament" continues in use, to some extent, in both religions, and also in Islam, signifying its foundational role.

The sources that came together to produce the Old Testament were diverse. They were all powerfully and intimately connected to this people's recollections and experiences of their encounters with God. The people had a passion to tell that story, beginning with the divine encounter experienced by all humanity, represented by Adam and his family, and then their own communal and familial memories of the experiences of the family of Abraham, Sarah, and Hagar, followed by Moses and the slaves escaping to the desert in hopes of forming a new kind of country, and a variety of subsequent experiences in their quest to work out that destiny, including the Davidic monarchy, the division of the kingdom, the exile in Babylon and the return.

Summaries of that story abound, including my own attempt to tell it through the eyes of Jews, Christians, and Muslims, or through "Abraham's dysfunctional family" in *Noah's Other Son: Bridging the Gap Between the Bible and the Qur'an*. The great story of the Bible and its people is crystallized in a kingdom-building dream by David for Jews, in personal and corporate redemption in Jesus Christ for Christians, and in God's final revelation in the Qur'an given to Muhammad for Muslims.

There will be no attempt to retell that story here, but rather to set forth over a hundred years of scholarship concerning the Old Testament compendium of stories revered by all branches of this family: Jewish, Christian, and Muslim. In particular, this is done through a colorful diagram showing how a welter of sources was skillfully edited together into the Bible, the bestseller of all time. It is a foundational document of three religions and of Western culture, and a cornerstone of the world civilization that is emerging in the twenty-first century; therefore it deserves continued and growing attention.

Modeled in many respects on the similar diagram depicting the opening chapters of the New Testament that has been helpful to Christians for over seventy years now, my Old Testament diagram appears on the cover. The New Testament diagram by Allan Barr is included by permission on the back cover. A prototype of a "Diagram of the Revelations of Allah in the Holy Qur'an" occupies a similar place, with a full prototype appearing as a two-page spread near the conclusion of this publication.

Allan Barr chose white, pink, yellow, and blue as all the best colors for printing such a diagram representing Mathew, Mark, Luke, and Q, with a tiny note in green for a couple half verses of Mark omitted by the others. I have selected pink, green, blue, and yellow as effective and dramatically attractive in representing the J, E, D, and P sources of the Pentateuch, as explained in the introduction above and in the text that follows. In my Old Testament diagram, gray denotes minor editorial touches by the redactor who edited the whole compendium in its final form and as we have it in our Bibles.

There are many written commentaries on the Four Document Hypothesis (or simply the Documentary Hypothesis) and hundreds of variations, major and minor, in assigning verses to each of these sources. I do not attempt to adjudicate between the scholars who have made undoubted advances on the original, and I essentially limit myself to the delineations made by Julius Wellhausen in 1884, based in significant part on the work of his mentor, K. H. Graff in 1866. Mistakes there may be, and improvements are always welcome in this field of study, but it is the Graff-Wellhausen version of the Documentary Hypothesis that was the watershed in the development and acceptance of critical techniques, equipping students and scholars with the tools to understand and go further.

So in the diagram, I basically adhere to the original Graff-Wellhausen assignments of authorship, as delineated by the color code, and as summarized in a table by Stanley B. Frost in 1960. There are some exceptions when both *The Interpreter's Bible* and *The Anchor Bible* agree with the exceptions, and significant departures only where Richard Elliott Friedman convincingly overrules the other two in his turn-of-this-century masterworks on the subject, *Who Wrote the Bible?* and *The Bible with Sources Revealed* (2003), adopted with his acquiescence.

In this investigation there may be a tendency to sometimes lump Jews and Christians together with respect to critical techniques that they developed, not always jointly but certainly in tandem with each other. Jews and Christians are eager to share these techniques with Islamic scholars who have already signaled their interest. Jews and Christians are also increasingly intrigued by the traditional scholarship of Islam and eager to gain insights into the Qur'an for a range of reasons: to gain new information from this ancient lore about the *Sitz im Leben* of their own scriptural heritage, to experience spiritual growth inspired by a related scriptural tradition, and to improve familial relations within the still-dysfunctional family of Abraham, Sarah, and Hagar.

From the Qur'an and the Hadith we learn about Mary's parents and her priestly vocation under the sponsorship of her uncle, Zechariah; we learn details about the Bible's mysterious Sabeans; we learn of Noah's fourth son, Canaan; we learn the names of women in the Bible like Pharaoh's wife/daughter, Asiya, who adopted Moses; we learn of Potiphar's wife, Zulaika, who entrapped Joseph; and we learn of Bilqis, the Queen of Sheba. From Islamic Scriptures we obtain a view of Gnostic writings and of material from the Gospel of Thomas that is similar to a vogue in both current secular literature and the media. There are even Islamic images reflecting the Gnostic and other hetrodox views of the Christian Messiah.

Possibly the most exciting aspect of Qur'anic study with the aid of critical techniques is a growing appreciation of the Qur'an as a template of scriptural compilation. It is an accessible model of scriptural formation from the last major culture to spring from the ancient Middle East, indeed from the same Abrahamic family as the Bible, and one in which reliable information about scriptural development has never disappeared from public view.

To illustrate the model, Muslims believe Muhammad was illiterate, making it probable that nearly all surahs of the Qur'an were written down by the women of his household, one of whom was entrusted with its preservation and transmission to the world. We will examine her story. The Hadith is a later collection presenting conversations, acts, and habits of the Prophet of Islam as recorded by his Companions, including many women, some of whom are to be documented in this investigation.

Study of these materials does not rely on archaeology, secondary sources, or conjecture. Islamic primary sources, under rigorous reevaluation by Islamic scholars today, have a potential to reveal whole new paradigms that may now be applied to biblical texts as Jews and Christians consider the scriptural roles of women among the prophets, priests, apostles, and companions. These matters will be examined from the perspectives of the scholarly community in the whole extended family, in such a manner that laypeople and students will be brought completely into the conversation.

While what we can share is the main subject of this endeavor, it might be appropriate to touch briefly and simply on the essential ways in which Jewish, Christian, and Muslim understandings of Scripture differ. For Jews, the Word of God became community, in a people for whom ethnicity, language, and religion are fused. For Christians, the Word of God became flesh in Jesus of Nazareth, the Messiah or Christ, the Savior of the world. For Muslims, the Word of God, kept in heaven on a golden tablet, became the words of the Qur'an. These traditions of Abraham's family are closely related, but we will benefit more from what we can share if we understand and appreciate one another's perspectives.

2

Identity Theft?

F OR MANY CENTURIES, THROUGH the Middle Ages and beyond, Jews and Christians believed that Moses wrote the first five books of the Bible, a sacred tradition enhanced by the much-later pious addition of his name in the title of each book. These books are often called the Pentateuch, meaning "five scrolls." They form the essence of the Hebrew Torah and even the King James Version of the Bible refers to them as the First, Second, Third, Fourth and Fifth Books of Moses, though none of the Hebrew manuscripts bears such a title. Muslims also generally accepted the tradition that Moses wrote the Pentateuch.

The Pentateuch itself does not give any indication that these books were written by Moses, and although the book of Deuteronomy purports to be four speeches by Moses, the rest of this collection uniformly speaks of him in the third person as if he were someone different from the writer.

To illustrate, in Numbers 12:3 we read, "Now the man Moses was very meek, more than all men that were on the face of the earth." If Moses actually wrote that, he was certainly not meek. Either the statement is untrue, or Moses himself did not write that verse. Or take Deuteronomy 34 where we have an account of Moses's death and burial. We have heard of people who have written their own obituaries, but no one else has ever described their own funeral and remarked that the grave has been lost sight of "to this day" (v. 6). Moses could not have written this, nowhere does the Bible say he did, and there is no need for believers to suppose or pretend that he did write these books. But that takes us to the intriguing question of who did write these books, and why.

Biblical "criticism" or analysis is one of the world's most engaging detective stories. There were hints of its pursuit in the early centuries of the Common Era, but not enough to establish a pattern. A medieval Jewish physician named Isaac ibn Yashush presented the problem of ascribing authority to Moses to the court scholars in Muslim Spain. He pointed out that a list of Edomite kings appearing in Genesis 36 gave the names of monarchs who lived long after the biblical account of Moses's death. He suggested that this must have been written by someone who lived after Moses. A medieval Spanish rabbi named Abraham ibn Ezra gave Isaac the nickname "Isaac the Blunderer" and suggested that the book written by ibn Yashush should be burned.

But the genie was out of the bottle, and the question would not go away. Even Ibn Ezra continued to have doubts of his own, as could be found in his later writings. He alluded to a probable "alternate" author who wrote about Moses in the third person, described places that Moses had never been to, and used terms that Moses would not have known. He was not willing to make this claim outright though, for he wrote, "If you understand, you will recognize truth . . . and he who understands will keep silent." This nervousness about critiquing the Scriptures or analyzing them overmuch was not overcome until our own era. The Bible was usually kept under lock and key through the Middle Ages, and its secrets were only revealed progressively, until today when we can let the Bible speak on its own terms. The study of the Qur'an is into a similar pattern at the present time.

The next to take up the question about the authorship of the Pentateuch was a Protestant Reformer, Martin Luther's colleague, Andreas Rudolf Bodenstein, known as Carlstadt. He drew attention to Genesis 12:6, where we read that "the Canaanite was then in the land," obviously a part of Genesis written by someone after David had rid the area of the Canaanite inhabitants, who were still there when Moses would have been writing.

Carlstadt was followed by the Spanish Jesuit Pereira, who raised a similar question about the story in Genesis 14:14, where Abraham pursues Lot's captors "as far as the city of Dan." He concluded this must have been written after the Hebrew conquest, since Dan was known as Laish in the time of Moses. This discrepancy would be like a document purporting to be written by one of the Dutch founders of New Amsterdam but somehow calling the place New York, an absolute giveaway that the document came after the British conquest.

In 1651 the English scholar Thomas Hobbes came right out in his *Leviathan* with the conclusion that someone other than Moses must have written the Pentateuch. In the same century, Baruch Spinoza, a Dutch philosopher who was expelled from the Jewish community for his pains, and yet another Roman Catholic priest, Richard Simon, severely reprimanded for his findings, studied the matter in detail. Both came to the conclusion that the Pentateuch was composed of several separate documents edited together, but neither quite realized that there could have been several separate writers. Until the middle of the eighteenth century, the pieces of the puzzle were being identified, but no one was able to put them together.

Then in 1753, a French physician, Jean Astruc, poring over the evidence, noticed something about the divine names "God" (*Elohim* or *Eloh* in Hebrew) and "Jehovah," (more correctly spelled as *Yahweh* and written as LORD in many English translations). The names were not used indiscriminately, but a block of verses using "God" would often be followed by a block using "LORD." Astruc was able to distinguish two major strands of material, and scholars began to call these two authors E and J, for *Elohim* and *Jehovah*. They were different enough to indicate two authors or editors, and Astruc later postulated the existence of more possible "sources" of documents that make up the Pentateuch as we know it. At least two other European scholars came to essentially the same conclusion.

Immediately after this conclusion was established, a number of things made sense for the first time. Why had Genesis 6:19 said that two of every sort of creature went into Noah's ark, when Genesis 7:2 said that seven pairs of clean animals entered? How else do we explain that Abraham had trouble with the king of Gerar over his wife, Sarah, and that then read of the identical situation occurring respecting Isaac, his wife, Rebecca, and the king of Gerar? Similarly, why would Abraham be involved in a dispute that led to a well being called Beer-Sheba in Genesis 21:31, and Isaac be involved in a dispute with the same result, the naming of the well Beer-Sheba, in Genesis 26:33? And did Joseph's brothers sell him to Ishmaelites (Gen 37:27), or did Midianite traders find him in the well and sell him in a transaction unknown to his brothers (Gen 37:28)? These and dozens of other seeming discrepancies are easily resolved when we recognize that two or more tribal folk-story versions are involved here, woven together in a richly textured fabric.

Somebody had edited a collection of ancient documents together with the same skill that the writer of the Gospel of Luke employed in gathering materials from different source documents to produce the final work. In the opening of the Gospel of Luke, the writer acknowledges the investigation and use of various sources and eyewitness accounts regarding the life of Jesus Christ (see Luke 1:1–4), and it is now clear that we have something very similar in the monumental production of the opening books of the Old Testament.

These tribal recollections, eventually written down and edited together, present God's Word as a many-faceted diamond, with depth and beauty reflected from many angles, despite natural flaws in its intricate parts. Humanity's connection with the Divine was consistent, however remembered, and humanity itself had a role in bringing these gems to light, into the era of written literature of the most sacred kind.

For Jews and Christians, the development of this understanding of how their Scriptures came into existence has involved a deepened appreciation for the ways in which God has entrusted the transmission of the Divine Word to the whole community of believers, as well as to its divinely inspired prophets and leaders, each in their definitive roles. The final editor of the Pentateuch treated the sources with the greatest respect and was used by the Holy Spirit to transmit the material to us. We must read it with both respect for the sources and the guidance of the Holy Spirit in understanding and applying the meaning of the message revealed to us by the Word of God as conveyed through the words of the people who wrote, edited, and preserved these Scriptures.

As we shall see later in this investigation, reading does not refer to mere private digestion or to the study of words, but also to audible expression and experience. Considered variously as a sibling of Christianity and Islam, almost their parent in certain respects, or even a grandparent in terms of antiquity of the tradition, Judaism has perhaps the greatest range of experience with reading and expressing the word of God. Some of my favorite examples in these regards are cited by Karen Armstrong on pages 188 and 189 of her insightful *The Bible: A Biography*. The quotations are not principally from her, but with obtuse documentation that can be seen better there than here, she tells the stories of two less mainstream though influential strands of Jewish experience, when Kabbalism encountered the Hasidic tradition.

> One day, the Besht [Israel ben Eliezer (1696–1760, leader of the Hasidim, "the pious ones")] was visited by Dov Ber (1716–72), a learned kabbalist who would eventually succeed him as leader of the Hasidic movement. The two men studied Torah together and became immersed in a text about the angels. Dov Ber approached the passage in a rather abstract way and the Besht asked him to show respect for the angels they were discussing by standing up.

As soon as he rose to his feet, "the whole house was suffused with light, a fire burned all around, and they [both] sensed the presence of the angels." "The simple reading is as you say," the Besht told Dov Ber, "but your manner of studying lacked soul." A common-sense reading, without the attitudes and gestures of prayer, would not yield a vision of the unseen.

Without such prayer, Torah study was useless. As one of Dov Ber's disciples explained, Hasidim must read scripture "with burning enthusiasm of the heart, with a coercion of all man's psychological faculties in the direction of clear and pure thoughts on God constantly, and in separation from every pleasure." The Besht told them that if they approached the story of Mount Sinai in this way, they would "always hear God speak to them, as he did during the revelation on Sinai, because it was Moses's intention that all Israel be worthy of attaining the same level as he did." The point was not to read *about* Sinai but to experience Sinai itself. (Armstrong, *The Bible: A Biography*, 189)

3

Interrogation

THESE OBSERVATIONS ARE BASED on simple but crucial forensic techniques. We become familiar with these classic methods of critical analysis as we first examine the Pentateuch and Synoptic Gospels (the first three books of the New Testament) with the aid of tools developed for that purpose. These tools have been honed over the course of the last one hundred and fifty years in particular, and now it is said that we have come to the end of the critical era, as scholars, pastors, and spiritual leaders look more for how we should live out the meaning of the texts than for their provenance or origin. Scripture does have more for our lives than its authorship, context, or even its original purpose. We will revisit the importance of traditional critical understandings, even in a postcritical era, but first let us introduce a final critical enterprise, a technique new to many of us, called rhetorical criticism.

Plato, the Greek philosopher, was among the first to use rhetorical criticism as a technique of investigation. In the *Phaedrus*, Plato has Socrates examine a speech by Lysias to determine whether or not it seemed authentic to Socrates, based on the way it sounds. Does it ring true, and is it therefore credible on that basis, regardless of the strength of the argument? Undergraduate students of classical Greek are often called upon to translate a tiny work called *Ion*, in which Plato has Socrates interviewing requesting various people to compare the poems of this illiterate sailor, Ion, to their knowledge of his normal speech in his home port—as possibly a proof for the existence of the Muses, whose words Ion was now presenting in his new status as village poet. It seemed clear that it was not their old friend talking, so the poetry seemed legitimate and genuinely from a quasi-divine source.

Rhetorical criticism analyzes verbal artifacts such as words, phrases, and songs—even indications of emphasis and tone—to discover how they work: how they instruct, inform, entertain, move, arouse, perform, convince, and, in general, persuade their hearers, including whether and how they might impact a wider audience. In short, rhetorical criticism seeks to understand how words affect people. The Qur'an is without doubt a most important example of words in recitation as the vehicle for God's self-revelation through human vehicles. Its evocative tones resonate in an experience of the holy that frequently seems to surpass the meaning of the words. The Qur'an is memorized in Arabic before being understood simply because of its calming and empowering affect on the one who recites it.

The discipline of rhetorical criticism has been used to analyze various literatures but has only recently been applied to biblical studies under the influence of American scholars such as James Muilenburg, Phyllis Trible, George Kennedy, Wilhelm Wullner, Vernon K. Robbins and Ben Witherington III—and especially Walter Brueggemann. Brueggemann is known to many from his appearances in Bill Moyers's PBS television series *Genesis*, at the turn of the new century and by his twentieth-century bestsellers, including *Cadences of Home* and *The Bible Makes Sense*. Brueggemann popularizes the techniques of rhetorical criticism and makes them accessible to the public, even while attributing the revival of this discipline mainly to Muilenburg. The roots of rhetorical criticism, one of the most exciting contributions to studies like this investigation, and a technique we will attempt to apply, may be of interest here especially as we approach the Muslim contribution in this field.

> It is commonly recognized in Scripture study, and more particularly in Old Testament study, that James Muilenburg is the primary figure in the emergence of rhetorical criticism as an identifiable undertaking. Muilenburg was trained in literary studies before he came to Scripture studies, so that he approaches the texts with knowing literary and artistic sensitivity. He knew, at the outset of his biblical scholarship, that nothing is accidental in literary articulation, but that artistic intentionality generates always fresh interpretive possibility. In 1968 he presented his discipline-defining lecture titled *Form Criticism and Beyond*, in which he proposed rhetorical criticism as a practice of reading texts in ways that paid careful attention to detailed rhetorical matters that marked turns and accents. He understood that it is the detail of the text and the precise cadences of speech that matter to the intention of the text. Thus he paid special attention to the repetition of words and sounds, to conjunctions and prepositions that turned statements

in odd ways, to the intentional use of the great freighted words of faith, and to the careful and judicious placement of the divine name in the text.

Muilenburg's work can only be appreciated if it is seen in the context of dominant interpretive methods in his day, which were largely preoccupied with historical questions. In that dominant mode of scholarship, it is not an overstatement to say that little attention was paid to the text in its utterance. (Brueggemann, *Cadences of Home*, 58)

The Bible has always been important in silent, private reading and in public reading aloud but has rarely been studied by professionals from the approach of the audible sound, at least not with the aid of scholarly tools. Muilenburg was researching his method at the very time my classmates and I were struggling with the methods that sought to expand our understanding by examining what had happened behind the text, and in reconstructing the historical and archaeological evidence. No one then anticipated the urgent necessity of taking the Qur'an into account, or the way in which it would come into our agenda in the twenty-first century.

Students in the 1960s might have been warmed by a greater ability to relate the text, as they heard it daily in the chapel, applying its sound to studies in the classroom and the laboratory. Undergraduate students today, seminarians, and laypeople studying the Bible in the congregational setting, will be even more appreciative of this new development in the changing circumstances of the religious institutions to which they belong.

The context of the twenty-first century now more accurately mirrors the scriptural story: the disenfranchisement of the Jewish people throughout much of their history; the persecuted minority role of the dynamic Christian church in the Roman Empire, and elsewhere more recently; the denigration of Islam by the rest of the family, thanks to both Western prejudice and the actions of Islamic extremists; and the stress that faithful Muslims experience in our time. We can relate to the speeches in Scripture, whether to Ezra's reading from the Pentateuch for the first time in public as the Judean society rebuilt, or the book of Revelation's offering comfort and final justice to persecuted Christians in Rome. Words on a page do not have the same impact as words in an audible cry from the heart.

The main spoken addresses of interest in the Pentateuch are those by Moses, in particular the series of his purported speeches in the book of Deuteronomy. Students and other readers are invited to undertake "close readings" of these speeches, that is, to read aloud, deliberately, with close attention to each word and each phrase as it might have sounded when delivered, not merely as written. Having examined these speeches, readers might compare them to a similar experience of Moses's speeches in the other books of the Pentateuch. Moses may not have literally written any of them, but are there "trace particles" of Mosaic style, emphasis, meaning, and purpose; or do Moses's speeches come from two entirely different sources, with either source or neither source being Moses; do the sources present identical, similar, or different agendas?

To get a sense of who is who and what is what in the Pentateuch, readers can then go on to examine and compare speeches by others, such as Abraham, Jacob, and Joseph, or Sarah, Hagar, and the other women, to get a sense of the personas of the characters, of the authors, or both. Parables of Jesus that move us, like the Good Samaritan or the Prodigal Son, can bring tears to our eyes, but have that effect less when we read them silently and more when we hear them, read them aloud, or recite them. As a result, we get a feel for the authenticity of Jesus that some of the scholars of the so-called Jesus Seminar, poring over the written texts, may find difficult to understand.

The place where Christians and Jews have cherished this rhetorical experience is in the Psalms, which continue in virtually all traditions and denominations. The content of certain psalms is frequently questioned, and occasionally students and others wonder why they remain a prominent part of weekly worship. But it is precisely because of the traction they gain in the human heart through audible communal expression and aural impact. The intention now is to expand something of the same encounter with the Divine to other elements of Scripture.

In *A Pathway to Interpretation*, Walter Brueggemann introduces a new criterion for Old Testament studies, with specific examples to enable readers to apply the techniques of rhetorical criticism to specific Bible passages in ways that draw out their meanings, providing a bridge between the eras of critical scholarship and postcritical biblical studies. That new criterion is a successful blending of ancient rhetorical principles with the devotional approach illustrated by the Kabbalist and Hasidic leaders in the last chapter. Other critical techniques are included as a subtext in this approach, which is illustrated with copious examples.

So rhetorical criticism deserves consideration in our investigation, without overshadowing the presentation of the original Graff-Wellhausen material, as a clear example of the ways in which higher criticism continues to enrich the field of biblical study. I am especially anxious to include it because of its affinity to the growing interest in "lower criticism" of the Qur'an, where the actual sounds of the Scripture are universally acknowledged to be part of the experience.

Muslim scholars are far ahead of others in this regard, with a whole body of material presenting frequent reference to the different tone and style of Muhammad when he speaks for God in the Qur'an as compared to when he speaks in his own voice, as quoted in the Hadith. The Qur'an is not so much for reading as for reciting and hearing, and this may also be more of our biblical heritage than has been realized until recently.

On my wall I have certificates dated 1906 and 1923, when my grandmother and my mother were recognized by the Presbyterian Church for their accomplishments respecting the memorization and recitation of Scripture as children in two bygone generations when people memorized whole books of the Bible. It was an entirely different religious environment from the one in which I, my children, and my grandchildren grew up. Rhetorical criticism is a tool we will attempt to apply to our investigation in modest ways at least.

4

Prime Suspect

IN HIS 1990 BESTSELLER, *The Book of J*, Harold Bloom asserts that the J material was written up by just one writer, a collector of the sacred stories of the kingdom of Judah. He gives that writer the stature of Homer, Shakespeare, or Tolstoy, and he puts forth the revolutionary idea that the author of J was probably a woman, quite possibly a daughter of King David. In proposing a daughter of David as the author of the J document, America's great literary critic confesses that the concept is possibly "fiction." Actually, all guesses, even educated guesses, as to the personal identities of any of the contributors to the Pentateuch are speculative, including the notion that Moses wrote the whole thing. But perhaps there is more to Bloom's idea of female authorship in the Pentateuch than many, including Bloom himself, care to recognize.

The Bible itself recognizes a role for women who were storytellers and songwriters. In the Introduction to the Anchor Bible commentary on Ruth, Edward Campbell lays the groundwork for an understanding that has evolved since 1975. He begins by citing Hermann Gunkel's assertion that many of the "legends" in the Old Testament have a defined style that suggests there must have been a class of professional storytellers, like those in the surrounding Arab culture that have bequeathed their tales to the world through *Arabian Nights*. Campbell goes on the ask who those storytellers might have been and answers that they were countryside Levites and "wise women." He documents this role of the Levites in Scripture and continues:

> The other possibility, that the story-tellers were wise women, is not as easy to document. We start from the story in II Samuel 1–20, in which Joab selects a wise woman from Tekoah as the one to weave a story for King David, which turns out to be allegorical, in order to persuade him to bring Absalom back to court . . . One cannot

help wondering, then, whether this woman was chosen precisely for her quick wits and for her reputation for telling stories well. A story within a story, and a wise woman at the center of it!

Still within the Court History of David (II Sam 9–20) there appears another wise woman, the one who persuades the town of Abel-beth-maacah to turn over the rebel Sheba to Joab (20:14–22) . . .

Finally, there are the words of the "wisest" of the women around Sisera's mother, in Judges 5:29–30 . . . Women as singers in Israel are a well-documented phenomenon, especially in victory and mourning song (Miriam in Exodus 15:21; Deborah in Judges 5:12, Jephthah's daughter in Judges 11:34).

. . . May these women, especially these "wise women," be a locus of the story-telling art in ancient Israel? (Campbell, *Ruth*, 22–23)

André LaCocque, in his commentary on Ruth, provides a sustained argument regarding the female authorship of the book. And he does the same for Song of Songs in *Romance, She Wrote!*

Richard Elliott Friedman claims that the document we know as J was actually compiled or written by a woman. At the very time Friedman was working on *Who Wrote the Bible?* Carol Meyers was writing her landmark feminist analysis, *Discovering Eve*. This distinguished biblical archaeologist at Duke University goes so far as to say concerning the story of Eve, "The artful crafting of that simple yet powerful narrative is inextricably linked to the life experience of the Hebrew author. The world around him (or her?) contributed to the choice of words, characterizations and motifs" (Meyers, *Discovering Eve*, 4).

After presenting evidence that the author of E was almost certainly male, in his fuller answer to this question, Friedman writes:

The case is much harder to judge with regard to J. Originating at—or at least reflecting the interests of—the Judean court, it came from a circle in which both men and women had a certain status. That is, even in a male-led society, women of the noble class may have more power, privileges and education than males of a lower class. The possibility of J's being by a woman is thus much more likely than with E. There is really nothing in the E story to compare with the J story of Tamar in Genesis 38. It is not just that the woman Tamar figures in an important way in the story. It is that the story is sympathetic to a wrong done to this woman, it focuses on her plan to combat the injustice, and it concludes with the man in the story (Judah) acknowledging her rights and his own fault.

> This does not make the author a woman. But it does mean that we
> cannot by any means be quick to think of this writer as a man. The
> weight of the evidence is still that the scribal profession in ancient
> Israel was male, true, but that does not exclude the possibility that
> a woman might have composed a work that came to be loved and
> valued in that land. (Friedman, *Who Wrote the Bible?* 86)

Could it be that, intrigued with the notion of female authorship in the
Pentateuch as it became public, Bloom brought all his abilities in literary
analysis together in taking a stab at this theory—giving it the benefit of
well-honed literary skill, unerring instinct, and seasoned intuition? We are
now in a position to add forensic credence to Meyers's question, Friedman's
conjecture, and Bloom's instinct, and to possibly shed light on this issue
from another source entirely.

The dating of J to sometime after 900 BCE, perhaps soon after Solomon's
reign, is widely accepted. The author was certainly someone who treasured
the stories of the kingdom's origins, and Bloom speculates that she shared
David's patriotic vision and nation-building kingdom-building agenda. He
notes that the J material actually does contain much more about hearth
and home and women's concerns than do E, D, or P. Bloom observes that
J also discusses the circumstances of wealthy, educated women in ancient
times who had particular opportunity for writing, while the leading men of
the time were engaged in conducting business, governing, and waging war.
These observations will be placed in subsequent chapters alongside similar
indications from the oldest Islamic documents we believe may have been
penned by women.

The royal household was clearly the most literate venue in the kingdom, with the editing and production of the books of Psalms and Proverbs,
in whatever proportion we may actually assign these tasks to our subject's
father and brother, David and Solomon respectively. Literate males at court
may have had greater input in accounting and the writing of records, but it is
the internal rhetorical evidence in the literature that may eventually seal the
argument in favor of a female author or editor of the stories. Carol Meyers
has established the profile of ancient Israelite women in their households,
including the prevalence of religious and other homespun oral traditions.
In an e-mail to me, on reviewing an early draft of this material, in late 2008
she wrote:

> The ancient story-telling art that produced the family stories of
> Genesis, which J wrote down, may have been women. J may have

created an overall style and coherence to those narratives, but she was almost certainly working from existing oral tradition, produced by female storytellers. The reason that there are so many female characters in Genesis (and not all that many in the rest of the Pentateuch, except for J sections in the first 2 chapters of Exodus) is that Genesis deals with individual families, whereas the rest of the Hebrew Bible deals with collective Israel or with the elites (priestly and royal families). It's not just that the rest of the Bible is sexist; it's that the subject matter has a national orientation, which leaves out ordinary women (and men!).

These points will be supported by the newly appreciated Muslim paradigm of frequent or even usual writing of Scripture by women, with some of Bloom's points merely indicating her likely identity or family connection. For the moment we will focus on the author of J as if she were the daughter of David, even though the case we will make is not strong in itself without the support of the Muslim template and probabilities in the other parts of the Bible yet to be considered.

The author of J was a literary genius with unmatched powers of irony and characterization, as shown throughout her work. But in our viewing her work on the "Diagram of Sources of the Pentateuch," something else about her subject matter jumps off the chart, something unique in ancient documents from all sources, biblical and otherwise. Without this diagram, her clear focus on the profile of women has not been as widely observed as it might have been. For example, the opening creation story in chapter 1 of Genesis comes from P, with a generic inclusion of all elements of the universe. But alone in the creation accounts from primitive sources around the world, Genesis 2, from J, tells the story of the first woman, the figure of Eve as the prototypical wife and the mother of all. This itself is remarkable; but unforgettable portraits of a range of other female characters amount to written evidence akin to what is called gender speech in these forensic investigations.

Gender speech represents the cutting edge of rhetorical analysis at this moment in literary criticism, in biblical studies, and elsewhere. Gender speech, as a tool of rhetorical criticism, is so fresh that it is known by several names so far: sociolinguistics, gender language, and gender phonetics being the main alternatives.

In many languages, and across most language groups, independent of masculine and feminine nouns and pronouns, there are separate and distinct rhythms, inflections, and special words that are used by only one gender. Recent studies illustrate traces of this trend in all languages, English and Hebrew included. Females frequently speak in a pattern that is distinct from the speech of males, a distinction that sometimes carries over into writing styles in ways that can be documented.

Nancy Bonvillain gives examples of this fact in the Japanese language in her landmark study, *Language, Culture and Communication*, which, admittedly, is limited to certain parts of the Japanese countryside.

- The word "eat" is *taberu* when spoken by a woman, and *kuu* in the mouth of a man.

- "Delicious" comes out as *oisii* from the lips of a female, and it is *umai* to a male speaker.

- The "stomach" where the food winds up is *onaka* to a woman and *hara* to a man.

- Some "water to wash it down" is *ohiya* and *mizu* to the respective genders.

In *An Introduction to Sociolinguistics*, Alan Bell and Janet Holmes illustrate this reality beginning with indigenous languages in New Zealand. In the following example there is a distinct form of speech when males are speaking to other males, as compared to a common form when females speak, or when males address females:

"Dear" is *ba* in common parlance but becomes *ba-na* when addressed from one male friend to another dear friend.

"Person" is *yaa* in the shared language but becomes *yaa-na* when it is "mano a mano," as we say.

Bell and Holmes also have a chapter called "Politeness Strategies in New Zealand Women's Speech," which illustrates how this practice has transferred over into English in that mixed culture. The investigation has not progressed very far in the study of English generally, but the following examples have been vetted by my grandchildren, and are offered to the reader to determine if the gender of the speaker can be identified:

> What a beautiful home; you should be very happy here.
> Nice place; must have cost you a fortune.
>
> Cool shirt, dude.
> That's a lovely blouse.

That's a nice car. I love the color.
Nice wheels!

Shiny shoes, man!
I like your shoes; where did you buy them?

My examples, of course, are from colloquial speech, not literary language. But such differences in linguistic register between male and female speakers, narrators, or authors may also appear in folk stories when they are written down. Even more helpful is an interesting insight given to me by my daughter Indira, who has worked with men and women in various corporate executive-development programs. Indira has pointed out typical differences in communication styles between men and women, which sometimes become a focus for coaching.

> In communicating with others, women leaders are often coached
> to be more individually assertive because they tend not to take
> credit for what they have and are achieving. They will tend to use
> the word "we" and very rarely the term "I," even when it is their
> own individual work they are discussing. With men, the difficulty
> is reversed. Men are often coached not to inappropriately overuse
> the word "I," and make much more use of the term "we," which is
> more a signal of a collaborative, team-playing approach.

Obviously the discipline of gender-speech analysis is in its early stages in English, and I believe the same may be true in respect to biblical Hebrew. Work remains to identify female speech markers in biblical Hebrew (beyond "content" and "it sounds like a woman"), but even now we can begin to analyze the J document from these elemental perspectives of sociolinguistics or gender speech. When we do, it appears increasingly possible that Harold Bloom's well-informed instincts and educated intuitions are correct, regardless of certain deficiencies in established norms of biblical criticism. J was indeed in all probability written by a woman, judging by the content and the ironic tone of voice in the text, as may be observed in what follows.

5

Lineup

THE FOLLOWING WORD PICTURES and female portraits are all from sections everyone identifies as from J, and nothing similar is found in E, D, P, or anywhere else in the literature of the ancient world. While this material is indeed skillfully edited and blended into the larger compendium, it is incredible that after over a hundred years of working with what I call the documentary evidence, no one has yet taken sufficient note of the unique intensity and the exclusive extent of this interest in women and women's concerns, not even the illustrious Dr. Bloom. This distinction in the J material stands out clearly when charted in the "Diagram of Sources of the Pentateuch."

Below is a list of female characters introduced or uniquely detailed by the J document.

THE WOMEN OF THE J DOCUMENT

Eve

Unique among stories of human origins, the description of Eve contains the powerful paradox of a woman in a subordinate position contending with the challenges of life represented by the serpent and the tree of knowledge, who then gets blamed for all that unfolds as a consequence of those challenges. Perhaps she blames herself, but this is an ironic tone of voice that colors each of the female portraits by David's unnamed daughter. Without references to the contrary, we may assume that the name Eve, Mother of us all, came from the inspired mind and pen of our author, to match up with the name of Adam.

Eve's Daughters

They are not named, but they are included as a reminder of the constant female presence (Gen 5:4), unlike all other records. Our author does this in each generation of the stories of famous men she has inherited from the oral history of campfire stories, which she is about to collate into this first prototype of Scripture.

Adah and Tzilah

The generations continue until she reaches the wives of Lamech (mythically the four-times great-grandson of Eve), the first female names given to her by history in a whisper (Gen 4:19–22). These two are the mothers of musicians and metal workers, among others, and their names are enshrined here to make the point that such inventors were as much children of their mothers as of their famous fathers—again that ironic whimsy.

Sarah

There was enough known about Sarah in relation to her husband that the author can actually paint a full portrait: a sour woman, with good reason. She was barren and exploited, laughing in derision at God, but able to somehow hold her own in spite of everything.

Hagar

Here the ironies of life are painted in full color. The woman who is despised in the biblical tradition is the one to whom God makes the promise of matriarchy (more offspring than can be counted . . . Arab nations and Muslims), every bit as extravagant as God's promise of patriarchy to Abraham, but a promise (Gen 16:10) the world is only now beginning to recognize and perhaps appreciate.

Keturah

In old age, Abraham married a young wife who gave him several times as many children as Sarah and Hagar had (Gen 25:2). As Jews, Christians, and Muslims may know, the six sons of Keturah became the ancestors of the tribes of Arabia (1 Chron 1:32–33). I have benefited immensely from the worthy study, *Hagar, Sarah and Their Children: Jewish, Christian and Muslim Perspectives*, by Phyllis Trible, Letty Russell, and others. It is the author of J, however, who reflects the consciousness that Abraham had far more children by other women than the two given birth by Hagar and Sarah. Someone needs to write a book about the children of Keturah, who have fallen between the cracks.

Lot's Wife

We all know this story, and the ironies escape no one, but the skillful portrayal of this woman in a few deft phrases takes a scrap of history or memory and makes it memorable.

Lot's Daughters

This despicable pair accepted God's grace, only to seduce their drunken father and produce offspring who became the enemies of the Israelite people, and of King David, to whom our author is loyal almost to a fault, as seen by the portrayal of this pair. Indeed, any tribe or nation with whom David fought came in for rough treatment from the author of the J material.

Rebecca

We know Isaac's cunning wife especially well through her maneuvering role in gaining the birthright for her favorite son. She knows the ability of her sons, and in order to further the best interests of the family, Rebecca, like many disempowered women after her, had to work subtly and sometimes with cunning. Our author understands this as no male author could ever grasp.

Rachel

Jacob's favorite wife brings this same cunning to the service of her husband and her own future in safeguarding the sacred artifacts during their escape from her father. These *teraphim* may have been household idols representing her father's family deities. More than family heirlooms, they had a power that Willard Oxtoby compared with the "corporate seals" of the family business. Jacob loves Rachel in a special way, and she produces the heirs to the promise. The Bible reports that the tomb of Rachel, the mother of the people, had its own site in Bethlehem, some distance from the rest of the family, all interred with Abraham and Sarah at Machpelah. Rachel is a key figure in modern Judaism and various Jewish and even Christian streams of Kabbalah, in which modern feminists make pilgrimage to that traditional tomb site, revered also by Muslims.

Leah

Jacob's first wife offers enough irony for both sisters and their competing surrogate concubines, but there is some pathos about Leah, always trying harder but never quite succeeding. Many women could relate to her.

Dinah

Our author did not have to dig hard to find the story of the rape of Dinah, since the aftermath had seared the kingdom, but she drew out the irony from the communal recollection that Dinah was loved by the Egyptian prince who ravished her, and possibly that Dinah loved him, or might at least have happily shared his throne, had it not been for the murderous fury of her brothers.

Tamar

All these ironic tones reach their climax in the risqué story of old Judah's daughter-in-law. Widowed and passed on from one son to another as each of these ne'er-do-wells dies without heirs, Tamar is finally offered Judah's youngest son, a boy of greater promise. Reneging on the arrangement up to the death of his own wife, Judah is fooled by Tamar into taking her for a sacred prostitute, to console himself in his grief. He cannot pay just then, so he offers his signet ring, his family bracelet, and his monogrammed staff as security. When he sends payment, the prostitute cannot be found. But when he hears that his daughter-in-law is pregnant, he is ready to have her executed, until she presents his security and his heirs: the twins Perez and Zerah. Tamar is cunningly resourceful. She takes control, and God is with her as she turns the tables on her more powerful exploiter. It is hard to picture any man writing this account, even if inspired by God. The story does not rank with the stirring accounts of patriarchal leadership, but it does portray a situation in which a woman ironically masters the odds. The inference is clear that the Spirit of God is with women and blesses them, even in a way that has sometimes seemed ironic.

Zulaika

We get the name of Potiphar's wife from Islamic sources, and she confesses her sins in the Qur'an—new to many of us. The author of J is interested in women of all sorts, and in every kind of situation, though her political bias emerges whenever she has the outline of a story about women from the enemy side.

Jochebed

Our author did not know the name of Moses's mother. That comes to us in Exodus 6:20 and Numbers 26:59, two fragments from what the documentary evidence identifies as the book of Generations, an older genealogy broken up in pieces by the P group or by the final editor (sometimes called the redactor), who used pieces of it to link sections of material from J, E, and P. But typically only the author of J bothers to tell us of the mother's striving against all odds to save her son, and of a sister's hiding in the weeds as her brother is taken into the arms of the princess (Exod 2:1–4). This girl steps forward with an offer of assistance and gets her mother the job of caring for her own son (Exod 3:7–9). Irony indeed!

Miriam

The girl is Moses's sister, strategizing to protect him as a baby, and remaining his loyal supporter through most of his life, despite a falling out. She is not even mentioned in the famous genealogies, but the author of J is not going to let this woman be forgotten. Miriam accompanies herself with a hand drum in the Song of Miriam after the Israelites' successful crossing of the Red Sea (more accurately translated "Reed Sea"). The song led by this sister is joined by other women dancing, singing, and beating their own hand-drums in a remarkable scene of a kind not pictured elsewhere in Scripture (Exod 15:20–21).

Ankesupaten

Egyptian records tell of a princess who married the future pharaoh, Tutankhamen, at a time when he needed an heir to secure his own right of succession and the future of the throne. Some speculate that this is the princess who took Moses out of the Nile in the story reported in J. Tutankhamen was simply too young to produce an heir, and in some such circumstance, in spite of a decree by the ruling pharaoh, an Israelite baby may well have been plucked out of the Nile by that princess named Ankesupaten in Egyptian records and called Asiya in Muslim lore. Moses was adopted into the royal family as the son of the princess, a prince to pass off as belonging to the royal family. This speculation notwithstanding, only the J document refers to the adoptive mother of Moses. The ironies abound in all these examples of women persevering against all odds.

Zipporah

With a name that means "bird" in English, the future wife of Moses was one of seven daughters of the priest of Midian, where Moses fled after his altercation with the Egyptian authorities. Zipporah's role is simply to reconnect Moses to his Semitic family roots, completing his evolution from prince to prophet, priest, and patriarch. There is always a woman in the picture in the J accounts as they appear in Genesis and Exodus. Always the role is secondary, or veiled, but it is frequently determinative for families.

As recently as 1996, in her fine book *The Five Books of Miriam*, Ellen Frankel launched a creative quest to more fully appreciate these women. *The Five Books of Miriam* was followed in 2001 by a scholarly analysis of the women in the Pentateuch as part of a survey of all biblical women in *Women in Scripture*, edited by Carol Meyers. But nowhere in the ancient literature of the world is there such a collection of female portraits, both those deserving of renown and those connecting the story through relationships with fathers, sons, husbands, and brothers.

GENDER SPEECH

A close reading of each of these J episodes lets us hear a poignancy in an ironic voice that can come only from a woman who relates to her subjects as a woman. She would be the one whose writing skill exceeded that of even her brother, King Solomon, who gets credit for the sayings he may have uttered or quoted, whether or not he personally wrote any of them down. She writes wistfully, possibly during the reign of her nephew, the inept Rehoboam, on whose watch her father's kingdom is divided into Judah and Israel: the southern kingdom ruled by Rehoboam and the northern kingdom ruled by his brother Jeroboam and ruled by their successors in each kingdom, until both kingdoms crashed.

Is it possible that there was an oral tradition of women's stories that were passed on from generation to generation and finally put into writing by a female member of David's literary household? On February 24, 2004, the *Washington Post* carried a report of a Chinese written and spoken language known only to women, the first of several startling revelations about this hitherto-unknown enduring tradition. *Nushu*, the household script, served generations of Chinese women in various provinces and across classes through centuries of male-only educational systems. Almost obliterated during the Communist Cultural Revolution, and limited now to very elderly traditionalist women and very young intellectual feminists, *Nishu* stands as the gold-standard example of secret women's literature with a wealth of songs, poems, ancient diaries, and recorded women's folk stories. (That such a women's-only language existed, especially a language of this scope, might appear to some even less likely than the existence of female authors during the time of David.) What we are indeed suggesting as a possibility among the women of the royal household in ancient Jerusalem is not as dramatic as the Chinese example, but not less possible or less probable than the similar tradition among women in the aristocratic households of ancient Arabia, recorded in the Islamic literature we shall examine later in this investigation.

I place much of our study under the rubric of gender speech to note that both the content and the style of J appear to reflect a female author, if not a feminist agenda. This is a prelude to an equally startling observation about one of the authors of the New Testament, an observation original to this investigation and even more specifically dependant on the forensic techniques of rhetorical criticism.

I believe *The Book of J* identifies the Bible's first author and one of its greatest, and Bloom presents us with the full grandeur of her literary creation. No believer questions the divine inspiration of this material in the hands of this author, but we are immediately impressed that if she was a pencil in God's hand, the editors who put J together with E, D, and P were the palette in God's studio. Fortunately the techniques of biblical criticism allow us to peer beneath the surface to almost identify the genius who crafted the J collection of great stories, enshrining the role of women in Scripture and leaving enough evidence for us to work with, if we can recognize it.

To some, perhaps restricted by their own patriarchal thinking, the whole idea still seems difficult to appreciate, and in spite of his reputation as a critic of highest standing, Harold Bloom himself may not have had the tools of rhetorical criticism to prove the theory first alluded to by Meyers and advanced by Friedman. Even Bloom's mentor and late contemporary critic, Northrop Frye, much of whose career was dedicated to biblical criticism from a literary perspective, never brought such tools to bear as developed in the more narrow confines of seminaries, by specialists from Muilenburg to Walter Brueggemann, Phyllis Trible, and others.

Though we depend on other critical techniques to determine the date and the location of the J document in hoping to pin down the identity of the author, almost in spite of himself, Harold Bloom has made what is now an increasingly supportable case in regard to the identity of the person who put all those divinely inspired and long-cherished folk tales into writing. Overall the stories do center on the patriarchs, and in this regard J resembles E, D, P and dozens of other such documents outside the Bible from the ancient Near East. But J alone has the content and the tone of a work that we can reasonably assess as written by a woman, and the conjecture that she may be a daughter of King David is now less far-fetched than most people thought at first. It is simply a great pity that other failings overshadow the one idea of great merit in Bloom's *The Book of J*, that idea itself borrowed from Richard Friedman, a scholar whose biblical credentials are equal to Bloom's credentials in the other literary genres he has so completely mastered.

In the current postcritical era there have been several attempts to determine if and how the Scriptures do indeed ever address women's concerns, and my own denomination, the United Church of Canada, has published a quarterly journal titled *Women's Concerns*. Evangelical publishing houses have even published specific women's Bible versions of the Scriptures, addressing women's concerns from their own perspectives in the margin notes. How much could we add if we were to mine the mother lodes of female writers of Scripture, of whom there might be several? Is there any serious reason to reconsider our assumptions over the last several centuries in that regard? I believe there is.

If Moses was literate, he certainly did not write in Hebrew, which was not developed into a written language until almost five hundred years after his lifetime. Aside from his doodling in the sand while accusers slunk away from the woman taken in adultery, we have no knowledge of any literary ability on the part of Jesus, though it is clear that he could read. Moses and Jesus, one the transmitter of the Torah and the other the great teller of stories, depended on other men and women to write down the torah and the gospel stories. Just as Moses and Jesus may have been illiterate in a functional sense, Muhammad was himself illiterate, as we know.

Muslims everywhere acknowledge that Muhammad's "household," which was often entirely female, produced the written text of the Qur'an. Small parts may have been done under his roof by Zaid, his secretary later in life. But even Zaid was more involved with the early texts of the Hadith than with the Qur'an itself. Muhammad left explicit instructions as to the honor due to "the People of the House," the women so easily overlooked in

Islamic cultures. The women of Muhammad's household, in the last culture of the ancient Near East that came to us whole and intact, provide a clear and natural model for what may well have happened in the households of King David in the Old Testament and St. James in New Testament.

Gender prejudices have prevented Jews and Christians from seeing the fact of women's importance in reference to their own Scriptures, but the Muslim community's prejudices have been focused elsewhere while they have sometimes regarding writing to be part of "women's work," especially since, in the cases cited so far, women did the stenographic functions but not the dictation. Modern examples of the same aristocratic tradition in Islamic societies will be provided in due course, but Muslims have always acknowledged the possibility of the role of prominent females in compiling and producing Scripture. This is a sufficient surprise to Jews and Christians that it will require more complete treatment in a later chapter dealing with critical traditions in Islam. The topic is introduced here to facilitate the beginnings of a new appreciation for the veiled women who produced and compiled Jewish and Christian Scriptures somewhat earlier in an essentially similar culture.

6

Arraignment

A FTER DR. JEAN ASTRUC's demarcation of J and E in 1753 came a productive period of ferment, especially in the Protestant theological
schools of Germany. One scholar would put forward a hypothesis about the
authorship of the Pentateuch, and this would be seized upon and attacked
unmercifully by the remaining defenders of the Mosiac authorship on the
one hand, and by rival scholars with new theories on the other. For over
a century this sifting and refining went on with every jot and tittle coming under scrutiny by scholars who loved God and cherished the words of
Scripture, always seeking to broaden as well as deepen their understanding
of every phrase.

Finally in 1884 a great servant of the Word, named Julius Wellhausen,
built a careful word-by-word study of the whole issue, based on his revisions of an 1866 attempt by K. H. Graf and the theories of Wellhausen's own
mentor, W. M. L. de Wette. Known as the Graf-Wellhausen Hypothesis, as
the Four Document Theory, or simply as the Documentary Hypothesis, the
conclusions of this study are accepted as a definitive turning point in the
quest to understand the origins of the Pentateuch, at least in the seminaries
of most Christian denominations and in many of the colleges of Judaism.

Almost no one today agrees with all the finer details of what I call the
documentary evidence as first propounded by Wellhausen, but the idea that
the Pentateuch is composed of four documents, or now more properly defined as four "sources" of material, has almost universal acceptance. Debates
continue about the composition of each strand of this material; about
whether it began as an oral "campfire" tradition, as a document or as several
documents; who edited them all together, and why. Questions remain about
the order of composition, J, E, D, and P, or possibly J, E, P, and D.

These questions and other "objections" to the documentary evidence will be considered shortly, because the debate has been productive. Before entertaining objections, however, we should confirm our understanding with some illustrations that will assist those who do not read Hebrew, but who possess common sense and literary experience.

The evidence for the basic hypothesis is strong and obvious, once the key is available. For example, Canada has two official languages—English and French. But if history had turned out differently and English had become singularly predominant, for example, a national collection of heritage documents might still contain poems, songs, and other references to both God and *Dieu*. Any knowledgeable student of Canadian history would be able to separate out such documents and discover a consistent pattern of historical, spiritual, and cultural traditions from the French Canadian "tribe." That is basically what happened in biblical analysis when the J and E sources were first identified on the basis of the use of the divine names, Jehovah (or *Yahweh* in Hebrew) in the southern kingdom of Judah, and Elohim (and Eloh or other appellations containing *El*), as used in the northern kingdom of Israel.

Once the first elements of the documentary evidence became clearly established, the other sources of material could also be more clearly defined. For example, were the roots of modern American culture to be published today using materials and speeches from English playwright William Shakespeare, Austrian immigrant Arnold Schwarzenegger, Christian evangelist Billy Graham, and African American poet Maya Angelou, all edited together by topic, almost anyone could pick out the Early Modern English spellings, the immigrant's grammar, the salvation agenda of the evangelist, and the lyrical cadences of African American aspirations.

The four sources of material in the Pentateuch are almost that obvious, and there is little debate about which verses are to be ascribed to J, E, P, and D, though each of them obviously has subtexts and sources of their own. After a few courses in Hebrew, a fully engaged seminarian can peel away the encrusted layers of the Pentateuch with confidence, revealing a virtual treasure trove of theological gems from four basic sources, with a fifth hand evidently editing the material and linking the sections with old genealogical and dating records and the occasional theological footnote. This study is intended to assist the beginning scholar to do this in English and the general reader to appreciate the analysis.

We have already identified J and E, and Astruc's theory stood up under rigorous examination, though there is still continuing and expanding discussion about the nature and the agenda of each source before it was blended into the whole. There is evidence that J is older, probably written down in the era some time after the year 900 BCE, but using materials that were then up to a thousand years old. J came from the southern tribes of Judah, as we can tell from its stories, and seems intended as a national history pointing toward the Davidic monarchy and the temple establishment at Jerusalem as the fulfillment of God's plan.

In contrast, E has its origins around the campfires of Israel in the north, a more pan-Semitic society with its continued use of *Eloh*, the generic name for God we have come to recognize in its Arabic form as *Allah*, still used to this day by Arab Christians and other Semites. The heroes of E are northern. Another difference between J and E is that E refers to the holy mountain where Moses received the Ten Commandments as Mount Horeb. J has its southern heroes and references the same events on the mountain it calls Mount Sinai. E, though compiled slightly later than J, appears to contain material as old as J, possibly preserved by Levites, the quasi-priestly hereditary religious order descended from Moses. They were intensely loyal to the legacy of Moses, as compared to the members of the temple priesthood in Jerusalem, descended from Aaron, who promoted the more intensely nationalistic legacy of David. Careful reading of the Pentateuch makes it apparent that E is the precursor to the publication of D, just as P builds on the ethos of J. It is possible to read between the lines that E supports the political existence of the separatist northern kingdom of Israel and points to all Israel's first capital at Shiloh during the conquest era, a continuing Levite bastion, as the most ancient and legitimate national shrine in a theology of centralization. Similarly, the temple priests in Jerusalem pointed to their capital as part of a centralizing theology.

After the fall of Israel in the north, decimated by the Assyrian Empire under Sargon II in 721 BCE, the Levites from Shiloh were among the refugees streaming into Judah and Jerusalem. Their first act was to ingratiate themselves by publishing a combined JE document, uniting the history of the north and south as one people, with J remaining the dominant element but with E stories, material, and theology as a supplement and supportive balance.

Shortly thereafter, a Levitical author, whom Friedman identifies convincingly as Baruch, the secretarial scribe to the prophet Jeremiah, published an annotated version of the most sacred treasure of the Levitical tradition: the ancient Deuteronomic Code. This forms the bulk core of Deuteronomy as we have it today, material purported to have come directly from Moses in some manner. Deuteronomy may have originated as an oral tradition coming from Moses himself (as suggested by various scholars between Astruc and Wellhausen), memorized, recited, and written early as Hebrew emerged into written form, and identified by the letter D in the documentary evidence. This almost-complete draft of Deuteronomy is quite certainly the law book "found" in the temple in 621 BCE during the renovations sponsored by the young reformer, King Josiah (2 Kings 22). This was some three hundred years after J and E had first been penned, at about the time the people needed a more concise summary of the teachings of Moses to get them back on track. It was the populist "old-time religion," as promoted by the Levites. D has a style and even a theological emphasis all of its own, and it is perhaps the easiest of the four documents for students of Hebrew to identify.

Finally, according to the documentary evidence, running through all the other books of the Pentateuch, there is a fourth obvious and distinguishable stratum of material in a more highly polished style of Hebrew than either J or E. This sophisticated source uses *Elohim* as the name for God all through Genesis and only switches to *Jehovah* at Exodus 6:2, precisely when God reveals that name to Moses in this stratum. This document, prior to the blending of the four, is full of such theological sensitivities as that, and is greatly interested in matters of ritual and ceremony. It records genealogies and statistics, both of which are given spiritual significance, and its whole tone reflects a mature and lofty theology.

This source supplies the opening of Genesis, most of the second half of Exodus, including the description of the tabernacle sanctuary in the desert wilderness (not even mentioned in J, E or D), all of Leviticus with its instructions for worship, and most of Numbers, with details about the sacred community. It is referred to as the Priestly source and given the initial P to refer to the group of priestly scholars who developed it, not finally at the end of the work, as we now suspect, but as the Aaronide priesthood's lofty response to the JE compilation. It gives the universal context of the creation story and the theological significance of the epics and legends reported in JE, almost certainly before Deuteronomy made its belated public appearance. This was an era of theological writing in Hebrew that can only be compared to the philosophical outpouring in Greece referred to as the age of Pericles, about a hundred years later with Socrates, Plato, Aristotle, and others. The motives of the Aaronide priesthood and the theopolitical program of the Levites will be considered further, once we have established the rest of the compilation sequence of the Pentateuch.

Welhausen thought that the J, E, D, and P documents or, more correctly, the "sources," were finally combined by the Priestly Source—the last of the four—possibly working as a team during the Babylonian captivity (597–538 BCE). More recent forensic research, internal to the texts, puts the final edit under the control of just one person, possibly soon after the return of the Judeans to Jerusalem. This would have been possible under endowments provided by the Persian king, Cyrus, to Ezra as recorded in the Bible and elsewhere.

This dedicated priest, in firm control of his assistants and colleagues, was determined to unify and codify the life of Israel, perhaps almost to the point of fanaticism, but seizing the moment to integrate all traditions into one law, one Torah. The writing or speaking style and the Hebrew syntax used by the writer of certain parts of the books of Ezra and Nehemiah bears the strongest resemblance to the final editorial touches added to the text of the Pentateuch, identified on our cover diagram in grey, where they stand out in comparison to the mass of that material.

7

Cross-Examination

THIS IS ALL RICH material with profound theological significance, which is sometimes merely intrinsic to the source and sometimes drawn out by the editing redactor, R. The redactor conducts the symphony with J as the wind section, E the percussion, and P, the Priestly source as the theological continuo, or like violins maintaining a background theme in an orchestral production. When we reach Leviticus and Numbers, it is as if the backgrounded violins take over. These two books of the Pentateuch give significance to minute sacramental procedures, including proper vestments. While some "listeners" of the Pentateuch enjoy the soaring strings of detail, other listeners find unbearable the tedium of the third and fourth movements (the Deuteronomistic History and the Priestly source). However, these movements feature lively details about sanctuary cities for refugees and about prohibitions against mixed marriage.

In the early years of the documentary evidence, P was first thought to be from the era of the captivity in Babylon, perhaps before the return to Jerusalem in the sixth century BCE, and produced by the priests of a rather elite community of Judeans. That community was the Jerusalem aristocracy, civil service, and temple priesthood who had been taken into captivity in 584 BCE, when the southern kingdom of Judah fell to the then dominant Babylonian Empire. These Jews, who rose to positions of prominence under the Babylonians (a status befitting their education, culture, and moral rectitude), were among those entrusted to run the Persian Empire once the Babylonians were defeated.

It is more recent studies, crowned by the detailed analysis of Richard Elliott Friedman, that indicate this group may have included the priestly party that wrote or compiled the material we call P, but that they had done this work a generation earlier, as a single document while still in Jerusalem.

According to Friedman, it was their intention to protect their prerogatives as the temple priesthood and to counter the growing influence of refugee Levites from the north during the reign of King Hezekiah. Fleeing the collapse of the northern separatist kingdom of Israel, the Levites, descended from Moses, were welcomed by the royal household in Jerusalem as a counterbalance to the powerful temple priesthood, descended from Aaron.

The Levites soon produced the popular combined JE scroll to win a place for northern tradition in the southern kingdom of Judah and eventually adopted young King Josiah as their putative fulfillment of God's promised Messiah after the model of David, whose elevation to a status equal to Moses they now accepted. P appeared as a more priestly and sacrosanct version of the JE storyline, and the Aaronide priesthood kept its options open in the matter of promising a Messiah. Their priestly motif and temple-centered theology were carried forward by the prophet Ezekiel, even into exile in Babylon, including his sacred dreams of a return to Jerusalem. Meanwhile the Levitical prophet, Jeremiah, languished in his own exile in Egypt.

How did the P material come to the group of priests who produced it? Had it been written down in Egyptian hieroglyphics and kept secret until rewritten in the well-developed Hebrew of an era sometime after J and E? Was it private oral tradition among the priesthood for a thousand years, as the Deuteronomic Code of Moses may have been among the Levites? Could it have been based on temple rituals that had tabernacle precedents in the desert and which could now be reconstructed? Was it all a dream on the part of priests inspired by God to imagine and record what worship should have been like during the wilderness experience, and with hints from J and E thrown it to authenticate its antiquity? Or with the elevation of the temple in Jerusalem, was some combination of all of the above responsible for this particular compendium of worship, ritual, and religious law—elements of which have endured down to the present: for example, in the vestments of a Catholic priest, Anglican altar procedures, and in the seating arrangements for the choir in a Baptist church?

This seesaw between quasi-priestly Levites and the Aaronide priesthood in the documentary evidence gathered many scraps of folklore and all elements of Israelite theology, with a potential significance far beyond the sum of their parts if somehow they could be brought into a hybrid compendium. God inspired not merely an author or a school of authors, but a people who together articulated the Word through an inspired process in which their troubles were as influential as their blessings in hearing and recognizing the divine voice.

Only a national crisis of the greatest magnitude could facilitate the unlikely eventuality of the reconciliation of these diverse materials: J, E, P, and D. Not that God necessarily plans our disobedience and disasters, but the Holy Spirit seems able to use even this ugly raw material for blessing. God did this in the eyes of many with the establishment of the State of Israel in response to the Shoah or Holocaust of the twentieth century. The decimation of Judah; the destruction of Jerusalem and its temple; and the enslavement of its aristocracy, civil service, and priesthood by the Babylonian empire under Nebuchadnezzar in 584 BCE was an event of just such a magnitude. The establishment of the written Torah/Pentateuch is indeed an ancient example of blessing and hope that can emerge for a people even after disaster.

It would be hard to exaggerate the impact of the Babylonian exile, except to say that it ranks with slavery in Egypt long centuries earlier, with the brutal persecution of Jews and Christians by the Romans in later centuries, and with the Holocaust long centuries later; and in all three cases the final resolution was proof to the Jewish people that God is able to lead people out of their deepest despair into unimagined blessing when they trust God. This might be one of the Jewish people's important messages to the world.

Judean exiles rose to special prominence in the Babylonian administration, partly because it was the cream of Hebrew society that was taken captive for the purpose of expanding the administration of a growing empire. When Persia eventually defeated Babylon, the new rulers initially co-opted the Jewish administration to administer its own expanded territory. We know of some of the experiences of life in captivity as they are reflected in stories like those in the books of Esther, Daniel, and Ezekiel.

Then, after more than a generation in captivity, the Persian king, Cyrus the Great, decided to ask these people, still homesick for Jerusalem, to return there to set up a buffer state between the Persians and their only other rival, Egypt. God's grace was apparent in psalms that proclaimed, "We were like people in a dream" when this happened. Significant numbers of aristocrats, civil servants, and priests, with their children and families, returned and together with Levites, peasants, and others who had not been exiled, rebuilt Jerusalem with generous grants from the Persian treasury.

The rebuilding of the civic society was only moderately successful under the aristocratic Zerubbabel, and the governor Nehemiah failed to complete the restoration of the temple, at least during his first term. Somehow the soul of the community did not return, and reports reached the Persian court that since religion had been the paramount characteristic of this people, the rebuilding would not be complete without the temple.

A second major royal grant, authorized by King Cyrus, persuaded several thousand priestly families to join the return under the leadership of Ezra, with the specific purpose of restoring the temple to its former glory and reestablishing the religious life of the people on its ancient traditions. Ezra evidently took this as license to hire all the help he needed from among the priestly class to undertake the compendium of the religious resources we know as the Pentateuch or Torah. Tradition has it that there were fifty priestly scribes working section by section under Ezra's supervision and editorial control, perhaps getting organized even before they left Babylon.

Once they got to Judah, legend has it that Ezra established the *Knesset HaGedolah*, "The Great Assembly," a representative spiritual governing body. The task eventually became a national undertaking involving virtually all the people, including the assembly of all citizens to hear the first reading of the compendium in the public square before the temple in a scene described well in Nehemiah 8. The texts to be blended were certainly complementary, even despite contradictions on the surface.

The value of J was beyond question in presenting the divine origins of the covenant between this people and God. E would help integrate the remnants of the lost tribes of Israel, citizens of the defunct northern kingdom, now dispersed throughout the Persian Empire and beyond, into the program of the return to Jerusalem. E also contained valuable historical records not available from any other source, and, indeed, these had already been blended into one JE edition.

D had standing as "The Book of the Law" and either had a direct connection with Moses, or was an appropriate, inspired, and widely accepted summary of Moses's teaching that was "found" or reintroduced when needed. It was popular and well known, so that it needed to be included as a solid block, not integrated or edited in any significant way, except perhaps to give a token presence to the other source traditions in the final chapter. The main task was to integrate P in a way that might enhance J and E material, smooth out any obvious disjointed portions, and bring the old-time populist material within a priestly theological framework without diluting or distorting the core of the P document.

It might have been possible to take J and call it the book of Genesis, to make E the book of Exodus, to use P as a Leviticus and Numbers rolled into one, and to anchor it all with Deuteronomy; but there were problems with this. J and E had already been edited together after the fall of the northern kingdom to provide a unified sacred history and to begin to smooth out some of the conflicting information. It just seemed better to make an integrated whole by adding some of the P theology and literary style to make a better job of JE—with a dash of P here and there in the new scrolls of Genesis and Exodus. JE would have been one scroll for at least a generation; but with the addition of P material, its length became too hard to manage, and the birth of Moses seemed like a suitable juncture for a break. So the book of Exodus begins with Moses's birth. Likewise the addition of more ancient material from J and E wherever needed authenticated the lengthy P material in Numbers. Unfolding circumstances left few cynics, however. Leviticus stood alone and unmixed as the core of P, reflecting the priestly agenda of Ezra.

The center of pure P was the tiny scroll of Leviticus (which could have been more naturally added to Numbers). Placing a P chapter at the opening of the whole Pentateuch in Genesis and some P at the end as the penultimate verses in Deuteronomy is the unique Brian Arthur Brown rationale and understanding of the construction of the Pentateuch. It is not very different from most other summaries of the structure of the Pentateuch, and I am merely attempting to stand on the shoulders of other critics. Richard Elliott Friedman would not agree with my delineation of sources, since he sees the R hand of Ezra in a few verses of Leviticus; and Stanley Frost did not see the verses assigned to P at the end of Deuteronomy.

The priestly school may have been a brilliant team, possibly all of one mind and one spirit; but, as we say, a camel is a horse put together by a committee. A project of this magnitude needed a guiding genius with the motive, means, and opportunity to make it happen smoothly—practically a "Second Moses," which is exactly what ancient tradition called Ezra. The priests returning from Babylon were all of Aaron's line, and no indication of a role for the Levites in this work is apparent, except that they are mentioned as being present at the conclusion. Ezra was obviously conscious of the fact that the earlier Levite success in combining J and E had been due in large part to their fair and respectful balance of material, and he may have impressed them in turn with his own balance. Respectfully concluding with the beloved Deuteronomy, possibly reedited ever so slightly in exile for important reasons yet to be discussed, Ezra thereby acknowledges its place as the anchor of the entire work and the last to be published.

Ezra's motive was the renewal of the spiritual life of the Judean people, an all-consuming passion, in his case. The means were provided to him by the policy of Persian monarchs who first sought to reestablish the nation of Judah under Zerubbabel and Nehemiah as a buffer between themselves and Egypt, and who later increased their support to ensure the spiritual development recognized as the heart of this nation. This reflects the enlightened Persian policy of gaining the loyalty of subject groups by respecting their priorities—economic priorities in some cases, cultural priorities in others, and religious priorities in the case of the Judeans.

As remarkable as it seems, Ezra's accomplishment in sacred literature in this context is not more amazing, for example, than the revival of the dead language of Hebrew as the everyday parlance in modern Israel that took place in a similar return that lasted through most of the twentieth century CE. The importance of the revival of Hebrew in the twentieth and twenty-first centuries is another subject to which we must return.

The later rather jumbled material in the biblical books of Ezra and Nehemiah conveys a confused chronology of the ancient return era, but it seems clear that Ezra took a period of a few years (possibly 458–444 BCE) to have everything in place before presenting the "New Revised Version" of the Scriptures before the people. Their hearts were prepared, the community was filled with anticipation, and the material had every *i* dotted and every *t* crossed, except for the few rough edits we have noted, lo these many centuries later.

Then Ezra declared the Torah closed to further additions or revisions, ascribed the whole to Moses, and assembled the people to hear it read for the first time in the new format. This well- staged public event is so moving that the account in the book of Nehemiah should be read more often as a greater part of the consciousness of the Christian community at least, and possibly by Jews and others.

The Republican Party in the United States takes pride in referring to itself as "the party of Lincoln." In Canada, some Conservative Party strategists picked up the idea and began to refer to themselves as "The Party of Sir John A.," referring to Sir John A. Macdonald, the first prime minister of Canada, and, to many, the leading figure of the 1867 Confederation which led to the peaceful and democratic evolution of Canada as a country. Sir John A. Macdonald died in 1891, so, one hundred years later, when this same Conservative Party published its election platform under the title, *The Policy of Sir John A*, everyone appreciated the point that the party was still running on a policy designed to hold the country together during a time of stress. No one accused them of forgery or plagiarism.

There was never any intention to pass off the 1991 publication as if it were actually written by Sir John A. Macdonald, but every attempt was made to claim legitimacy for the national unity platform of the Conservative Party by identifying it with Macdonald's policies and even quoting him wherever possible. Everybody knew John A. MacDonald had been dead for a hundred years, but nobody disputed the right of the Conservative Party to claim to be speaking in his name.

This was similar to the masterstroke that Ezra employed when he published the final edit of the Torah under the name of Moses during the rebuilding Judean society after a second period of slavery. The Torah, or "The Teachings of the Law" consisted of the five books of the Pentateuch, in which the four sources of material we know as J, E, P, and D are skillfully woven together into five composite documents, each approaching the maximum length of a scroll. It was not a stretch to claim that all the material had come down from Moses, given the high esteem that the traditions of these priests and Levites commanded, and given the fact that both priests and Levites were immensely pleased to see the prominence of their cherished materials in the national compendium.

There is no evidence that Ezra actually said or wrote that all five scrolls had been written by Moses. But the implication that they were indeed the books of Moses was clear from the day Ezra and his assistants read out the completed Torah, or Pentateuch, referred to as "the law of Moses," to the assembled people of Jerusalem: the event described in the Bible in Nehemiah 8:1–8. The five scrolls assumed that ancient and sacred characterization, with considerable justification, and were so regarded in all the centuries that followed. They may be so regarded by us with appropriate understanding.

How did the Judean community and later Christians explain this development? In the apocryphal book of 2 Esdras, written some years later, we read that the original scrolls of the Pentateuch were burned when Nebuchadnezzar, king of Babylon, invaded Jerusalem, and that they were simply rewritten by Ezra (2 Esdras 14:21–22). The early Christian church explicitly accepted this explanation of the events described above, as we read in the writings of Irenaeus, Tertullian, Clement of Alexandria, and, most important, St. Jerome, the translator of the Bible into the Latin

Vulgate, an edition of Scripture that served most of the Western church for a thousand years.

Such pious myths supporting Mosaic authorship for the Pentateuch do harm only if they limit the ability of the whole people of God to recognize its own role in the ongoing transmission of this work in progress. The role of the people of God is akin to the role of Ezra. And the Pentateuch is a work through which God continues to address each reader and listener afresh, engaging a commitment not only to live according to the Word but to take responsibility for transmitting it to others and to succeeding generations.

8

Objection!

TOWARD THE END OF the twentieth century, there was a brief loss of confidence in the documentary evidence as "fragmented" became the buzzword to describe both the sources and the Documentary Hypothesis itself. By the end of that century, confidence had been restored. The cover notes summarizing a 1998 book by Ernest Nicholson, provost of Oriel College, Oxford, describes the situation well.

> Despite innumerable studies from at least the time of the Reformation, it was not until little more than a century ago that one hypothesis concerning the origin of the Pentateuch, the so-called "Documentary Theory" formulated by Julius Wellhausen, established itself as the point of departure for all subsequent study of this topic. This has remained so until recently, but during the past twenty-five years the study of the Pentateuch has been once more in turmoil, and new theories have proliferated. This book arises from conviction that much in current Pentateuchal research needs to be subjected to rigorous scrutiny and that much, indeed, is radically mistaken. Professor Nicholson argues that the work of Wellhausen, for all that it needs revision and development in detail, remains, the securest basis for understanding the Pentateuch. This book is not a mere call to go 'back to Wellhausen,' for much in the intervening debate has significantly modified his conclusions, as well as asking questions that were not on Wellhausen's agenda. But the Documentary Hypothesis should remain our primary point of reference, and it alone provides the most dependable perspective from which to approach this most difficult of areas in the study of the Old Testament. (*The Pentateuch in the Twentieth Century*)

Having withstood an onslaught of contrary opinion from both fundamentalists dedicated to Mosaic authorship, and sincere contrarians determined to explore all the options, the Documentary Hypothesis has now been established as the documentary evidence of the origins of the Pentateuch, a phrase that will be used henceforth, as it is increasingly through this investigation.

This judgment notwithstanding, the criticisms of the late twentieth century have served to advance the argument and to continually refine the basics. Possibly the most widely circulated negative critique of the documentary evidence was a midcentury bromide presented in Hebrew as eight lectures by Umberto Cassuto and published in Hebrew, not widely circulated in English or other languages until that late-century debate described above about the validity of the documentary approach. His famous eight lectures were published in 1941, translated into English in 1961, and eventually widely circulated.

Cassuto rejected two key elements of work that had evolved from Wellhausen: that the Pentateuch had its origins in separate documents combined by an editor into the final text; and that the four sources of the Pentateuch had been composed between 950 and 550 BCE, with the final redaction around 450 BCE. Cassuto taught that the Pentateuch was written down as a single, unified text in the tenth century BCE and not thereafter altered in any significant way. Much of his evidence was linguistic—modeled on the theories of the integrity of the Homeric legends. He also argued that the divine names Yahweh and Elohim reflect different purposes rather than separate sources, with Yahweh referring to God as Lord of Israel and Elohim, or simply Eloh, referring to the God of the world. Cassuto's theory was worthy of consideration, on the face of it.

A few scholars, such as Rolf Rendtorff and John Van Seters, supported Cassuto. Despite a willingness to consider all the options by the time Cassuto's speeches were circulating, the vast majority of scholars carefully worked through his arguments and eventually found them lacking. However, even Cassuto has left us with something: the awareness that in using *Eloh*, a more generic and regional name for God, Israel's most common word for the Deity was closely connected to *Allah* (also rendered *Alah* or *Elah*)—the name for God employed by all Semitic peoples in the region, by those that the Bible identifies as descendents of Noah's son Shem—Semitic.

The more substantial roots of the era of disaffection with respect to the documentary evidence, as we may call it now, were found with several other respected scholars of Cassuto's generation: Hermann Gunkel (1862–1932) and his younger contemporaries, Sigmund Mowinckel, Martin Noth, and Gerhard von Rad, who were all still writing and teaching when I was in seminary at McGill University in the 1960s. Their followers fleshed out their possible objections to the documentary evidence, but what finally remains is a kernel from each that continues to inform our understanding.

Gunkel illustrated conclusively that the so-called documents were not the work of individuals and suggested that they may never have been published as documents at all. For example, in the opening chapter of Genesis, the material we identify as the Priestly source is actually closely dependent on pre-Israelite Babylonian creation myths.

Long before rhetorical criticism had come to our attention, Mowinckel drew linguistic comparisons between songs in the Pentateuch and the Psalms, noting how the cadences of the Song of the Sea and the Song of Miriam in Exodus 15 closely resemble the style and meter of the psalms of David. Noth and von Rad shook up Wellhausen's notion of the unity of the Hebrew people in the Pentateuch by their discovery in the book of Joshua of a society of Israelite warlords, which society we might compare with present-day Afghanistan: united in religion, but in hardly any other way.

Hermann Gunkel's theories are now mainstream and are even taught to teen Sunday school classes, who love all the research into the Gilgamesh Epic and Hammurabi Code. But it is presumed that the Israelites were influenced by these from their neighbors at an early time, and that the priestly school reworked them theologically according to Israel's experience of God's grace and mercy.

Sigmund Mowinckel's connection between the Psalms and the portion of Exodus coming from the J source fits neatly into our current speculation that the same persons in David's household wrote down his psalms and also composed or collected the J material. Noth and Von Rad simply provide a covenant theology shared by a variety of tribes connected through the Abraham, Isaac, and Jacob family of the covenant, either mythically or by blood. Most people in these tribes had ancestors who shared in the remarkable exodus of slaves from Egypt. They also participated in the powerful things that happened to this diverse group in the desert, which they could not but attribute to divine intervention.

The upshot of all this is that technical experts now universally refer to Wellhausen's "documents" as *sources*, with materials from the J source frequently delineated as J^1, J^2, J^3, for example. We will see this when we come to discuss the Mosaic material in Deuteronomy, which I call D^1, the original Deuteronomic Code of Moses. Annotations by the Levites who preserved and cherished it we might call D^2, and tiny but significant revisions during the Babylonian-exile era (possibly by one of their number as a refugee in Egypt—perhaps even by the same Levitical scholar who had made the D^2 annotations) we might appropriately designate as D^3. There is even a D^4, as we shall see.

The original Hebrew campfire stories about Abraham, Isaac, and Jacob, and the women's domestic traditions from Eve to Sarah and Hagar were a thousand years old, and some source material from surrounding cultures was even older than that, but had been memorized and recited for dozens of generations. Alex Haley's *Roots: The Saga of an American Family* documents a similar phenomenon in African society as recently as 1976. Favorite stories could be collected when writing began in Hebrew, and theological spin could be placed on other ancient sources then woven together into a narrative, a sacred history, given the faith experience of the Israelite people and the attention of the writers to the guidance of the Holy Spirit. A current example of this kind of "cut-and-paste" technique is the production of the stage musical and motion picture *Mamma Mia*, which creatively strings together unrelated songs by the popular 1960s group Abba, making a highly entertaining storyline from their music.

The collectors, authors, or editors of JE, and the R compiler of J, E, D, and P are people we have come to trust because their testimonies about the ways of God resonate with our experience. They did not just make up biblical narratives or choose certain stories because they could be combined in an entertaining way. They worked out of their own faith experiences, which shine through even the most tragic stories. They opened themselves to the Spirit of God to be inspired with the story God wanted the world to hear. These Scriptures do not fade away or disappear with the passing of centuries or even millennia, because they still ring true to people of each succeeding age.

However, these Scriptures, arising from communal sources, are not complete until they are written and edited once more in the hearts of believers, who are doing nothing more than the original producers of the Scriptures did under God's guidance. These stories are works in progress, incomplete and containing both misunderstandings of God's ways and the dawning realization of God's way with each individual. The Bible itself gives examples of this evolution in understanding, as in the case of Job, itself possibly the very oldest narrative in Scripture and also from a source before or outside the early Hebrew sources.

Objection!

The comments at the beginning of this chapter about Ernest Nicholson's work on the legacy of Julius Wellhausen and other current scholars notwithstanding, it is an American, Richard Elliott Friedman, who has the final say on these matters at the conclusion of the reassessment era and into the twenty-first century, presenting a positive testimony to validate the documentary evidence. The point is often made that each scholar stands on the shoulders of a host of others, and if that was even true for Julius Wellhausen, it is also true of Professor Friedman; but his turn-of-this-century works—especially *Who Wrote the Bible* and *The Bible with Sources Revealed*—should be required reading for anyone serious about intricate nuances of the latest assessment of the documentary evidence. Also, Friedman writes for scholar, student, and general reader.

Having devoted a lifetime of focused scholarship to this specific topic, Friedman sides early on with those who have some lingering questions; but he makes it clear that his answers result more in modifications to the documentary evidence than in a replacement of it. In providing evidence, Friedman is like an expert witness who gives informed opinion that the jury feels sure it can trust. Friedman moves from larger matters like an earlier date for P (placing it in Jerusalem before the exile) and concludes Ezra's compendium, the Torah or Pentateuch, with D for reasons that are finely argued but not as obvious.

Resisting the impulse to make Friedman into the second bookend in an era that began with Wellhausen, we shall endeavor to stand on Friedman's shoulders also, to illustrate how each scholar and student has a role to play. For example, just from reading and study, it is my personal conclusion that Ezra, as the redactor, favored the P source in theology, and I am not the first to make that observation. Wellhausen believed that P was the last documentary source to be compiled, whereas Friedman and others now would have us understand the D was last, based on internal textual evidence. Has no one noticed that Deuteronomy is also last in the Pentateuch?

It was Ezra who placed D last in the Pentateuch, simply because it was compiled last and published last, and that determines its order of placement within the documentary evidence. Coming from Moses, or at least containing speeches by Moses, Deuteronomy required a preeminent position to validate and summarize all that was contained in the first four scrolls. If P was written before D was published, and R (Ezra) knew that, then this possibility also, in addition to the subject matter, dictated the order of both the Pentateuch and the documentary evidence to be J, E, P, and D. This is as

Friedman and others would now have it, but it was Ezra, not Friedman or any other current scholar, who made this decision.

Internal textual evidence may require a change to Wellhausen's J, E, D, and P order, but such evidence is superfluous, unless we are oblivious to the obvious. If he knew Deuteronomy was actually the last of the four sources to be published, it was Ezra who placed it last and left it reasonably intact. It is as simple as that. However, Ezra then placed a chapter from P, his favored material, at the opening of the first scroll, and a whole scroll of P material, known as Leviticus, at the center, to give the priestly material the prominence he felt it deserved. To this matter and a matter we now return.

P is also scattered through the other scrolls for all the good reasons we have considered, but segregating one tiny scroll of pure P material and making it central was deliberate in my view. It would have been easier to amalgamate Leviticus and Numbers, making one scroll just longer than Exodus and just shorter than Genesis: a proper and convenient length. So in my diagram it may be noticed that Leviticus is P material, unmixed with other sources. I have rejected the view of Friedman and many others that Leviticus has some R verses added by the redactor. I favor of a Leviticus that is purely priestly. The evidence for other material in Leviticus is not strong in any of the commentaries. If there is similarity between those few verses in Leviticus attributed to R and such insertions elsewhere in the Pentateuch, it may be that R picked up these phrases from P in the Leviticus section that he admired so much.

Friedman's position on Deuteronomy is that there is no reason to doubt that the Levites of the north had maintained material from the Mosaic period, either orally and memorized, or written as early as is feasible. I would add that this could possibly have been in a proto-Hebraic written form. This material would be the Deuteronomic Code (Deuteronomy 12–26), including the Ten Commandments, plus an ancient blessing near the end of the scroll. This material is shown in bold on the diagram and could be referred to as D^1. Friedman presents the Levites as releasing an annotated version soon after arriving in Jerusalem as refugees, following the collapse of the northern kingdom of Israel, notes that we show as D^2 in regular print on the diagram.

When first published, the annotated Deuteronomy reflected the belief that the Divine should be worshipped in a particular earthly sanctuary or temple that was to be regarded as eternal. (The Levites had transferred their allegiance and feelings of loyalty from Shiloh to Jerusalem. For the Levites, patronized by David's successors such as Hezekiah and Josiah, the messianic monarchy would always occupy the throne of David.)

Then those who treasured this scroll and its theology of the central shrine experienced what seemed like the ultimate tragedy in Babylon's defeat of Judah; in the decimation of Jerusalem; in the destruction of the temple and the torture, enslavement, and ultimate murder of the monarch they regarded as God's anointed. There were seemingly few prospects for returning to rebuild the Holy City and temple, or for the restitution of the messianic monarchy. This negative picture was reinforced by Jeremiah, the prophet of doom, who fled with many of the Levites and others as refugees to Egypt, while the high priests, the remaining aristocracy, and civic leaders were transported to Babylon, to a dread fate followed by a future only a merciful God could have in store. It was in moments of deep despair that the penultimate editing of Deuteronomy took place. Deuteronomy does not lose faith but, as Friedman illustrates better than anyone, presents God's worship in a heavenly sanctuary and hints of God's messianic promises with references to a universal kingdom and an eternal king, an overlay of material that we show in italics and which we might call D^3.

Minor verse insertions from the other sources (J, E, and P), added by Ezra, give all sources a connection to the final days and hours of Moses, giving us D^4. This inclusive design of Deuteronomy 34 makes it the only chapter in the entire Torah/Pentateuch to include all four sources identified by Wellhausen represented in one chapter of the Bible. Deuteronomy concludes as we have it in all our Bibles, basically unchanged in two and a half millennia.

All these document compilers contributed to God's revelation in ways far beyond their personal understanding, producing a Torah that is much more than the sum of its parts, especially when finally edited by Ezra into the compendium of the Pentateuch, surely one of the most outstanding and successful literary undertakings in the entire history of the world. We continue to advance in understanding, with the guidance of the Holy Spirit and the aid of textual critics, working within the framework of evidence in which we can have confidence.

At this point another example presents itself, demonstrating how, by faith, we continue to stand on the shoulders of our leading scholars. Critics are said to be at their best when they can show in a text meanings that the author did not intend. I am not a critic, but I once discovered such an unintended meaning in a text I was reading.

I wrote something for another publication about how Professor Friedman had connected the earliest glimpses of messianic theology in Deuteronomy to the more universal and eternal understandings of the Messiah accepted by Christians and understood by Muslims. I e-mailed my piece to him and got, among other things, his reply to this point, to the effect:

> You wrote, "Richard Elliott Friedman refers to the impact his recent revisions of the Documentary Hypothesis might have on Christian messianic theology as being universal and eternal." I have to tell you that I have no idea what you're referring to. I don't remember ever writing anything about this.

I reread the section of *Who Wrote the Bible?* to which I thought I had been referring, and he was right. I had read what he had not written, and as a Jewish commentator, he had been entirely within his own faith and his area of expertise in referring to a development in a specifically Jewish understanding of universal expectations and eternal dimensions. He was making observations that, to him, had no wider implications. When I, as a Christian, read Friedman's understandings of those Scriptures (whether or not he would agree with my inclinations), I might take his words one step further, as referring to Jesus Christ. Just as I might bring Friedman's views from Judaism into a Christian context, so Muslim readers might similarly alter Christian visions of Jesus and eternity. The Qur'an, of course, presents Jesus as Al Masih six times, and while there are differences with the Christian view, the universal and eternal aspects of his messianic role are similar.

The documentary evidence is perhaps the best example imaginable of this function of critics, as each generation of Pentateuch writers found more than the earlier producers intended or imagined. The documentary evidence sheds light not only upon the question of who wrote the Bible but also upon why they wrote, not just on their own purposes for doing so, but also on God's purpose. God inspired a thesis in the heart and mind of one author (J), to be answered by an antithesis from another author (E), producing a synthesis from editors (JE). Then the process was repeated with JE as the new thesis, answered by P and edited by R, Ezra, in a new synthesis. The final redactor of the Pentateuch blended more than one synthesis into a Torah beloved by Jews and presenting a portrait of the Messiah that possibly none of the individual writers or editors saw.

For centuries, Christians have been partners with Jews in academic disciplines related to biblical study, even when everything else was strained between them. We hope to extend assistance to our Muslim colleagues in the present process, and this presentation ultimately concludes with illustrations of how Muslims will also assist Jews and Christians by sharing "what the Qur'an reveals about the Bible."

It has taken most of eight chapters to present simply what we know now about the Torah or Pentateuch, but this is worthwhile both in itself and to lay the groundwork for considering first the New Testament and finally the Qur'an and the Hadith. Facts presented in the legend of my diagram are influenced by evidence that many scholars present, but total agreement on every detail is not required to move the argument beyond a hypothesis to a position beyond reasonable doubt, a certainty we will attempt to find in the New Testament also, and eventually in both the Qur'an and the Hadith, using much the same methodology.

To look ahead in anticipation, while we have become more certain about how some of these dynamics operated from before the dawn of history down to at least the time of Ezra, we are still in the process of learning about others. We should introduce one such possibility before leaving the Hebrew Scriptures: a possibility to which we have but briefly alluded.

We are beginning to recognize a template for scriptural development and production that is different from our traditional picture of all Scripture's being written down on a scroll or tablet by the hand of one great prophet or priest. It is a model that comes to us also quite profoundly from Muslim sources: from the last great culture of the ancient Near East and indeed also from the family of Abraham, Sarah, and Hagar. The Qur'an is presented audibly or verbally as inspiration from on high to Prophet Muhammad, but just as the first surah was recited by him and then written down by his first wife, Kadijah, the bulk of the Qur'an was possibly written down by wives and daughters in his household. Muslims believe Muhammad was illiterate making it likely that nearly all the surahs, or chapters, of the Qur'an were written down by the women of his household, with perhaps a leading role being assumed by Hafsah, who was later entrusted with its preservation and transmission to the world, a point worth developing in reference to earlier Hebrew Scriptures in particular.

The Hadith presents conversations, actions, and habits of the Prophet of Islam as recorded by his Companions, both male and female. Determining authorship of these materials does not rely on secondary sources or conjecture. Islamic primary sources, under rigorous reevaluation by Islamic scholars today, have the potential to reveal whole new paradigms that may now be applied to biblical texts.

Mounting evidence shows that in the region known today as the Middle East, educated women had much more influence than we had imagined in the tent complexes of socioreligious potentates at the time of Mohammed and before. In fact, the nomadic societies of that time are considered to have been matriarchal, a step beyond the royal court in this regard, but, again, the such roles for women were limited to the leading families.

We know a bit about Naqiya-Zakutu, the literate Semitic wife of Sennacherib, who rebuilt and administered the city of Nineveh as a new capital for her husband. Perhaps the clearest recorded example of this influence of women is the tent complex of Muhammad. If women exerted influence in Muhammad's tent complex, then why not in the palace of King David and in the Jerusalem home of St. James, a leader of the early church in the eastern Mediterranean? This female role can be observed among Arabic Bedouin today, but primarily in the households of leaders, a situation similar to the role of women in the compounds of illiterate Afghan warlord/parliamentarians, who depend on educated local or foreign wives for computer literacy, even in a society where education is denied to most daughters of the common people.

A good example of this role in more modern Arabic society might be seen in the part that Queen Noor of Jordan played with respect to her writings for the Hashemite monarchy as the wife of King Hussein. It will not do for critics to suggest that there is no evidence of this pattern of women's influence in the Bible. The powerful influence of educated foreign wives in the courts of Solomon, Ahab, and others is well documented because of the crises that occurred, but influences of Israelite or Judean aristocratic women and even of sympathetic foreign wives, might not have been less, even if anonymous or unacknowledged.

This pattern of women's influence throws a whole new light on assumptions about certain writers of Scripture who have hitherto been judged by norms relating to Western women, whereas we are still learning of the roles of biblical and Muslim women. Even if many psalms were indeed "composed" by David, there is no evidence whatsoever that he personally put pen to paper and wrote any of them down. We do not know what role close companions and family might have had in the final writing of any psalms that he or other male or female liturgists did compose. We do know that much of the writing is anonymous or veiled.

Likewise, the book of Proverbs, traditionally said to be from the lips of Solomon, may come to us from the hands of his wives and sisters, like a woman who quite likely could have written the Book of J. Note also the reference to the teachings originating with the unknown King Lemuel's mother in Proverbs in 31:1. Similarly, the book of Ruth comes from the royal household's family memory of David's great-grandparents, and the books of Chronicles correct the records of Samuel and Kings to the liking of David's household. For that matter, both Ecclesiastes and the Song of Solomon might be reviewed to consider who did the actual writing.

Applying this procedure to the norms of the Qur'an, we might find that if the New Testament "Q" document came from a writer in the household of St. James, it was probably from the hand of a female member of his family—perhaps from his own wife or a sister, or perhaps even from the pen of Mary Magdalene, the much-speculated-about female companion of Jesus, who might have come under the protection of James in such a culture, and joined his household. Were she the widow of Jesus, as hinted in gnostic writings and promoted in the modern media, she would come under the protection of her brother-in-law, James. We will not pursue such speculation here except to note that the universally accepted Gospels attribute considerable wealth to this Mary who helped finance Jesus's ministry. Mary Magdalene is an example of the resourceful women with a degree of power in biblical times.

The Epistle of Priscilla (Hebrews) would have arisen likewise out of the household of the wealthy Christian businessman, Aquila. We should look for similar patterns in anything in the Scriptures that is anonymous, even in Job, with the prominence given to his daughters, or Esther, the story of well-connected women in high places. The rule might become, "If it is anonymous, it may be assumed that the writer is a woman."

Additional evidence in this regard remains to be presented in future chapters. The Qur'an may be the most authentic entrée into the world of the Bible available to us in this area. As such insights are developed we are entering the next stage in the quest for scholarly understanding of Scripture among those eager to hear and experience the Divine Word.

PART 2

Opening the Christian Scriptures

ΚΑΤΑ ΜΑΘΘΑΙΟΝ

1 Βίβλος γενέσεως Ἰησοῦ Χριστοῦ υἱοῦ Δαυὶδ υἱοῦ Ἀβραάμ.

2 Ἀβραὰμ ἐγέννησεν τὸν Ἰσαάκ, Ἰσαὰκ δὲ ἐγέννησεν τὸν Ἰακώβ, Ἰακὼβ δὲ ἐγέννησεν τὸν Ἰούδαν καὶ τοὺς ἀδελφοὺς αὐτοῦ, 3 Ἰούδας δὲ ἐγέννησεν τὸν Φάρες καὶ τὸν Ζάρα ἐκ τῆς Θαμάρ, Φάρες δὲ ἐγέννησεν τὸν Ἑσρώμ, Ἑσρὼμ δὲ ἐγέννησεν τὸν Ἀράμ, 4 Ἀρὰμ δὲ ἐγέννησεν τὸν Ἀμιναδάβ, Ἀμιναδὰβ δὲ ἐγέννησεν τὸν Ναασσών, Ναασσὼν δὲ ἐγέννησεν τὸν Σαλμών, 5 Σαλμὼν δὲ ἐγέννησεν τὸν Βόες ἐκ τῆς Ῥαχάβ, Βόες δὲ ἐγέννησεν τὸν Ἰωβὴδ ἐκ τῆς Ῥούθ, Ἰωβὴδ δὲ ἐγέννησεν τὸν Ἰεσσαί, 6 Ἰεσσαὶ δὲ ἐγέννησεν τὸν Δαυὶδ τὸν βασιλέα.

Δαυὶδ δὲ ἐγέννησεν τὸν Σολομῶνα ἐκ τῆς τοῦ Οὐρίου, 7 Σολομὼν δὲ ἐγέννησεν τὸν Ῥοβοάμ, Ῥοβοὰμ δὲ ἐγέννησεν τὸν Ἀβιά, Ἀβιὰ δὲ ἐγέννησεν τὸν Ἀσάφ, 8 Ἀσάφ[1] δὲ ἐγέννησεν τὸν Ἰωσαφάτ, Ἰωσαφὰτ δὲ ἐγέννησεν τὸν Ἰωράμ, Ἰωρὰμ δὲ ἐγέννησεν τὸν Ὀζίαν, 9 Ὀζίας δὲ ἐγέννησεν τὸν Ἰωαθάμ, Ἰωαθὰμ δὲ ἐγέννησεν τὸν Ἀχάζ, Ἀχὰζ δὲ ἐγέννησεν τὸν Ἑζεκίαν, 10 Ἑζεκίας δὲ ἐγέννησεν τὸν Μανασσῆ, Μανασσῆς δὲ ἐγέννησεν τὸν Ἀμώς, Ἀμὼς[2] δὲ ἐγέννησεν τὸν Ἰωσίαν, 11 Ἰωσίας δὲ ἐγέννησεν[3] τὸν Ἰεχονίαν καὶ τοὺς ἀδελφοὺς αὐτοῦ ἐπὶ τῆς μετοικεσίας Βαβυλῶνος.

12 Μετὰ δὲ τὴν μετοικεσίαν Βαβυλῶνος Ἰεχονίας ἐγέννησεν τὸν Σαλαθιήλ, Σαλαθιὴλ δὲ ἐγέννησεν τὸν Ζοροβαβέλ, 13 Ζοροβαβὲλ δὲ ἐγέννησεν τὸν Ἀβιούδ, Ἀβιοὺδ δὲ ἐγέννησεν τὸν Ἐλιακίμ, Ἐλιακὶμ δὲ ἐγέννησεν τὸν Ἀζώρ, 14 Ἀζὼρ δὲ ἐγέννησεν τὸν Σαδώκ, Σαδὼκ δὲ ἐγέννησεν τὸν Ἀχίμ, Ἀχὶμ δὲ ἐγέννησεν τὸν Ἐλιούδ, 15 Ἐλιοὺδ δὲ ἐγέννησεν τὸν Ἐλεάζαρ, Ἐλεάζαρ δὲ ἐγέννησεν τὸν Ματθάν, Ματθὰν δὲ ἐγέννησεν τὸν Ἰακώβ, 16 Ἰακὼβ δὲ ἐγέννησεν τὸν Ἰωσὴφ τὸν ἄνδρα Μαρίας, ἐξ ἧς ἐγεννήθη Ἰησοῦς ὁ λεγόμενος Χριστός[4].

17 Πᾶσαι οὖν αἱ γενεαὶ ἀπὸ Ἀβραὰμ ἕως Δαυὶδ γενεαὶ δεκατέσσαρες, καὶ ἀπὸ Δαυὶδ ἕως τῆς μετοικεσίας Βαβυλῶνος γενεαὶ δεκατέσσαρες, καὶ ἀπὸ τῆς μετοικεσίας Βαβυλῶνος ἕως τοῦ Χριστοῦ γενεαὶ δεκατέσσαρες.

18 Τοῦ δὲ Ἰησοῦ Χριστοῦ[5] ἡ γένεσις[6] οὕτως ἦν. μνηστευθείσης τῆς μητρὸς αὐτοῦ Μαρίας τῷ Ἰωσήφ, πρὶν ἢ συνελθεῖν αὐτοὺς εὑρέθη ἐν γαστρὶ ἔχουσα ἐκ πνεύματος ἁγίου. 19 Ἰωσὴφ δὲ ὁ ἀνὴρ αὐτῆς, δίκαιος ὢν καὶ μὴ θέλων αὐτὴν δειγματίσαι, ἐβουλήθη λάθρα ἀπολῦσαι αὐτήν. 20 ταῦτα δὲ αὐτοῦ ἐνθυμηθέντος ἰδοὺ ἄγγελος κυρίου κατ᾽ ὄναρ ἐφάνη αὐτῷ λέγων, Ἰωσὴφ υἱὸς Δαυίδ, μὴ φοβηθῇς παραλαβεῖν Μαρίαν τὴν γυναῖκά σου, τὸ γὰρ ἐν αὐτῇ γεννηθὲν ἐκ πνεύματός ἐστιν ἁγίου·

THE
GOSPEL ACCORDING
to S.Matthew.

CHAP. I.

1 The genealogie of Christ from Abraham to Ioseph. 18 Hee was conceiued by the holy Ghost, and borne of the Virgin Mary when she was espoused to Ioseph. 19 The Angel satisfieth the misdeeming thoughts of Ioseph, and interpreteth the names of Christ.

* Luke 3. 23.

HE booke of the * generation of Iesus Christ , the sonne of Dauid, the sonne of Abraham.

* Gen. 21. 3.

2 * Abraham begate Isaac , and

* Gene. 25. 26.
* Gen. 29. 35.
* Gen. 38. 27.
* 1. Chro. 2. 5. ruth. 4. 18.

* Isaac begate Iacob, and * Iacob begate Iudas and his brethren.

3 And * Iudas begat Phares and Zara of Thamar, and * Phares begate Esrom, and Esrom begate Aram.

4 And Aram begate Aminadab, and Aminadab begate Naasson, and Naasson begate Salmon.

5 And Salmon begat Boos of Rachab, and Boos begate Obed of Ruth, and Obed begate Iesse.

* 1. Sam. 16. 1. and 17. 12.
* 2. Sam. 12. 24.
* 1. Chra.3. 10.

6 And * Iesse begate Dauid the King, & * Dauid the King begat Solomon of her *that had bin* the wife of Vrias.

7 And * Solomon begat Roboam, and Roboam begate Abia, and Abia begate Asa.

8 And Asa begate Iosaphat, and Iosaphat begate Ioram, and Ioram begate Ozias.

9 And Ozias begat Ioatham, and Ioatham begate Achas, and Achas begate Ezekias.

* 2. King. 20. 21. 1. chro. 3. 13.

10 And * Ezekias begate Manasses,

and Manasses begate Amon, and Amon begate Iosias.

11 And ‖ Iosias begate Iechonias and his brethren, about the time they were caried away to Babylon.

‖ Some read, Iosias begate Iakim, and Iakim begat Iechonias.

12 And after they were brought to Babylon, * Iechonias begat Salathiel, and Salathiel begate Zorobabel.

* 1. Chro. 3. 16, 17.

13 And Zorobabel begat Abiud, and Abiud begat Eliakim, and Eliakim begate Azor.

14 And Azor begat Sadoc, & Sadoc begat Achim, and Achim begat Eliud.

15 And Eliud begate Eleazar, and Eleazar begate Matthan, and Matthan begate Iacob.

16 And Iacob begate Ioseph the husband of Mary, of whom was borne Iesus, who is called Christ.

17 So all the generations from Abraham to Dauid, are fourteene generations : and from Dauid vntill the carrying away into Babylon, are fourteene generations : and from the carrying away into Babylon vnto Christ, are fourteene generations.

18 ¶ Now the * birth of Iesus Christ was on this wise : When as his mother Mary was espoused to Ioseph (before they came together) shee was found with childe of the holy Ghost.

* Luke 1. 27.

19 Then Ioseph her husband being a iust man, and not willing to make her a publique example, was minded to put her away priuily.

20 But while hee thought on these things, behold, the Angel of the Lord appeared vnto him in a dreame, saying, Ioseph thou sonne of Dauid, feare not to take vnto thee Mary thy wife ; for that which is conceiued in her, is of the holy Ghost.

21 And

9

Discovery

THE HEBREW TEXT OF the beginning of the first book of the Pentateuch (called *Bereshit* in Hebrew) was faced in part 1 of this book with the Jewish *Tanakh* version, called Genesis in current English usage. The Arabic text of the opening of the Qur'an will be similarly matched by *The Sublime Qur'an* in English to open part 3 below. The first page of the New Testament opens this part of *Forensic Scriptures* in the original Greek, but the twenty-first-century English version that may become standard has yet to be translated. The English version employed here is one that most English-speaking Christians have never seen. It is the original 1611 edition of the King James Authorized Version, an ancient predecessor of the Standard Version most people think of as the King James Version. Since then, the Standard, Revised Standard, and New Revised Standard Bible Versions have all played roles, along with other "contemporary" versions. This presentation of the original KJV may help explain the necessity for newer versions, but the utmost care is required in presenting this precious heritage.

In regard to the Hebrew Scriptures, for example, there came a time when a tradition of pious devotion became so strong that in temple and synagogue, and especially in private conversation, the name of *Yahweh*, as revealed to Moses, was not to be pronounced at all, lest the commandment about using God's name in vain be transgressed. This was about the time when the Masoretic version of the Hebrew Bible first added diacritical marks or vowel symbols to the original consonants—little accents resembling punctuation marks, to aid in pronouncing the words of a language that employs an alphabet with only consonants.

In the scrolls of the Torah, whenever the strict Masorete transmitters came to *Yahweh*, or *YHWH* in Hebrew, they added the vowel marks for *Adonai* instead, to remind themselves to avoid pronouncing *YHWH* and to use *Adonai*. The custom of referring to God as *Adonai* was not real-ized by the first Protestant translators of the Bible into European languages, who came up with an amalgamated word using the consonants of *YHWH* and the vowels of *Adonai* to produce a new name for God: "Jehovah" (*J* and *Y* represent the same sound in many languages). The word "Jehovah" as a translation of *Yahweh* was an accidental invention of the Protestant Reformation that endured, to the amusement of the rabbis in Europe, but is a name for God that has stuck among the devout.

This is a benign example of how the lack of critical abilities can lead to unfounded religious traditions; such traditions are present in all faiths. About a hundred years ago a new church of Christians known as "witnesses" proclaimed that not only is "Jehovah" a name for God, but that it is God's only name! In fact, of all the biblical names we use for God, technically speaking, "Jehovah" is the only one that is not authentic! This amusing story may equip readers and students to appreciate the contribution of biblical criticism to some of the more vexing problems in the text. Might Muslims devoted to the well-preserved original text of the Qur'an find some freedom of interpretation by reexamining the diacritical marks added to that text, also at a somewhat later time and under changing influences?

For many years the best ancient text of both Hebrew and Christian Scriptures was the Codex Vaticanus, an old and well-preserved manuscript from the fourth century, which was used officially for Roman Catholic translations. Then in 1844 Konstantin von Tischendorf, a German bibli-cal scholar, found an older manuscript, Codex Sinaiticus, at the Russian Orthodox monastery of St. Catherine at Mount Sinai (supposedly on the rubbish heap). He presented it to the czar, whose family lost it to the Com-munists. The Communists did not value it, of course, and sold it to the British Museum in 1933, where it became widely available to translators. A new era in Bible translation began on the basis of this more ancient, au-thentic text, but even more exciting discoveries were to come.

In 1947 a fifteen-year-old Bedouin boy named Muhammad Ahmad el-Hamid threw some stones up into a Palestinian hillside cave to scare out a goat. He heard the sound of breaking clay pottery. Upon investigation, he made the single most surprising find in modern biblical pursuits: the discovery of the Dead Sea Scrolls. These ancient manuscripts, hidden in the year 70 of the Common Era, included complete scrolls of some Hebrew Scriptures in near-perfect condition and portions of all others except for

Esther. The accompanying documents also shed light on Judean sectarian practices and the context of early Christianity.

Wild rumors ensued that the Dead Sea Scrolls proved that the Jews never crossed the Red Sea, and tabloid headlines at the grocery checkout counter screamed that the Essene monks in the desert community had been homosexuals, including Jesus and John the Baptist. These rumors were compounded by the passage of years in which Israeli authorities would not release these manuscripts. Financing from Christian seminaries, led by faculties of divinity at McGill University and at the University of Chicago, gave Christian scholars a role in what appeared to many at first as a cover-up. The Vatican and other players contributed to the confusion. There was a nervous determination to control the outcome or at least to have an orderly release of information.

When the information did become public, the most amazing aspect of the discovery was the realization that the Scriptures used by Jews, Catholics, Orthodox, and Protestant Christians have a textual integrity that is solid. Exposure to these more ancient texts did not reveal any significant changes in the biblical storyline or content. Rather, it provided an opportunity to refine the wording of new translations in a way that was eventually truer to the overall message of these religions about virtue, justice, and loving compassion. The result was a more inclusive and intuitively valid text, which was at the same time more scholarly and accurate in terms of the fine details of the original writings. The best scientific methods of the twentieth century had combined with the suspicious watchfulness of all the participants to give everyone complete confidence in the texts when they were finally published to the world. The originals are now publicly displayed with great care in the controlled environment of the Shrine of the Book, a museum built for the purpose in Jerusalem. The Dead Sea Scrolls demonstrate that contrary to charges from New Age critics and modern cynics, nothing significant in the biblical texts has been changed by ignorant scholars, corrupt church officials, or Satan himself.

In 1945 another Muslim made a discovery just as significant for Christians as the Dead Sea Scrolls had been. But this second discovery was eclipsed by the first until most of the Dead Sea Scroll documents got published, some comparatively recently. An Egyptian farmer named Muhammad Ali and his brother had been digging for fertilizer in a potash deposit in the desert. They uncovered a jar a foot tall and eight inches wide, crammed with small tract-like booklets. Coated with slime and encased in mud that took decades to remove by scientific methods, the Nag Hammadi Library, as it is called, contains significant writings of gnostic Christians.

The gnostics were a Christian sect whose beliefs, as traditionally stated by other Christians in the church, were that the material world is a bad illusion and mortal flesh is deceptively evil. In contrast to the gnostics, orthodox Christians believe this is not a bad world, though the church has always acknowledged human sin and our capacity to despoil the creation of a good and loving God. In Genesis, as God completed each "day" or era of creation, God stood back and pronounced over each thing, "Behold, it is very good."

Gnostic views were expressed in writings published in the second century in the name of those associated with Jesus—writings such as the Gospel of Mary and the Gospel of Philip. Two of the gnostic documents of interest lately, especially in New Age spiritual circles, are the Gospel of Thomas and the Gospel of Judas. There are also the Sophia (Wisdom) of Christ, the Acts of Peter, the Revelation of Peter, the Revelation of James, the Gospel of Lazarus, and others, forty-five books in all, contained in thirteen volumes, each the size of a small paperback.

Many seeking an alternative to fundamentalism or authoritarian church dogma have attempted to rehabilitate the image of gnosticism. Gnostics appear to have contradicted the emphasis on "faith" based on cohesive teachings as worked out by the believing community, as opposed to their preference for a personal spiritual journey on the part of each individual. This was a problem for the early church, which was trying to create a cohesive unified faith somewhere between the extremes of such nontraditional Christian expressions, which were not only diverse but frequently anti-Semitic, on the one hand; and other spiritual, religious, and secular traditions on the other.

The earlier existence of these gnostic writings has always been known about, occurring in fragments and quotations from documents and letters produced in the early church during nearly two hundred years of struggle on these issues. The church, in finally overcoming gnostic influences, rejected the gnostic writings, banned them, and ordered all copies to be burned. But what might we guess would happen when the authorities tried to destroy documents that some group regarded as precious? Quite naturally, someone hid a collection or "library" of these writings!

After their discovery in 1945, it took twenty years for the world to fully appreciate that the Nag Hammadi library contained authentic Coptic translations of Greek writings by the gnostics, published at a time when gnosticism was rejected in the church, after seriously rivaling orthodox Christianity and almost taking over. Again, with this discovery, there was panic in certain conservative quarters in the modern Christian church. The rumors were that the Nag Hammadi documents would dethrone the pope with information about early church government or even prove that Jesus had been married to Mary Magdalene. Hints of his love for her did actually lead to fictions like *The Last Temptation of Christ* and *The Da Vinci Code*. Close examination of the Nag Hammadi documents, however, has merely enriched the study of Christian Scriptures, many of which were penned at the beginning of the controversy, as answers to the gnostics. Writings in the Nag Hammadi library are valuable in the sense that it is easier to understand the answers in the Bible when we know the questions. Such discoveries have continued to justify the confidence of the church in its primary sources. There is never anything to fear from the truth. Blind faith is never as thrilling as faith with eyes wide open. The ancient debate may be repeated, and whatever value gnostic Christianity may offer the modern world will be discussed in relation to the Scriptures that were written in defense of orthodox belief.

Gnostic views continued to spread through underground channels right up to the time of Muhammad and beyond. They often surface in popular media today, animated by discomfort with clumsy or defensive presentations of church dogma and by the rediscovery of these ancient gnostic texts. The gnostic view of the Messiah (that he possessed all knowledge, that the cross was bogus, and that he did not die for anyone's sins) bears several hallmarks of the Messiah as presented in the Qur'an. It is not suggested that the Qur'an was therefore based on gnostic sources. Indeed the orthodox Muslim view is that much of what is revealed in the Qur'an was revealed by Allah previously to others, who preserved it sometimes faithfully and sometimes in corrupt and garbled texts. In this case, the Qur'an may be able to shed light on what the main competing version of Christianity believed about the Messiah.

10

Documentation

PEOPLE SOMETIMES ASK WHY only such documents as the Old Testament, the New Testament, and the Qur'an come to be regarded as
authentic or "holy" Scriptures, while other brilliantly written spiritual material does not attain this status. In the last several centuries, the Book of
Mormon by Joseph Smith, the *Writings* of the Bahá'í movement, and the
Guru Grantha of the Sikhs came close to such recognition or achieved it
in their own smaller circles. In liberal circles of the twentieth century *The
Prophet* by Kahlil Gibran and the "Letter from Birmingham City Jail" by
Martin Luther King Jr. qualified as Scripture in the minds of some for a
short time. New Age "revelations" in the last couple of decades that aspired
to such acceptance included *The Celestine Prophecy* by James Redfield and
A Course in Miracles by Helen Schucman, attaining almost cult status for a
brief period. No one disputes that God speaks to individuals and significant
groups in ways stretching from these writings through classical music to a
sunset over the ocean.

But in addition to the approval of spiritual authorities at crucial moments, Holy Scripture may be said to be self-authenticating in certain
important respects. Scriptural accounts of people enduring plagues; of nations punished in war, sexism, or racism; and other scriptural accounts of
how God seems to act in various times and circumstances may for some
people cause problems with the Scriptures as received. But then a psychia-
trist like Carl Jung may come along to explain plausibly that these battles
and scourges in Scripture can be understood as reflections of what happens
inside the psyche of each person in the course of life. Critics say the science
in the Bible does not add up exactly, and the history is faulty, leading whole
societies to almost jettison their holy books for a time, only to find the
next generation believing more fervently than the previous. Church leaders

explaining away the mystery to make the Scriptures more believable, find children turning to *The Lion, the Witch, and the Wardrobe* by C. S. Lewis or to J. K. Rowling's Harry Potter series to recover a sense of mystery, until the Holy Scriptures are made accessible simply as they are. Of course, when the Scriptures are restored to their essential role as engaging and foundational resources for life, they may be read and understood alongside contemporary expressions of the spiritual and ethical journey of humanity. Fairy tales and children's stories have always had a role in developing the imagination, but they cannot become substitutes for Scripture, which always has a depth beyond the current ability to simply explain.

Self-authentication involves the instinctive turning and returning of millions of people, generation after generation to that which they recognize intuitively as sacred. Periods of "enlightenment" come and go and often look foolish or shallow in retrospect. The "revolution" always revolves back to its starting point, if we understand the meaning of that word. The books of compelling writers in one generation are auctioned at estate sales for twenty-five cents a pound to the next generation, who have moved on in their own way. Ancient mythologies are studied for psychological understanding in institutions of higher learning, but the Scriptures alone endure in every generation and in all social strata as current resources for living and understanding the meaning of life as it comes to us from God. An intelligentsia is usually waiting in the wings, smugly certain that this will be the last such generation.

In these regards, in spite of predictions to the contrary, the twenty-first century is already no different than the twenty centuries that preceded it. At least since records have been kept following the invention of the printing press, and well before then by estimates, the Bible is far ahead as the perpetual bestseller. As "number one" every month, every week, and every day, it is not even reported in the popular media. In the twenty-first century, the Qur'an has moved up to become ranked as the perpetual number-two bestseller, largely unreported, perhaps for similar reasons. Either sophisticated media critics are embarrassed at this phenomenon, or they also fall into the common assumption that the high standing of Scripture is surely about to end, as has been predicted on record since at least the first modern encyclopedia, published during the French Revolution.

In the year 70 CE, the city of Jerusalem was destroyed by the Romans, who were wishing to be finally rid of this rebellious remnant of Judeans. As a stubborn people who refused to assimilate, the Jews (and their Christian offshoot sect) were already threatening the official religion of the Empire, a patriotism that was expected to be supreme in the lives of all citizens. The Israelites had been dispersed before, as when the Assyrians decimated the northern kingdom of Israel in 721 BCE, resulting in the scattering of the lost tribes of Israel and the refugee arrival in Judah, as described previously. This time, with the destruction of Jerusalem by the Romans, there was an absence of political leadership. The spiritual leaders from the long-restored southern kingdom of Judah met in the village of Jamnia, fifty kilometers, or a day's walk, from Jerusalem, to see if there was a way to face this crisis and to remain united as a people. They provided pastoral care for the refugees and consulted daily for more than a decade.

The rabbis in session at the Council of Jamnia had to decide between either lying low until someday Jerusalem and its temple might be rebuilt (knowing that had happened before) or recognizing that this Diaspora might endure, at least for generations, and make some provision for spiritual life and Jewish identity. When they had been in exile in Babylon, the priests of an earlier era had launched a scriptural project of immense proportions, which was part of what made the eventual return so successful. That Scripture, the Torah, became codified out of the necessity to recall the temple rituals, based on erstwhile desert tabernacle precedents, plus the historical legends, all of which bound the people together. That precedent came up time and again during the deliberations that went on for several years at Jamnia.

In the face of the mighty Roman Empire, the rabbis at Jamnia came to the conclusion that Jerusalem and its all-important temple could not be rebuilt in the foreseeable future, a decision probably made final when in 135 CE the legions of Emperor Hadrian decimated a brief Jewish attempt to reoccupy Jerusalem under the rebel Simeon bar Koseba. Something was needed to permanently represent God's presence in their midst.

They decided to turn to Scripture once again, to make an agreement about which writings were holy, and to include them alone in an official Hebrew extended compendium of Holy Scripture. They had more sacred writings than just J, E, D, and P, now edited together into the Torah of Genesis, Exodus, Leviticus, Numbers, and Deuteronomy. They decided to add to it selections from the whole body of their literature, including the writings, speeches, and oracles of the prophets and other "writings" to replace the temple itself in the lives of the Jewish people. The consensus about which books were holy enough to be included was possibly developed sometime late in the first century CE at Jamnia, but not recognized until after 135, when the Jamnian convocation disbanded, at which point the Hebrew Bible as we know it became accepted by Jews around the world, who welcomed this expanded Scripture as a virtual temple.

However, by this time the mainly Jewish Christian church was using a larger collection of Jewish books called the Septuagint as its Old Testament. In completing his translation of the Scriptures into the vernacular Latin in 405 CE, St. Jerome segregated the extra books into a section he called the Apocrypha, meaning "hidden." A thousand years later, the churches of the Protestant Reformation reverted to the official Jewish list that they considered to be more authentic as authorized by the rabbis at the Council of Jamnia. This accounts for the difference between Protestant Bibles and those used by most Catholic and Orthodox churches today.

The New Testament, as the specifically Christians Scriptures, had an even more twisted path toward acceptance of an authentic list or "canon." The Gospels came into use individually as teaching aids, consisting of the stories of Jesus and the saving events of his life, death, and resurrection. The Epistles or Letters of St. Paul were addressed to specific churches or individuals to settle spiritual questions and as administrative guides. They were not intended for wider circulation, but copies were distributed as they became cherished among Christians. The so-called Catholic Epistles by Peter, James, and John were general letters intended for circulation in the growing Christian community at a slightly later time, but none of them were designed to be part of a collection either. Other writings, such as the Apocalypse of John and the Apocalypse of Peter as well as the epistles known as Barnabas, 1 Clement, 2 Clement, and the Shepherd of Hermas were circulating. Also circulating without any particular authorization through the second century were items like Jude and the Didache (a canon law or church manual).

The impetus for establishing an official canon list came from the Gnostic Christians, still largely within the church. In 144 CE, Marcion published a list of what he considered to be Christian Scriptures from a Gnostic perspective. It consisted of ten letters by Paul, no Old Testament, and the Gospel of Luke stripped of all Jewish references. For his efforts he was kicked out of the church. He founded his own church, and the Gnostics began the separation that would lead to their demise after a lengthy struggle with orthodoxy over the Jewish roots of Christianity and the church's affirmation of the essential goodness of creation.

As part of the campaign of orthodox Christianity against Gnostic Christianity, Justin Martyr was the orthodox theologian who engaged Marcion in dialogue in 160 CE, referring to the "Memoirs of the Apostles," Matthew, Mark, Luke, and John, plus the Apocalypse or Revelation of John, as all being acceptable Scripture for the Western Church, then headquartered in Rome. This list of the four Gospels became widely accepted in the Western Church and was almost immediately adopted (minus Revelation) as the first Christian Testament in Syria by Tatian, Justin's powerful disciple, who was the leading theologian of the Eastern Church.

Work on an official list continued in the first Christian seminary at Alexandria in Egypt from about 180 CE onward, especially after Clement became its principal. The criterion was established that Christian Scriptures would be limited to writings by the apostles, including St. Paul, for all the apostles had died, and their testimony was to be recorded. In some sense, it was felt that just as the Old Testament had replaced the Jerusalem temple, the New Testament should replace the apostles. More work at the second seminary in Caesarea under Origen authorized the larger Septuagint as an Old Testament for the growing Greek-speaking membership of the church, with notations about which books were official Jewish Scriptures, about which already were being quoted in Christian Scriptures, and about which were unauthorized but valued as background study.

By 350 CE, Cyril, the bishop of a smaller but influential Jerusalem recently rebuilt, was strictly enforcing a canon or list including the four Gospels, the Acts of the Apostles, twenty-one epistles, including all the Pauline and Catholic Letters as we have them, but not the Revelation. In 363 at Laodicea a council of thirty bishops from across the church recognized the leadership of Jerusalem in this matter and ruled that only Cyril's list and the Old Testament could be read as Scripture in the churches. This was widely accepted until 367 when Athanasius, the theologian and historian of the church under persecution, added Revelation in his lectionary for use in the church at Rome once again.

Most churches accepted his list, though it was not confirmed until the Council of Hippo in 393 and the Council of Carthage in 397, both meeting in North Africa. The bishops of the Syrian Church dissented both times, and to this day that church does not include Revelation in its canon. Ancient churches have made alterations to the generally accepted canon: the Armenian Church still has a book of 3 Corinthians, the Coptic (Egyptian) Church includes 1 and 2 Clement (Clement was their famous seminary principal), and the Ethiopian Church appends a number of prayers, ceremonies, and church rules to canonical Scripture.

In 1975 I had the privilege of performing a wedding for dear friends and parishioners, a mature couple who ran an antiques dealership in Dawson Creek, at Mile Zero on the Alaska Highway in northern British Columbia. As payment for my performing the ceremony, they offered me a Bible, which I agreed to accept despite having many copies already. Upon opening and examining my gift, I discovered an original copy of the Bishops' Bible published in 1568, two generations before the Authorized King James Version.

I was absolutely astounded. It seems that a freak snowstorm in the balmy southern city of Victoria had prevented out-of-town dealers from attending an important estate sale auction that featured the heritage possessions of a family that had brought to Canada books that were already old back in the colonial days. My friends bid on book lots by the shelf, relatively unopposed, and acquired one of the two copies of what is called the Bishops' Bible in this country, almost by chance. Since they had been hoping to find an appropriate gift for me, they believed it was a Godsend intended for their minister. It has become a most precious possession of our family.

While Shakespeare was still a child, the Bishops' Bible had been authorized by Queen Elizabeth I and Archbishop Matthew Parker. The Bishops' Bible is not highly regarded as a translation, but fortunately, whole sections were lifted from Miles Coverdale's 1538 Great Bible, as authorized by King Henry VIII. The Great Bible, a copy of which was chained to the pulpit of every English Church, was Coverdale's revision of the first English Bible, produced by William Tyndale in 1525, which itself brought to fruition the earlier unpublished translation by John Wycliffe, produced by the Oxford scholar translating "on the run" through Europe before the Protestant Reformation had been secured.

The fifty-four translators of the King James Version were instructed to use the Tyndale Bible as a template, though, in fact, they derived inspiration from this whole cluster or family of translations with respect to English language—especially from the Coverdale sections that had been made popular by the Great Bible and the Bishops' Bible. In contrast, Shakespeare quoted the equally correct but stiffer 1560 Geneva Bible, a translation by English Calvinist exiles in Europe. The language of the Wycliffe-Tyndale-Coverdale-Bishops' family of Bible translations was already archaic in the

time of King James, but the enduring legacy of the translation he authorized was its natural descendant: the Authorized Version kept the sublime
majesty of that most noble and worshipful form of the English language—a
Bible version derived from Reformers who had put their lives on the line
(several had been burned at the stake for their efforts) and emulated by the
King James translators in their more precise rendering.

This legacy has extended through the (British) Revised Version of
the KJV, the (American) Standard Version, the (Canadian and American)
Revised Standard Version, and the (Universal) New Revised Standard
Version, released by ecumenical bodies over the last couple hundred years
at about forty-year intervals. The scholarship has been unmatched, but the
sublimity of the language eventually seemed compromised through this era
of critical analysis. Many expect this deficiency may be remedied by the
next translation in this series now anticipated by about the year 2020 from
the Bible Translation and Utilization Committee of the National Council of
Churches in the United States. That translation will seek to recover a more
lyrical emphasis as found in a variety of more poetic evangelical versions,
which currently suffer from an excess of colloquial language that may not
serve the English-speaking world over any extended period of time.

Of great interest to me is the fact that that my original Bishops' Bible
still has the leather straps and metal hasps used to lock the Bible after its
public reading. From the beginning of the Protestant Reformation, the
Bible was to be read aloud in public worship in the vernacular, national
languages of Europe, but it was not until the time of King James that every
Christian was given free access to it. In most communities, only the clergy
could actually read, and the fear was that as people learned to read and as
books became common thanks to the newly invented printing press, there
would be as many interpretations of the Bible as there were Christians.

But the church was also taking the lead in public education, and laypeople were being given increased responsibility and authority in Protestant
churches. Before long, the locks came off the Bibles. Bibles were dissemi-
nated to every home. The church began the common practice of Bible study
to provide the "official" interpretations and the scholarly understandings
of the text, to complement the guidance of the Holy Spirit in the heart of
each reader. Some of the predicted chaos came to pass with divisions in
the church and a proliferation of sects, led by people founding their own
"true" churches based on their private understandings of the Bible. Historically, such movements that have endured eventually produced scholars

who could read Bibles in the Hebrew and Greek originals, and such sects became churches with enhanced appreciation of the centuries of biblical scholarship they could easily inherit.

The locking apparatus on my Bishops' Bible illustrates that for the first fifteen hundred years of the Common Era, for most Christians, Scripture was experienced by hearing, not by reading. The aural experience of audible presentation has been overshadowed for almost five hundred years by printed copies read in private. This took place through a combination of factors, including the doctrine of "the priesthood of all believers" from the Protestant Reformation, the invention of the printing press, and the advent of public education. The fact that for most of Christian history, the Bible was heard rather than read by most people was seen as a disadvantage to these new propagators of the faith, but that may be only partially true. We now suspect, from the recitation of the Qur'an among Muslims and the revival of biblical Hebrew in the Jewish community, that the emphasis on private reading and subsequent stress upon critical analysis may have robbed the Christian community of something essential to the faith: the aural and vocal experience known by ancestors adept at memorization and recitation.

These skills have only slowly disappeared between the first Protestant generation, which still produced Bibles of aural majesty, to the generations of my grandparents and parents, for whom the memorization and recitation of Scripture was an important and common part of religious life and practice. The practice of memorization was completely abandoned with disdain by most Christian churches in the middle of the twentieth century as "mindless repetition of words without meaning." The interest was in understanding rather than reciting, as if a choice must be made, but we are beginning to realize again that words have power. The aching void created by this change and the related lack of other aural experiences has been felt only as the new century opens, a time in which other branches of the Abrahamic faith family seem to thrive on these cherished practices. It is not even as if young people cannot recite. They can recite volumes of lyrics from popular culture but have not been offered the wisdom of the ages or the Word of God in this manner.

Meanwhile, we are continuing to unlock the Scriptures with the critical methods developed in the last century. Even the current postcritical era, with its renewed emphasis on the meaning of the Word rather than its history, is now only completely possible because we have verified and more properly understood the text. The ability to read the text more clearly, combined with the new emphasis on hearing the text (Jews in the original Hebrew, and Christians in new versions yet to be released) will be hallmarks of a new era. Rhetorical criticism has capped off the century dominated by critical techniques and has introduced a new era in which the aural experience of hearing the Scriptures recaptures something essential in church and synagogue. Jews and Christians have become aware of the fact that something was missing, partly through the emergence of the aural Qur'an in the consciousness, and partly through the combined scholarship of this family as a whole at the beginning of the twenty-first century, just as the fruits of rhetorical criticism were also becoming available.

Without sacrificing their aural experience, Muslims are now unlocking their cherished Scriptures in our time, employing a combination of older critical techniques of their own and an acknowledged adoption of the specific techniques developed by Christians and Jews over the last century or more, as we shall see. After verifying the techniques explained in reference to the Old Testament by applying them to the New Testament, this study will then conclude with several chapters that will illustrate these developments in the Islamic community. The application of critical techniques to the Qur'an will also have value to Christians and Jews, offering new insights from material within the family of Abraham, Sarah, and Hagar through the application of the techniques of analysis pioneered in the critical examination of the Bible.

11

Corroboration

SOME ANALYSIS OF THE Christian Scriptures is in order at this point. We have seen how textual analysis and criticism has worked in recognizing the sources of the Pentateuch. There is a similar exercise available to sincere scholars of the Christian Scriptures, both lay and professional, with equal value in appreciating the richness in the backgrounds of the first three New Testament gospels in particular. It is another detective story.

The texts of the gospels are sufficiently familiar in Western culture and even in world culture for readers to make their own observations, based on the best-known stories. This exercise does not even require language skills, because, although the gospels were all written in Greek, this particular investigation can be successfully pursued in English or in any other translation.

We begin with the question of where the gospels came from and why the first three of them look so much alike and yet have such important distinctions. The relationship between Matthew, Mark, and Luke is a puzzle often referred to as the Synoptic Problem.

The Gospel of Jesus Christ according to St. Matthew appears first in the New Testament, because it repeatedly points to the purported fulfillment of Old Testament prophecies concerning the Messiah. It opens with stories of the magi, astrologers visiting Bethlehem following the birth of Jesus, a hint of the Persian origins of this gospel. Like the Pentateuch, Matthew has four strands of material: a document we know as Mark's gospel that Matthew's gospel shares with Mark and Luke; another document shared with only Luke: a collection of sayings of Jesus unique to this gospel (possibly a portion written by Matthew himself during his mission ministry in the farther east); and finally the unique opening section that presents Jesus's genealogy (from Mary to as far back as Abraham), the birth and magi stories, and the flight into Egypt.

The second gospel in the Christian Scriptures is the one by Mark. According to 1 Peter 5:13, Mark was like a son to St. Peter, who had been a disciple, then an apostle, and finally the first bishop of the church in Rome. Papias, bishop of Syria, remembered Mark as Peter's interpreter in his missionary work. This leads to the natural assumption that when Peter died, the church turned to Mark to publish a collection of the stories of Jesus, since no one wanted Peter's stories about Jesus to be forgotten. As Peter's interpreter, Mark probably knew the stories by heart, and there is no significant reason to doubt that Mark was the author of this gospel. Both internal and external evidence suggests that the Gospel of Mark appears to be basically one document. There are no nativity stories and only a few verses about the resurrection. Mark's gospel is mostly a collection of the stories of Jesus that the world knows in direct, unpolished language, like a transcription of Peter's gruff style.

Luke tells us at the outset that he is the compiler of the third gospel, the one that bears his name, having gathered material from many sources and having interviewed eyewitnesses to the events of Jesus's life. One of those sources must be Mark, because virtually every word of Mark is reproduced almost verbatim, just as it is in Matthew's gospel. Luke has his own collection of parables not found in Mark—material from Jesus's ministry unique to Luke, though not written by him since, as we learn in his second volume, the Acts of the Apostles, Luke is a physician from Greece who became a Christian some years after the life of Jesus through the missions of St. Paul. There is also that document in Luke that has material in common with Matthew and, like Matthew, Luke too has a unique birth-and-childhood section. His genealogy is through Joseph all the way back to Adam—no magi, but shepherds and other authentic Palestinian figures.

John's gospel is sufficiently different in style, purpose, and content to ignore in the synoptic question, but why do Christians have those three "look-alike" gospels, and what can be gained by comparing them? The answer gives both a picture of the early church and the license for the church universal to present the essence of the gospel in the context of the lives of people in all the cultures of the world.

Mark gives the essence of the teachings of Jesus, and if we grasp that essence, the more esoteric stories and doctrines of Jesus's birth and resurrection may be seen in the fullness of their symbolism and as presentations of messianic credentials. It is as if those are subjects for believers, once they have accepted his teaching. Matthew focuses on the Jewish Diaspora from east to west and develops the messianic claim within Hebrew "proof texts," quoting Israelite and Judean prophecies and tracing the lineage of Jesus only within Judaism, beginning with Joseph and concluding with Abraham. Luke presents a gospel to the non-Judean world, not quoting Scriptures (which would be unfamiliar), but eyewitness accounts, which could then still be verified. Greek Orthodox tradition says that Luke knew Mary in her old age and painted her portrait in oils. That may have provided him with the connection to her and knowledge of her life that served as a basis for his writing about the time the angel Gabriel appeared to her with the revelation that she would bear the Messiah. (Gabriel is same angelic presence that is also described in other writings as having revealed things of great import to Daniel and to Muhammad.) Luke's genealogy of Jesus relates him to the whole human family, beginning with Joseph and concluding with Adam. These distinct emphases remain despite the fact that two-thirds of all three gospels are virtually the same, and in the case of Matthew and Luke, 80 percent of the material is practically identical.

We surmise that Mark's gospel was written between Peter's death in the year 64 CE and the year 70 CE, when Jerusalem was destroyed, because the text presumes that this city is still standing. Matthew and Luke both integrated Mark's writing into their longer works. They both are two-thirds Mark, one-sixth that other document they had in common, and one-sixth something unique to each.

We believe that Luke and Matthew were written at about the same time, some time after 70 CE, because these gospels refer to the destruction of Jerusalem. It would have taken a few years for Matthew and Luke to acquire copies of Mark if they were some distance away from Rome, and there is evidence that they were. Matthew and Luke must have been some distance from each other also, since neither of them had yet seen the work of the other. Why else would Matthew leave out the stories of the good Samaritan and the prodigal son, masterpieces of world literature; and why would Luke omit parables such as the ten virgins, the marriage feast, the laborers in the vineyard, and the talents if he had read them in Matthew? After all, Luke describes himself as a collector of sources.

We know from the book of Acts that Luke's audience was centered in the eastern Mediterranean and Matthew's audience somewhere in the Orient, possibly in Persia or even farther east, but there is more. Both writers had copies of Mark, but neither possessed the work of the other, as has been illustrated above; so how do we explain that another sixth of Matthew's gospel and of Luke's gospel are practically word-for-word identical but are not found in Mark? Source critics believe that this overlap proves the existence of another document circulating in the early church. It must have been in the possession of both Matthew and Luke, but unknown to Mark at the time he wrote. A copy of this document has yet to be found.

Source critics call this document Q (from the German *Quelle* meaning "source"), and since Matthew and Luke appear to have copied it meticulously, we assume that we have the whole of it. Q is a collection of information about Jesus, possibly originating as a supplement to Mark's collection of stories told by Jesus. Q includes such things as the temptations in the wilderness; Jesus's reply to questions posed by John the Baptist from prison; the conditions of discipleship; the mission of the seventy; some parables, such as the stories of the building on rock and of the talents; the Beatitudes (unexpected blessings announced by Jesus); and the Lord's Prayer, also known as the prayer of Jesus. All these are significant additions to what was available from Mark, and they appear to come from a source possessed by both Luke and Matthew.

Luke and Matthew (or the editor who finally put material by Matthew into the gospel that bears his name) both insert Mark's material to suit their agendas; but they do so respectfully, in large sections, as befits something from the "head office" of the church. The Q material is scattered more creatively into these composite documents, as if the writers of Luke and Matthew were not as beholden to the author. The material from these multiple sources may be represented graphically as a multicolored diagram. In side-by-side columns of gospel verses, Mark's material, Q, Matthew's unique material, and Luke's unique material are all assigned separate colors. The best known of these diagrams is the one by Allan Barr of Edinburgh, published in 1938 by T. & T. Clark, and included as a photo on the back cover of this book. This is Exhibit A in any dispute about the validity of critical methods of scriptural analysis, since even a child can clearly identify the strands of material and draw correct conclusions about such things as the order in which they appeared and the distinct agenda of each gospel.

All this is made simple by the diagram, originally produced by Professor Barr for his own students in Scotland. His work is based largely on the research of H. B. Streeter, published in 1924 as *The Four Gospels: A Study of Origins*. Streeter was a British New Testament scholar who occupies a place in its investigation analogous to that of Wellhausen in the study of the Old Testament. Almost by coincidence, Streeter too finds four basic documents behind the three Synoptic Gospels that were the center of his work: Mark, Q, Matthew's unique material, and Luke's unique material, and, again, some of them have subsources.

This analysis can be undertaken without the diagram by anyone with a photographic memory or a scissors-and-paste scrapbook, the kind of exercise assigned at seminary. An appreciation of the dynamics of the early church and the spread of the gospel is greatly enhanced by such studies. This is similar to the enhanced appreciation of Israelite history and God's dealing with people in the experiences of and the writing of the Pentateuch, which began to emerge once the basic hypothesis of the documentary evidence was first established. Now the documentary evidence is much more widely accepted, and is illustrated in the "Diagram of Sources of the Pentateuch." These enhanced appreciations of Scripture can guide Christian and Jewish believers in their current understandings and presentations of the faith, as may be seen in the following example.

The gospels agree that there were visitor witnesses to the birth of Jesus. On the basis of his research, Luke says they were shepherds. It is suggested that Matthew's unique representation of those visitors to his Persian audience as the more familiar magi was the license for early missionaries in Canada, for example, to present the nativity story in indigenous imagery. This style of evangelism is demonstrated in the Canadian Christmas carol titled either "The Huron Carol" or "'Twas in the Moon of Wintertime," in which God is given the name *Gitchi Manitou*, the Great Spirit of the native peoples, and the visitors are called wandering hunters and chiefs from afar.

This phenomenon has its parallels in Chinese, south Asian, and African figures in nativity scenes and on Christmas cards in those cultures.

12

Fingerprints

IN REFERENCE TO THE church and its relationship to the text of Christian Scripture, the discipline of "textual criticism" (the main branch of "lower criticism," or knowledge revealed from within the text) presents us with the delightful tale of the different versions of the Lord's Prayer. The story was pieced together by Christian scholars only after the finding of Codex Sinaiticus in Egypt by Konstantin von Tischendorf in 1844.

Prior to the invention of the printing press, used first for the purpose of speeding up Bible production, Bibles were mass-produced by monks in selected monasteries. Twenty or thirty brothers would sit in rows in a large room called a *scriptorium*, copying by hand as a reader dictated. When perhaps thirty Bibles were completed they would be shipped to churches requesting them, or to other monasteries and church institutions, including libraries and theological seminaries.

Occasionally a manuscript from one of the leading monasteries would be shipped to a new monastery, or one that was just going into the production of Bibles. If a copy with an error was shipped, and hundreds of copies were eventually made from it, that error would be repeated in all the copies distributed from that source. If the new producer were the only one in a certain country or region, the whole area would contain the error. As more copies were made, the church of that country might become insistent on its particular interpretation of the Bible, since all its churches had that version. There are a number of well-documented examples of this reason for variant texts, but none so clear as the case of the Lord's Prayer.

We do not know where Codex Bezae originated, except that it was in the Western Church, because it is in Latin. Scientific dating of its pages and analysis of the style of script confirm the tradition that it is from the fifth or sixth century, so it is ancient. In the Middle Ages it resided in the library of the Monastery of St. Irenaeus in Lyons, France. It came into the possession of the Protestant Reformer Theodore Beza, who wished to promote translations into vernacular European languages. He presented it to Cambridge University in 1581, and Cambridge named it after him.

Codex Bezae was then used as the basis for Bible translations into several European languages used by Protestants. An error existing in *Bezae* would be translated and incorporated into all the texts produced from it. Thanks to the new printing presses in Britain and on the Continent, the error would soon have thousands of copies and possibly be repeated for hundreds of years, even into various revised versions.

Picture the scene as it might have happened. The monks have been writing all day except for washroom breaks, chapel services, and meals. Late in the afternoon, some of them have writer's cramp, and the abbot, who had been reading, begins to get hoarse. They had finished the Old Testament, and began copying the New Testament that morning and were now up to the sixth chapter of Matthew. When he reached verse nine, Abbot Adrian read: "After this manner therefore pray ye," which the monks wrote. He continued: "Our father who art in heaven," which they wrote. At this point he might have said, "Carry on with that, brothers, while I get a drink and rest my throat."

Twenty monks kept writing, transcribing the words of the prayer they knew by heart. Except that when they said this prayer in chapel seven times a day, they added a doxology, a liturgical ascription of glory, as follows: "For Thine is the kingdom, the power and the glory, forever and ever, Amen." It was like another doxology, "Glory be to the Father" that many Protestant, Orthodox, and Catholic Christians still chant after reading a psalm.

Nineteen monks wrote the prayer, ending where Catholic and Orthodox Christians end the prayer to this day: "And lead us not into temptation, but deliver us from evil. Amen." Brother Michael, as we might call one of the copyists, exhausted and trying to complete the task in his beautiful handwriting, carried right on as he had done four times already that day in chapel, "For Thine is the kingdom, the power and the glory, forever and ever, Amen"—absent-mindedly forgetting that the doxology was not part of the prayer as given to the disciples by Jesus.

We can guess or imagine whose beautiful copy got shipped to Lyons, placed in the library, cherished, quoted on special occasions, and copied in their scriptorium. We now know which prized original, not even one of the copies, was acquired by a great Protestant Reformer, presented to

Cambridge, and used throughout Protestant lands as the basis for translations in Swiss, Dutch, and French Reformed churches, and by British Presbyterian, Puritan, and Anglican translators. It was Bezae, and this was the manuscript used most famously as the basis for the King James Authorized Version.

So for nearly four hundred years Protestants said a longer Lord's Prayer than Roman Catholics and wondered why Catholics did not know the whole prayer. In popular Protestant culture, from America to Australia, this seemed like proof that the Catholics had a defective tradition. After Codex Sinaiticus confirmed the accuracy of the Codex Vaticanus version, there was nothing Protestants could do except humbly admit that they were wrong.

It took a hundred years for this to be acknowledged, and Catholics included the ancient doxology from time to time, especially when there were Protestants present. In joint services of worship to this day, Catholics are generally gracious in the face of the Protestant preference, and Protestants continue with the longer version, even though in most other respects they are not as given to doxologies and liturgical flourishes as their Catholic friends.

Even more amusing, since Anglicans define themselves not as either Catholic or Protestant, but laudably as affirming both traditions, in some Anglican services the Lord's Prayer is said twice—once with the longer ending, and once with the shorter.

Just as many Christians may go on using the name Jehovah, Protestants may well continue to conclude the Lord's Prayer as if Jesus had spoken those last words as an "ascription of glory." What is of infinitely greater value is the insight that comes from renewed confidence in the text of Scripture, combined with the leading of the Holy Spirit in presenting the Word to the world in the twenty-first century.

These amusing examples illustrate how much we also owe to critical analysis of the Scriptures in more substantial areas of devotion and scholarship, including the investigation in the following chapter. Hopefully these examples of Christian error, presented humbly, may also encourage confidence in those now engaged in applying all manner of critical techniques to a reexamination of the Hadith, a treasured Muslim source that we have also to introduce subsequently.

13

Accomplices

THERE ARE DOZENS OF examples in the gospels of Jesus's interacting with women in everyday life, including questions, discussion, thoughtful consideration, debate, and even confrontation. He evinced an attitude toward women that shines through even into the very male-biased Greco-Roman early church culture in which the Scriptures were written down and collected. So, despite biases, we hear of women as part of a couple, as parents, or on the road to Emmaus, for example—images not common in other literature of the time, not present in his culture, and not always emulated by Jesus's followers in the church. This is only remarkable in that women were usually invisible to everyone else in those contexts also, but not to Jesus. On other occasions the women in Jesus's life were sisters, servers, companions, interlocutors, worshipers, wives, daughters, and others in individual or communal roles.

In some cases they remain nameless, as does the widow with her mite, or identified by the place they lived, but several are named. In many cases their actions but not their words are recorded, like the woman with an alabaster jar of perfume who washed Jesus's feet with her tears and wiped them with her hair (Luke 7:37–38), an act in public that would have alerted the "Taliban" of Jesus's day. Jesus responded to all these women, interacted with them, and spoke about them to others.

In more than a few cases, the women of the gospel stories have much to say and have their informed opinions reported, providing us with the opportunity to examine their speech from the perspective of rhetorical criticism, and with particular reference to gender speech. All that may be learned or appreciated from this exercise remains to be seen, but some initial observations could prove interesting and profitable.

An examination of the six longest and best-known speeches by women, or of conversations between Jesus and individual women appears to reveal a single speech trait that may be related to gender, and a tone in the material might be said to reflect something of a female identity marker. These examples may be listed before the trait and the tone are disclosed, and then considered in enough detail to suffice as at least circumstantial evidence in this initial rather cursory investigation. The speech presentations are as follows:

The Magnificat of Mary	Luke 1:47–55
The Woman at the Well	John 4:7–27
Martha Protesting Her Sister	Luke 10:39–42
The Canaanite Woman	Matthew 15:21–28
Martha at the Death of Lazarus	John 11:21–27
Mary Magdalene in the Garden	John 20:11–18

The linguistic trait that may be observed is the complete lack of female usage of conjunctions at the beginning of sentences. Both female and male speakers use them in many cultures, as when after a silence, one says, "So, when did you last see your parents?" The initial "so" is not related to anything previous and has no purpose except to enable the conversation to flow. In French, the word *alors* ("then") is used in much the same meaningless but effective way at the beginning of a sentence.

Since women in many quarters of Mediterranean culture in the time of Jesus did not traditionally speak out in public, it was not as possible for them to begin so smoothly, as if carrying on a conversation. In the biblical record, they always begin bluntly and somewhat awkwardly. We can see the use of these introductory conjunctions carried over into the Greek texts of male conversations as we have them in the Bible, in which tiny Greek particles of speech are obviously standing for something in the original Aramaic story, but the women always appear to blurt out their words.

In Greek, such introductory particles of speech are usually a meaningless *kai* ("and") at the beginning of a sentence, or a little untranslatable *de* signifying a beginning like "OK" or "Then" or "Now"—occasionally used to gain attention, or to begin speaking up. In English it is sometimes "but," "yes," or even "well," right out of nowhere. This is a frequent characteristic of both female and male speech in English, but it only appears in male speech in the gospel texts.

If this lack may be seen as a gender-speech trait in the gospels, it also relates to a tone in the material. Beginning with the Magnificat of Mary, the speeches of the women in the gospels are either very confrontational or sufficiently confrontational for that aspect to be observable. If Mary's Magnificat confronts the established order of society, the woman at the well is almost rude, Martha protests, the Canaanite woman is doggedly insistent, and Mary Magdalene boldly questions even the angels at the tomb.

Even in shorter quotations Jesus's mother, Mary, is blunt to him and to the servants at the wedding in Cana; the woman who touched the hem of Jesus's gown makes a bold statement that someone overhears; and the woman taken in adultery acknowledges the retreat of her accusers in a forthright manner. These women all have some kind of edge to their speech, partly because it took courage to speak to Jesus, even though they were affirmed in doing so. Moreover, they would not have spoken up at all except that there was an urgent need to confront some situation. These longer and shorter examples of gender speech may be taken as a beginning of overt feminism in religious literature, and their significance should not be understated.

Both in their manner and content, even the shorter speeches have an appearance that is distinct from male gender speech in the rest of the gospel material, just as we have seen in the six longer speeches. The clearest instance of these traits from the shorter speeches would have been the breathless report of the women concerning their experience of the resurrection, and the laid-back response of the male disciples. Unfortunately, we do not have the direct quotations in this case, but the reaction of the men in treating the women's report as "nonsense" captures the gender dynamics that are reflected in speech patterns here, elsewhere in the Bible, and still today in some studies.

Is there anywhere else in the gospels where these sociolinguistic traits stand out? Yes, there is one more outstanding example. While the identity of the writer is nowhere revealed, it is now possible to speculate with some confidence that the author of the famous Q document could very well be a woman. Q is largely a collection of "blurts" as compared to the more normal flow of gospel material.

The gender-speech trait of introductory words as described do not always appear consistently among men's speech in the gospels, but they are universally missing among women's conversation, giving their speech an awkward appearance. The gender-speech of males (beginning with a conjunction) abounds in Mark, in every other verse of chapters 3 and 4, for example. Even the English translations show telltale signs of the Greek manuscript, and the Greek shows clear evidence of the Aramaic original. The conjunctions are there in all the places where Mark is copied into Matthew and Luke, but they are totally absent in Q as transcribed into both Matthew and Luke. Indeed the breathless interjectory style in Q is identical to that in the women's speeches throughout the gospels, but in stark contrast to both the gruff, confident style of Mark and the polished, easy conversations in the material unique to both Matthew and Luke, all of which seem more to demonstrate masculine gender speech.

Moreover, Q is full of controversy and confrontation, the pattern we observed in the speech of women. The female author of Q is full of righteous indignation. Q opens with John the Baptist's preaching in the Judean desert, warning sinners and condemning hypocrites. This is followed by Jesus in the wilderness, tempted by Satan and confronting him at every turn.

Other contentions, confrontations, and controversies in Q include the sayings about the cost of discipleship and about the division of households, John's questions from jail about the mission, woes upon sinful cities, demands for signs, and warnings to be watchful. Confrontation and contention are not the only themes in Q, but they are pervasive, representing the agenda of women who had risked all for a faith that put values of compassionate love, social justice, and personal virtue to the fore. Along with this would be their concern for relationships with their Messiah and with one another that were now in jeopardy. This tone in the material coincides with the blunt, almost awkward manner of speech that is carried over into writing by the bold author of Q.

In Q, the woman's interest in family life is also portrayed in parables such as the wedding feast and the house built on a firm foundation, as well as in the teaching about forgiveness of a sinful brother. This material echoes the evidence presented by both Richard Friedman and Harold Bloom in their hypothesis regarding the authorship of J. The religion presented in Q is also entirely compatible with a feminine expression of spiritual life. Of such precious things from Jesus not even mentioned by Mark or anywhere in the other gospels, Q alone has the Beatitudes, the Lord's Prayer and the Golden Rule—not necessarily feminine, but consistent with traditional female values of care and compassion and virtue. And do women have culturally greater interest in intuitive and prophetic understandings about people and society—sometimes reflected historically in the role of the Wise Woman or Oracle or even the traveling fortune-teller, with her insights and predictions? It appears so elsewhere throughout the Bible, and we may note that Q leans strongly in that direction, as compared to Mark and the others.

Once again, it would take a remarkable woman to write such a document as Q, and she would need means, motive, and opportunity. Interior evidence suggests that Q is Jerusalem centered, and recent commentators like John Kloppenborg suggest that it is from members of what might be called the Galilean community there. If Q was written shortly after Mark, as postulated first by Julius Wellhausen, it may have been as a supplement to Mark, written at the other end of the Mediterranean. If Q is indeed first, as current speculation suggests, that could be the other way around.

The Christian establishment in Jerusalem was not yet separated from the temple, and under the leadership of St. James it became influential in both community and national life. Until the temple was destroyed in 70 CE, many Christians simply presumed that Jerusalem, not Rome, would remain forever the headquarters of the Christian church. So it appears in Paul's letters and in the fifteenth chapter of the Acts of the Apostles. Indeed, while in the gospels we read of Jesus's saying that he would build his church on the rock that was Peter (with no mention of Rome), both the Acts and the Epistles routinely defer to James as the administrative head of the church at Jerusalem. A document from Jerusalem would have reached Matthew and Luke quickly, especially if it had been meant as a follow up or a response to Mark's gospel.

St. James, the brother of Jesus, was bishop of Jerusalem. He had an image of something like an eastern potentate who governed the church with a strong hand, and who remained highly regarded in the wider community. He presided at the Jerusalem Council for the whole church in 49 CE. On the question of whether converts should be circumcised, James decided (over the objections of the other disciples) in favor of Paul and Barnabas, who opposed this practice. James's devotion to the Mosaic law made him popular with the Jewish authorities and, in keeping with his social standing, James is traditionally credited with the conversion of King Agrippa, who, according to the *Antiquities* of Flavius Josephus, was so displeased by the assassination of James by jealous Sadducees that he fired Annas, the high priest.

The stern writer of the epistle called James was nicknamed "James the Just" in the church, where as judge, he had a status above either Peter or

Paul. His was probably the only Christian household in which a woman might have the means and opportunity to write a tract like Q.

American readers may not relate to this image of St. James, which is well known elsewhere down through the Middle Ages and into modern times, since possibly only St. Mary and St. Peter have maintained "personality" in popular imagination. But St. James, St. Jago, or Santiago has maintained his character as the patron saint of imperial Spain, for example, where Guercino has painted him (now in the Harrash Gallery in Vienna) seated in the manner of an eastern potentate who does not rise to grant an audience. Attested by Dante to be buried in Spain, James is pictured in stained glass throughout that country as wearing spurs and the accoutrements of a knight at the top of the social order. A famous German print by Martin Schoen, Italian frescoes by Fra Filippo Lippi, and more stained glass in France all reinforce the image of this widespread persona. Rarely is James's image as completely reinforced as in England, where the social register headed by the royal family is called the Court of St. James, and foreign dignitaries present their credentials at St. James Palace before they ever get to Buckingham.

None of this is like the textual evidence favored by American scholars, but they too might concede some tradition of cachet to James when they hear Eliza Doolittle in *My Fair Lady* singing of her social aspirations: "I will go to St. James so often I will call it St. Jim's." Such folk traditions are increasingly used to supplement the likewise tricky evidence often adduced from the textual sources.

We understand that James was married and had children, but if Q was written soon after Mark and before Matthew and Luke, then James's children would have been too young for this work. My putative conclusion is that Q was written by the wife of St. James. She would have the resources and connections at hand, and she would have wanted to support his expectation that anything produced at Rome should be reviewed and supplemented by the church at Jerusalem. Further, she had the leisure to undertake the task. In addition, as quite possibly a prominent member of the Jewish aristocracy by birth, and given her husband's social standing, she almost certainly had the education and skill to do this, though without recognition, or in a "veiled" manner, so typical for her gender in the context of the times.

"Could this be so?" is a question at the heart of current investigations into the reasons why circumstantial evidence has traditionally been good enough to base inferences about the contribution of male writers of Scripture, even when the provenance is suspect; but the same has not been true for women traditionally and appears to be not yet equally true for women today. It is almost as if there is a fear of what the Reconstructionist Jewish scholar S. Tamar Kamionkowski calls "gender reversal" among biblical scholars, an apprehension seeming as real among older female scholars as among men.

At any rate, given what we know now about the veiled role of even aristocratic women like the putative author of J, we may easily appreciate the reason there is no extant copy of the document known as Q. Even such a highly regarded and widely used document falls into oblivion precisely because once it was subsumed into Matthew and Luke, Q ceased to have an identity as a separate document, since it had been written by a woman. This is in contrast to Mark, which while also subsumed into Matthew and Luke, did have an identity with its male author. Again the maxim, "If it is anonymous, it may be assumed that it was written by a woman."

As a matter of fact, just as recent scholarship continues to review the questions of Mark's authorship of the gospel that bears his name and even the location of where this gospel was written, so there is still a great deal we do not know about Q. For reasons indicated, we may never find a freestanding copy of this early gospel, but the very latest commentaries, like *Q, The Earliest Gospel* by John Kloppenborg, move the critical debate about Q's authorship forward by at last supplying convincing textual evidence of an intimate documentary link between Q and the Epistle of James.

While some today are even uncertain who wrote the letter that has always been ascribed to James, it does appear increasingly certain that the community surrounding James at the eastern end of the Mediterranean, and with its Jewish character, does have its own literary tradition. According to the International Q Project, Q is a part of that corpus, along with the Gospel of Thomas and other materials with an emphasis more on a kingdom of justice than on the personal "salvation" emphasis of the rest of the church. This communal justice emphasis will be a helpful part of the ongoing discussion with interfaith connections, particularly in the Jewish and Muslim communities, and may be especially welcome in emerging elements of the Christian community. Of course, these two emphases on personal salvation and justice are compatible and complementary: witness the blending of both Q and Mark in the longer gospels.

The Muslim template of female participation in such work makes it impossible to discard the probability that the Q portion of that Palestinian-Jewish-Christian corpus, which was never ascribed to one of the male apostles, and which was subsumed without comment into the others, was indeed written by a woman. The rhetorical remnants and linguistic traits of my own thought experiment merely support such an obvious conclusion.

14

Confession

THE FACT THAT WE do not have the name of the author of Q, while we have names associated with the other gospel documents, and the fact that no copy was preserved once it was incorporated into documents by male author/compilers are almost proofs that it was written by a woman. If not the wife of James, perhaps it was another woman who was particularly controversial or unappreciated in the very patriarchal early Greco-Roman church—a possibility that could be investigated by those increasingly persuaded of a deliberate attempt by leaders the early church to suppress the leadership roles of women like Mary Magdalene.

One basis of feminist criticism is a realization that the failure to recognize women as writers of Scripture and the denigration of their role in the early church was not merely due to benign neglect, or perhaps to temporary accommodation to the culture of the time, but to a conscious and deliberate campaign to eliminate female leadership, which occasionally challenged the dominant male hierarchy. The case for this position grows stronger by the decade but, again, is beyond the scope of this investigation into more basic evidence.

None of these observations is offered in a pejorative spirit, because we recognize the restricted role of women in that time, even while we begin to appreciate their influence and their contributions, particularly behind the scenes. For that matter, the precise role of women in the twenty-first century is still being debated, whether as identical to that of men or different, separate, even superior in many important respects. How this plays out will be determined, at least in some part, by a generous and grateful awareness of the part that women may have played in the writing of Scripture.

Even feminist Christian scholars, while longing for any proof that women were involved in writing the New Testament, might be inclined to reject my theory as "a stretch" because the traditional evidence is not available from other ancient writers. Yet this is my point when I say of any Scripture, "if it is anonymous, it may be assumed that it is written by a woman." This takes into account both the bias of the times and the template from Islamic writings and the Muslim world, in which leading women among the "People of the House" usually had roles connected to ideological and literary pursuits.

This template looks increasingly attractive and viable when applied to Hebrew and Christian Scriptures. The Islamic sources we are yet to examine in detail, and the modern situation, whether in the homes of Afghan warlord-parliamentarians or in corporations and other organizations, politics, and governments illustrate a template that can be applied both to Scriptures and to a review of gender-related aspects of modern life. This may be the situation, whether in the offices of Wall Street or in the interior workings of OPEC, in the White House (where no woman has been entrusted with overt leadership responsibility even yet) or in the secret, unknown labyrinth at the unrecognized core of the Saudi royal family.

However, just as Harold Bloom admits that his thesis may be speculative, I must acknowledge that my ascription of the authorship of Q to the wife of St. James is a "thought experiment" at this time. A thought experiment, from the German *Gedankenexperiment*, is more than a wild guess, but before it can be accepted, much more work needs to be done. When gender speech appears in written form, it is one of the sharpest and cleanest tools in the rhetorical criticism toolbox, but its use in scriptural analysis is in its infancy. Like Bloom's, my instincts may be correct, since one growing intuition in our time is that women played a far greater role in the early church than has been realized until recently. We need a Richard Friedman of the New Testament to take this investigation further, and such candidates abound in the seminaries today, and, of course, many of them are women.

In this connection, as we move beyond the consideration of women as mere accomplices in the writing of Scripture, perhaps it is time to revisit the thesis put forth by Adolf von Harnack almost a hundred years ago regarding authorship of the New Testament book of Hebrews by Priscilla. This is a thesis that stood on its own well before the more recent wave of feminist criticism appeared. We would revisit that thesis now with the expectation that sharp new tools like rhetorical criticism might produce more conclusive results.

Among the most highly regarded scholars of his day, Harnack believed that Hebrews was written by Priscilla, the wife of Aquila, her business partner and supporter of her teaching. They both had deep Judean roots and a keen Jewish Christian agenda. Priscilla was disciple and friend of St. Paul and a teacher of Apollos, who was a pastor and eventually the first bishop of the church at Ephesus. She is usually mentioned in the same breath as her businessman husband, but this may be only a device to permit the mentioning of her name as a female teacher who had the obvious admiration of St. Paul. Certainly, without Priscilla, Aquila would have no place in Scripture, so if she is that prominent, we might consider Harnack's evidence.

This brilliant scholar, whose training reflected a century of critical ferment in the German university seminaries, suggests four reasons why Priscilla should be acknowledged as the author of Hebrews:

1. It almost had to be a woman who wrote the book of Hebrews since the book is anonymous, and it was culturally impossible for a woman to be recognized as author. This solves the anonymity problem that has vexed church leaders since the fourth-century debates on canonization.

2. Priscilla's close and scholarly association with Paul (Acts 18:1–3; 1 Cor 16:19; Rom 16:3–4) would explain the Pauline concepts that caused many to ascribe the Epistle to the Hebrews to Paul, even though everyone admitted that the style eliminated him from serious consideration as the actual author.

3. Priscilla's instruction of Apollos (Acts 18:24–28) shows her scholarship, and Apollos's theology appears compatible with the theology of the book of Hebrews.

4. Hebrews 11 uncharacteristically includes many women in the list of the renowned persons of faith.

To look at Harnack's reasons in the light of further development of our understanding, we might flesh out his theories as follows:

1. The situation is similar to the possibilities of female authorship of J and Q, insofar as the anonymity required of women, whereas we can identify the male authors of the Pentateuch and the Gospels. The E document appears to be more a collection of northern materials authored and collected by Levites, P comes from the Priests of Aaron in Jerusalem, and D is ascribed to Moses, either in a documentary way, as memorized, or

as composed in his name. In the New Testament, all identified authors are male, and there are no anonymous authors except Q and Hebrews. The latter was anonymous, but to be included in the canon of recognized Scripture, Hebrews needed identifiable authorship. This the early church merely ascribed to its most prolific writer of epistles, even though everybody knew better. Any man having written Hebrews would have claimed it, even Priscilla's husband, Aquila. In fact, Hebrews is subsumed into the Pauline corpus in a manner analogous to the way in which Q is subsumed into Matthew and Luke.

2. In forensically considering Priscilla's influence on scriptural writings, we must also consider her influence on Paul. Whereas Matthew's gospel uses proof texts from the Old Testament to verify the messianic claims it makes concerning Jesus, Paul goes much further in using Israelite theology as a foundation for a fully developed Christology, summarized nowhere more completely than in the book of Hebrews. Paul calls Priscilla his "fellow laborer" or *synergos*, which suggests she may have been his colleague in certain respects, as well as a teacher to Apollos.

3. Additionally, while Aquila and Priscilla are mentioned in the Acts of the Apostles as the teachers of Apollos, she would surely not be mentioned at all unless she had clearly been the dominant partner in the teaching enterprise. One pictures a self-effacing Aquila, who himself is only mentioned to legitimize her teaching. In the Acts of the Apostles, Priscilla and Aquila are spoken of with her name first, an anomaly in the ancient world; this indicates her unusual status in the view of Luke, as the writer. This respect is echoed by Paul, who puts her name first in four of the six times he refers to this prominent couple, in spite of his frequent relegation of women to second place in deference to the compromise required in the cultural context.

4. Harnack's last point about the inclusion of women in the list of the faithful in Hebrews 11 may have reflected a conscious agenda of the Hebrews author, in much the same way that portraits of important women and honorable mentions of those behind the scenes may reflect one of the agendas of the author of the Book of J. Priscilla's list in Hebrews 11 does not flesh out the women in the deliberate fashion we see in J but includes them in a more normative literary manner. Along with women like Sarah and Rahab, who have verses of their own in Hebrews 11, women are presumed in context: Noah's household, Moses's parents, Pharaoh's

daughter, and the women who received their dead by resurrection. Such deliberate integration of women appears nowhere else in the New Testament, just as only J produces such portraits in the Torah.

To all Harnack's reasons for ascribing the authorship of the book of Hebrews to Priscilla we may now be in a position to add evidence from rhetorical criticism, if those who are expert in this discipline might take up the challenge. Does Hebrews "sound" like it was written by a woman? Suggestions that the emotional tone of Hebrews is more feminine, especially in the descriptions of Jesus, are in themselves inadequate; but tone, linguistic markers, and other elements that might be noted in close readings. Slow, audible and deliberate investigation may reveal something to either professional scholars or students in this new discipline.

In the earliest collections of New Testament Scriptures, such as the Chester Beatty Papyri, it seems passing strange that Hebrews follows the highly regarded Epistle to the Romans, whereas it eventually fell to lower status at the tail end of the Pauline corpus, possibly because of suspicions about its female or unknown authorship. Martin Luther contributed to the speculation about this Pauline–Priscilla–Apollos connection by suggesting that Hebrews was written by Apollos, whom we know to have studied under Priscilla. This possibility should now be reconsidered in light of what we are learning from Islam: that anonymous Scriptures can often be assumed to have been written down by women, unless signed by a man. If Apollos had written Hebrews, we would know that.

But again the question remains. Does Hebrews "sound" like it was written by a woman? The answer would be yes, or at least that Hebrews does not read like the writing of any man we know, so we might now assume that the writer is a woman. Hebrews certainly sounds like none of the men who wrote the other epistles: Paul, James, Peter, John, or for that matter, Clement, Polycarp, and others we know. This aspect of our theory requires attention by rhetoricians, and as yet there is no identifiable feminine marker like the "interjecting" or "blurting" style of women who wrote or spoke in the gospels. Once better established, the female authorship of Hebrews may provide markers to identify female authors elsewhere in Scripture, in ancient church circles, and elsewhere in classical and Koine Greek literature.

The Islamic evidence about the female authorship of Scripture is opening up a dynamic new enterprise, though it must be admitted that the Muslim "man in the street" has probably never even heard of this aspect of current scholarship, remaining oblivious to the primary sources in this regard.

In any event, as further study increasingly critiques and frequently supports our current understandings regarding the role of women in both Testaments, we can certainly add Priscilla to the list of suspects already identified. This is a frequent contention of *The Priscilla Papers*, a scholarly journal published quarterly since 1987 by Christians for Biblical Equality, a group devoted to questions of gender in Scripture (with a focus extending well beyond the book of Hebrews to also include investigations into the authorship of J, Ruth, and Esther), as well as other pertinent gender issues. This area of study began in the Protestant mainline churches some generations ago when the first women of the modern era were ordained. But in the twenty-first century this particular investigation is equally driven by the efforts of female Roman Catholic theologians and especially by women of scholarship in Baptist and other evangelical churches, such as those contributing to *The Priscilla Papers* and to more populist evangelical journals like *Mutuality*.

Perhaps the next step for someone with the requisite skill is the marriage of gender-speech research with *Nvivo* or some other computerized language-analysis tool, as long as we keep the spiritual objectives in mind. The possibilities are tantalizing as we link critical methods with the post-critical agenda, especially regarding the role and place of women in transmitting the divine Word in biblical times and in the present era. We may have a sufficient case at this point to at least suggest adding some sections and the overall mythos or message of the Bible to the important literary genre described as Women's Studies or Women's Literature.

PART 3

Opening the Muslim Scriptures

بِسْمِ اللهِ الرَّحْمٰنِ الرَّحِيْمِۙ -١

اَلْحَمْدُ لِلّٰهِ رَبِّ الْعٰلَمِيْنَۙ -٢

الرَّحْمٰنِ الرَّحِيْمِۙ -٣

مٰلِكِ يَوْمِ الدِّيْنِۗ -٤

اِيَّاكَ نَعْبُدُ وَ اِيَّاكَ نَسْتَعِيْنُۗ -٥

اِهْدِنَا الصِّرَاطَ الْمُسْتَقِيْمَۙ -٦

صِرَاطَ الَّذِيْنَ اَنْعَمْتَ عَلَيْهِمْ ۙ غَيْرِ -٧
الْمَغْضُوْبِ عَلَيْهِمْ وَ لَا الضَّآلِّيْنَ ۬

بِسْمِ اللهِ الرَّحْمٰنِ الرَّحِيْمِ

الٓمّٓ ۚ -١

ذٰلِكَ الْكِتٰبُ لَا رَيْبَ ۛ فِيْهِ ۛ -٢
هُدًى لِّلْمُتَّقِيْنَۙ

الَّذِيْنَ يُؤْمِنُوْنَ بِالْغَيْبِ وَ يُقِيْمُوْنَ -٣
الصَّلٰوةَ وَ مِمَّا رَزَقْنٰهُمْ يُنْفِقُوْنَۙ

وَ الَّذِيْنَ يُؤْمِنُوْنَ بِمَآ اُنْزِلَ اِلَيْكَ وَ -٤

CHAPTER 1
THE OPENING (al-Fātiḥah)

Stage 1
Part 1

1:1   In the Name of God,
•   The Merciful, The Compassionate.
1:2   The Praise *belongs* to God
   Lord of the worlds,
1:3   The Merciful, The Compassionate,
1:4   One Who is Sovereign of the Day of Judgment.
1:5   **You** alone we worship,
   and to **You** alone we pray for help.
1:6   Guide us to the straight path,
1:7   the path of those to whom
•   **You** have been gracious,
   not ones against whom **You** are angry,
   nor the ones who go astray.

*

CHAPTER 2
THE COW (al-Baqarah)

In the Name of God,
Sec. 1   The Merciful, The Compassionate
2:1   *Alif Lām Mīm;*°
2:2   that *is* the Book—there *is* no doubt in it,
   a guidance for the ones who *are* Godfearing:
2:3   Those who believe in the unseen
   and perform the formal prayer
   and they spend from what We have provided them
2:4   and those who believe
   in what was sent forth to **you**
   and what was sent forth before **you**
   and they are certain of the world to come.
2:5   Those *are* on a guidance from their Lord;°
   and those, they *are* the ones who prosper.
2:6   Truly those who are ungrateful,
   it *is* all the same to them
   whether **you** have warned them
   or **you** have warned them not;
   they believe not.

15

Custody

THE CASE THAT WOMEN *"wrote down"* the Qur'an becomes increasingly strong. The author is God, according to Islam, and the angel Gabriel was the vehicle of revelation, through Muhammad, the Seal of the prophets of old. The Prophet himself was illiterate, as is well known, and the Qur'an was given to him as recitations that he brought home, where members of his household and staff eventually wrote them down.

In the early years, all the Mecca surahs were transcribed by household members, all female, principally Khadiah, Muhammad's well-educated aristocratic wife, herself from a Christian family where literacy was then higher. Hers is a role of women in Islam that many Muslims wish to have more widely recognized today. In Medina, the writers would have been daughters like Fatimah and other wives like Hafsah, until somewhat later when Muhammad got a secretary for his administrative work.

The principal secretary was a man named Zaid, but his role in transcribing the Qur'an would be limited to later surahs. He joined the household as an adopted child and must have been taught to read and write by the women whom Muhammad frequently lauds as "the people of the house," a phrase reminiscent of one he received from Allah concerning Jews and Christians: "the people of the book." Admittedly, the image of Zaid (a male) participating in the task of writing would grow in early Islam, as patriarchy replaced the more feminine atmosphere of Muhammad's personal environment. But unlike the similar development in early Christianity, in Islam the documentary evidence attesting the writing by females remains available and easily accessible. As we shall see, there were at least five women among the People of the House (Muhammad's household) who were particularly distinguished by their literary accomplishments.

Further supportive evidence for the role of women in writing down and ordering the Qur'an comes from the natural ease of assigning custody of the original household copy of the Qur'an to Hafsah by her father, Muhammad's Companion, Umar the Great, the second caliph of Islam. He must have known that she did much of the original writing and knew more than anyone then living about the Qur'an. Why else would such an important task be given to a woman in an environment that had become increasingly dominated by males in the era immediately following Muhammad? The task of guarding the Qur'an was not a random honor assigned to someone who merely appeared trustworthy. It was a responsibility given naturally to one who had always been associated with this work, and who was most probably the main writer of most of the surahs. That this role was given to Hafsah, even when there was an obvious male who was interested and available, cinches the argument.

In any future questions (which there were) about what was really in the Medina Codex, the authenticity of the texts could be ascertained by the one who could recognize her own handwriting in many cases, who could recall the day she made an unintended inkblot, or who could recognize the piece of work done by another member of the household—even by Zaid in Muhammad's later years. For doubters, the verification work needed to establish these facts with greater certainty is to be done by responsible Muslim scholars, both male and female now. The Hadith has much of the evidence, and this work may be a crucial factor in the growing recognition of the role and influence of women in early Islam, an important part of the current Muslim agenda.

The Qur'an is not sacred Scripture to Christians or Jews, but the place of the Qur'an in relation to the Old and New Testaments is undergoing radical reassessment in the twenty-first century. The evocative power of the Qur'an as recited in the Muslim community is impressive enough to cause others of good will to question the recent centuries of negativity toward the Islamic Scriptures. Might the rejection of the Qur'an by Christians and Jews be as much related to fear and prejudice as to an objective view of authenticity of the material and its potential value to others in Abraham's family?

The growing appreciation of the Qur'an at several levels among Jews, Christians, and others indicates that in the first half of the twenty-first century at least, the influence of the Qur'an among non-Muslims might be compared to the influence of the Dead Sea Scrolls and the Nag Hammadi library in the last half of the twentieth century. The Qur'an is so much more than that to its Muslim devotees, as will be seen, but this is a starting place for the interfaith community, including the previously "hostile witnesses" within Jewish and Christian branches of Abraham's own family.

For many, the surprise about this is that the material in the Qur'an appears so biblical. Most Christians and Jews are in nearly total ignorance of the close relationship between the Hebrew Scriptures, the Christian Scriptures, and the Qur'an. Muslims believe that Jewish and Christian texts have become jumbled and garbled, but whether the rest of the family accepts that or not, even a cursory reading of the Qur'an makes it clear that it is like the third book in a series, ostensibly from the same source. Just as one cannot make complete sense of the New Testament without knowledge of the Old Testament, so no one can read the Qur'an without knowledge of the Bible stories.

The Qur'anic understanding of figures like Adam and Eve or of Abraham, Sarah, and Hagar is incomprehensible on its own, and the Muslim community has always acknowledged that. The Qur'an reads or recites as if the reader or hearer already knows the stories of Noah and Moses. David and Goliath are not introduced when their story comes up, because everybody who reads the Qur'an is expected to know that story already. They know the story of Jonah, which is brought up in the Qur'an in the same manner as the references to Jonah by Jesus in the Christian Scriptures, where familiarity is presupposed in exactly the same way. Most Muslims learn the Bible stories from summaries by Muhammad in the Hadith.

This new understanding of the relationship and the common roots of Judaism, Christianity, and Islam, based on their Scriptures, is an opportunity for scholars to contribute to the social reintegration that the members of Abraham's family are seeking, particularly in Europe and North America, where they live increasingly in close proximity. My earlier book, *Noah's Other Son: Bridging the Gap between the Bible and the Qur'an,* is an elaboration of this point. The title was inspired by the story, presented in the Qur'an, of a fourth son of Noah, who, in his youthful rebellion, spurns his father's warnings and refuses to get on board the ark.

> So the ark floated with them on the waves that were towering like mountains. Nooh called out to his son who had separated himself from the rest of the family: "O my son! embark with us and

leave your friends, the unbelievers." The son replied: "I will climb a mountain and it will save me from the water." Nooh said: "This day nothing can avoid the wrath of God except those upon whom He shows mercy." And the waves came between them and this son was among those overwhelmed in the flood. (Surah 11, Ayahs 42–43; Yusuf Ali translation)

Presuming prior knowledge of the scriptural stories, the Qur'an rarely disputes their content, except for a few ostensible corrections where it is felt that the Bible really got things wrong. Normally, accepting the biblical account as it is, the Qur'an simply proceeds to flesh out the stories with a wealth of additional material from ancient lore of what we now call the Middle East, filtered through the divine revelation of its significance to Muhammad in the incredibly moving verses recorded in the sacred text of Islam.

For example, the story of Noah's other son, whose name was Canaan, is a parable for our times when warnings of pandemics, climate change, and the consequences of greed go unheeded. It is also the template for a study of biblical stories of rebellion—from Cain, Ishmael, and Jacob to Jesus's parable of the prodigal son. This is but one illustration of the benefits of interfaith studies of the Scriptures in the Abrahamic faith family, and hence the inclusion of this introduction to Qur'anic studies in this forensic investigation.

As for rhetorical criticism, anyone who has ever heard the Qur'an recited would quickly acknowledge that the language of the Arabic Qur'an is among the most beautiful ever heard. At an increasing number of interfaith activities, Christians and Jews are beginning to discover that the only thing that compares with the Qur'an is certain sections of their own Bibles in a beloved translation. The Twenty-third Psalm and the Lord's Prayer make sense in any translation, but the beauty of language is found only in the King James Authorized Version, the "noble" form of English that is frequently compared to the Arabic of the Qur'an.

The Qur'an is made up of 114 utterances, almost like psalms given divinely, through an angelic spiritual connection of the kind also described more than two hundred times in the Bible. These experiences came to Muhammad over a period of twenty-three years, often unexpectedly, sometimes months or even years apart. Eighty-six of these recitations were revealed in Mecca, representing approximately two-thirds of the Qur'an. Twenty-eight such surahs or chapters, including several of the longest, or one-third of the sacred text, were presented to the Prophet later in his life at Medina.

Each recitation is validated in its authenticity by its own impact on the hearers. The impact of this collection of oracular prophecies has been so immense that its content has sometimes seemed secondary to its beauty. The contents are getting more scrutiny today than ever before in history, by Muslims and others, especially by Jews and Christians, both by critics and by those seeking to understand. Increasingly we also meet "progressive" Muslims who seek the deeper meanings in the text of the Qur'an by looking beneath the surface, a tradition that goes back to the earliest days of Islam, and indeed to Muhammad himself.

The Prophet may not have been literate in the academic sense, but there is no doubt that previous to and beyond the revelations from God, he had a tremendous interest in and a vast knowledge of things related to the Jewish and Christian religions in particular. This interest included substantial knowledge of the contents of the Scriptures of these religions. This information would have come to him orally through his extensive family, social, and business networks, all three of which included many Jews and Christians. He passed on his reflections on these Bible stories, interpreted through a Qur'anic filter, in the Hadith, which, while cherished as authoritative, were not regarded as part of God's direct revelation to him and through him.

There was a period of advanced Qur'anic scholarship in the fourth Islamic century (tenth century CE), before both Shia and Sunni schools began to cherish uncritically what they both consider to be absolutely complete renditions of the revelation to Muhammad. It may appear to outsiders that since then, until very recently, that Islamic scholars wishing to pursue questions about the textual context of the Qur'an or to analyze its contents have faced something not unlike the Spanish Inquisition, with fatwas and angry charges of blasphemy. The reasons for such sensitivity in this matter were covered in the preface to this book, but well-grounded and spiritually based scholarship has never threatened the Qur'an when properly understood.

This is especially true today, and we are discovering that since its texts have been so well preserved, Islam probably has little to fear from critical investigations like this one, or from other, far more searching critiques within the Islamic scholarly community. Treasures are pouring forth in the

Qur'anic fields of science, women's studies, social justice, and ethics. These gems are available not only to Muslims but as well to Christians and Jews, as new information with relevance to biblical studies. Well-entrenched Muslim traditions that are not truly grounded in the message or word of the Qur'an may seem to be under attack, but the Qur'an itself appears to be increasingly secure overall, and its beauty more widely appreciated.

Just as a dream written down in the morning rarely makes literal sense but may be laden with insight for those who can interpret its meaning, so it was, in a more cosmic sense, with the truths to which Muhammad connected as he was in a trancelike state (as he himself describes it) when he was seized by the Divine. As in a dream, these divinely rooted revelations may include images from many sources, used now afresh by Allah to reflect divine realities of a universal and eternal nature. These images may have come up in Muhammad's previous life experiences, much like other previous preparations had, such as his use of the Arabic language, for example, poetic to its core.

The words and images from Muhammad's life situation may have been arranged by God—winnowed, edited, and dictated from on high—but parts of the revelation can be clearly identified in relation the Prophet's own life experience, knowledge of which may aid in interpreting the revelation in this or that dream or trance. Muhammad never lost consciousness or awareness in these moments of high inspiration. His awareness of what these words from God meant is correlated to his knowledge of Syria, Yemen, other countries and peoples, and especially of Arabia itself. In the same way, John understood the Roman Empire addressed by God through angels in the imagery and the cadences of the book of Revelation. Daniel likewise understood all that God conveyed to him about Persia, Babylon, and especially Judah in the same way, with that same angel, Gabriel, fulfilling this role in the Hebrew Scriptures at Daniel 9:21. Indeed, as Gabriel speaks to Mary in the New Testament at Luke 1:26, the angel presumes that she has prior knowledge of the throne of David and of the kingdom to come. In all such cases, the revelation from the divine source, through the angelic presence, is radically new but presumes prior experience and knowledge of the world, both of its politics and its religions.

Muslims traditionally resist any inference that God used the language and life experiences that Muhammad brought to the moment, even if this does not suggest that the revelations are derived from "sources"; but this area is one in which Christians and Jews are currently excited in connection with what they can learn about their own Scriptures from the Qur'an when it repeats or describes something previously revealed in the Bible. Such hesitancy notwithstanding, Muslim scholars are publishing volumes to document these connections, such as the *Islamic Perspective* books on the Bible by Jay Crook in three massive tomes. In addition to the sacred meaning of the text, the Qur'an presents a wealth of reflection upon the ancient world from the perspective of a related tradition that remembered things and kept treasures long lost by the rest of the Abrahamic family.

This understanding could apply to images and material to which the thoughtful and mature Muhammad was exposed through the first forty years of his life, before the first revelation, and on through the series of revelations that came to him through his later years. If Muhammad's knowledge of Arabic was so obviously employed by Allah, what other preparations for receiving the revelations might Allah have provided to him?

Nestorian Christianity and other heterodox Christian traditions, especially those represented by his Abyssinian allies and by certain members of his own family, were well known to Muhammad. The Jewish Diaspora, including orthodox Jews and other Jewish traditions, was also a major influence in Muhammad's early search for truth. Orthodox Christian influence was all around him, in his own family, in Arabia, and wherever he traveled. Zoroastrian caravaners, like Muhammad's dear friend Salman, a Persian, could have brought even Hindu tales to his ears. The Hanif monotheists who preceded Muhammad rejected the idolatry of Arabian society and passed on ancient desert traditions about Adam and Eve and about Abraham, Sarah, and Hagar to him. The lore of the Sabeans, mentioned in the Bible but since forgotten, is now available only through the Qur'an, as filtered by Allah in the revelations concerning their beliefs. But Muhammad would have heard of all these traditions from practitioners.

In the same way that neither the welter of information from Mohammed's travels nor the Arabic and other stories that he absorbed were spiritually adequate for him, so the Arabic language is not necessarily religious except when God uses it as a vehicle of revelation. The religious traditions Muhammad encountered were not practiced in a manner reflecting the divine source of their inspiration, in Muhammad's experience, resulting in a renewal of that inspiration in which every line, phrase, word, syllable, and letter of the Qur'an inspired him as dictated from on high.

Muhammad's familiarity with the world and even with its religions did not guide, influence, or restrict the revelations of God to him any more than his knowledge of the Arabic language influenced the divine choice of words. Allah chose to use the experience, knowledge, and language of the Prophet as the raw materials for the beauty and true meaning of the treasure he chose to bestow on the world through Muhammad. In his view, and in the experience of his followers, the raw materials as found in the corrupt society of Arabia before Muhammad did not show forth the beauty or the meaning of the original revelations on which the divine words may have been based, but they do remain of interest to the rest of the family, even as described through a lens respecting the Islamic perspective.

In earlier chapters relating to Hebrew and Christian Scriptures, I offered guidance and recommended readings, fully amplified in the bibliography, for those wishing to pursue matters further. There is so much excellent material available about the Qur'an from well-qualified Islamic scholars that one would be hard pressed to know where to begin. However, since much of the best information is internal (intended for Muslim readers) or external by sympathetic Jewish or Christian interfaith scholars, I am limited somewhat and have made a choice.

In my opinion, the best piece about critical studies of the Qur'an by a Muslim scholar addressing non-Muslims is by Jane McAuliffe, a Canadian Muslim and a critical scholar who is currently the president of Bryn Mawr University in Philadelphia. McAuliffe has written many excellent books on interpreting the Qur'an, but a helpful next step for serious non-Muslim students and scholars beginning in this field is her 2004 presidential address to the American Academy of Religion: "Reading the Qur'an with Fidelity and Freedom." It is not yet available in book form but can be accessed online or in the *Journal of the American Academy of Religion*. In her presidential address, McAuliffe not only speaks to all colleagues (including Jews and Christians) on the subject of the ongoing extensive critical examination of the Qur'an. She also presents an assessment of resources appropriate for readers of this book, which is more complete than the bibliography I provide, in which information can be found to access her address printed as an article.

So were Muslim Scriptures written down by women? The evidence is not absolute, but, allowing for a traditional gender bias that Islam has shared with Judaism and Christianity, it may now be assumed that women, at the very least, did much of the transcribing. Islam has more available information about this than either of the other two traditions. For example, the traditionally preferred leaning toward an assumption that male scribes did this work is too flimsy to be credible in Islam, given what we know about the role of the "People of the House" and about the lack of male residents in Muhammad's household. Those Muslims who do see this simply do not wish to see the natural assumptions to be drawn from the situation. For Christians and Jews, the conclusion that women wrote down the Qur'an and possibly other Islamic works, based on evidence and contexts that have disappeared in their own traditions, represents a breakthrough that they have found impossible to make on their own, in spite of hints, scraps of information, and intuitions indicating the high degree of probability for female authorship of the earlier Scriptures.

The question of authorship or transcription is raised respectfully, though forcefully, after establishing that nothing in these critical investigations per se calls into question the divine origins of the revelations recorded in the Qur'an. The primacy of this point on the part of Muslim scholars and believers includes the conviction that echoes of similar words from other Scriptures are from previous revelations of the same material, rather than from "sources" that Muhammad somehow mimicked or copied. This conviction is no more radical that the belief of many Christians and Jews that what Moses received on Sinai, and what Jesus revealed in the Sermon on the Mount, are from God, regardless of similarities between the Decalogue and the Hammurabi Code, or between the words of Jesus and the Scriptures with which he grew up. Beyond this point, awkward as some questions may seem, nothing in Muslim tradition is too sacrosanct to question. For example, legitimate inquiry can be made about whether the golden tablet on which the Qur'an is written in paradise has words with diacritical marks or not, or about whether some of the "pencils" in God's hand were women who wrote down what was given to Muhammad to recite.

Khadijah was a self-respecting and independent businesswoman when she married Muhammad and appointed him as chief caravaner. He did not become the record keeper, correspondence secretary, or accountant; these positions she evidently kept for herself, given that we have no record of anyone else joining the household or the business at that juncture. No sons lived beyond infancy, but the high esteem in which Muhammad held his daughters (Fatimah in particular) would lead to a natural conclusion that from their mother they learned to write and keep records. After Khadijah's death, her daughters, as the "People of the House," carried on the family business and other responsibilities, shared now with new young wives, who apparently had the complete confidence of Muhammad.

After the death of the Prophet, Muhammad's secretary, Zaid ibn Thabit, was designated by Abu Bakr to collect the recitations that make up the Qur'an, and this he appears to have done between 644 and 656 CE. Zaid is often erroneously credited with writing down the verses of the Qur'an, but he was not even part of the household when the Mecca surahs were first transcribed. As an adopted child, and evidently brilliant, Zaid likely learned to read and write at home from the more-literate members of the household, since there is no record of his schooling elsewhere. Only during the latter Medina years might he have contributed significantly to the task of transcription.

Several male Muslim scholars with whom I have consulted have no fundamental objection to these conclusions in principle, despite an awareness that many details need to be given further consideration. They share an excitement that the obvious conclusion of accepting women as transcribers might contribute something substantial toward erasing the common misperception that the antifemale bias in Islam is fundamental. However, Laleh Bakhtiar, my tutor through several difficult parts of this study, has herself cautioned me. She writes in correspondence: "I have never heard that Hafsah actually wrote down the verses nor that she could even read and write. The Traditions state that the leaves, bones and other material that the verses were written on were given to her for safekeeping. This in no way implies that she actually wrote them down."

Her view represents much of the Muslim mainstream on this, but my point is this: Nothing says that Zaid actually wrote anything down either, or that any of Muhammad's male companions wrote down the verses; but someone did, and the clear sense of the context, with all the information that is available, suggests female authorship, if considered without bias.

During subsequent communications with Mahmoud Ayoub, the *éminence grise* of Islam in North America at Hartford Seminary, my suspicion that Dr. Bakhtiar was too modest in her assessment of the literary abilities of the women in Muhammad's household were confirmed. He verified that Khadijah was indeed literate according to the best scholarly opinion, and that Fatimah was certainly literate, even maintaining her own "mushof" or collection of Qur'anic verses that she used in private devotions, possibly while Muhammad was still alive, but certainly before the Qur'an was complete. Others among The People of the House who were unquestionably literate include three of Muhammad's younger wives: Hafsah, the eventual guardian of the Qur'an, Ayisha, a significant contributor to the Hadith, and Umm Salamah, also called "Hind," who is revered as "The Mother of Believers," and whose literary skills are especially well documented since she outlived all other People of the House into the era when the Hadith was being edited and produced.

Professor Ayoub assures me that the evidence for literate women in Muhammad's household is well documented, in contextual situations that I shall attempt to elucidate presently. If it were clearly established that King David and St. James were actually surrounded by literate women whose names and life stories we knew, and of whose contribution we were as certain as we are about any male contribution, the disciplines of Jewish and Christian feminist criticism would be elevated to a whole new level. Meanwhile, someone now should write a book about *The Women Who Wrote the Qur'an*, publishing full and proper documentation of these facts which have such obvious ramifications for Scripture in the whole family of Abraham, Sarah and Hagar.

Mahmoud Ayoub put this matter well to me: "It cannot be honestly said that the Muslim community kept up with the Qur'an in its treatment of women. Islamic family law is based on three sources: the Qur'an, the Sunnah [sections of the Hadith dealing with the actions and lifestyle of The Prophet] and 'urf, or cultural and social customs. It is this last source that prevailed because it gives the male so much power that often contradicts the Qur'an." Together, and with many others today, we hope that a new appreciation of women's contribution to Scripture may help to properly rebalance the relationship between men and women in Islam, in Judaism and Christianity and in the world.

In the matter of copying errors that led Protestants to adopt a longer version of the Lord's Prayer than Roman Catholics, it is true that we really do not know the names of any of the copyists, but we can safely surmise that they were Christians, likely male, working in a scriptorium associated with a monastic order. The evidence is circumstantial rather than forensic, but in the case of transcription of the Qur'an, enough is actually known for modern Islamic scholars to move beyond the circumstantial to reasonable conclusions. We don't know who transcribed the Qur'an, but it is more than surmising to state that such persons were Muslim, likely female, working at home as part of a respected entity, the "People of the House." On this basis, and on further evidence certain to be forthcoming, now that the issue has been raised, we present the Muslim template regarding the role of women in transcribing the Qur'an. This is a paradigm that may be applied to "anonymous" Hebrew and Christian Scriptures with a degree of considerable confidence, given the cultural similarity of the context. Among Jews, Christians, and Muslims there was a similar gender bias, which does not specifically denigrate the work of women but instead simply ignores it, in a manner not applied to works by men.

16

Handwriting

THERE IS PIOUS TRADITION among Muslims that every copy of the Arabic Qur'an in the world is identical. While there are no great differences, thanks to Hafsah, the fact that the original Arabic, like Hebrew, had no vowel marks, and that the methods of transmission varied in early years of rapid expansion, made it unlikely that all subsequent copies would be exactly identical. Pious traditions aside, this is not especially significant since the written copy of the Qur'an is not the real copy. The real Qur'an exists in heaven and is echoed on earth, not in writing but in sound.

In fact, setting aside the earlier confusion about which lists or canons of which collections were correct, so many versions of Hafsah's Medina Codex existed that in the fourth Islamic century (after 922 CE), it was decided to codify the variations. Since then, as every imam in the world knows, there have been seven official "variant readings" of the Qur'an, each of them with two recognized traditions of transmission, giving us fourteen versions of the Medina Codex alone, preserved and released by Hafsah as authorized by Uthman, who ordered the destruction of other original collections. Not all of the fourteen later versions are in general use today, but some are used for scholarly purposes and others liturgically. Still, despite small differences, there are no major or radical variations and no important issues outstanding with respect to the relatively short and well-preserved text of the Qur'an.

In early Muslim centuries there was an ever-evolving interpretation of the Qur'an by religious leaders in a centuries-old process called *ijtihad*. The decline of the process of *ijtihad* well before the modern era has led to the rigid and narrow interpretations of religious precepts that increasing numbers of Muslim thinkers today see as a prison. Not only is this approach restrictive; it is also unnecessary and counterproductive, though the public face of Islamic scholarship rarely exposes any emotion other than loyalty and conformity.

In addition to recognized variant readings of the Qur'an, there were also errors in hand copying in the Middle Ages, and modern printing-press errors, which produce clusters of slightly different versions of the Qur'an. Muslims of North Africa have always used a variant of the official text called the Warsh transmission, and official Turkish and Persian translations are normally used in worship in Turkey, Iran, and elsewhere among those communities, to the consternation of Arab purists. More and better translations are appearing in English and many other languages, capturing as much as possible the haunting ethos, the resonating intonation, and the evocative spirit of the Qur'an when read aloud. In the opinion of many, the true Qur'an is available only in Arabic for reasons intrinsic to its essence. The dominance of the Arabic original is not being challenged, but increasingly the translators are recognized as pencils in the hand of God.

In our own time, Laleh Bakhtiar is one of the many scholars who are bringing Islam into the twenty-first century through an insistence on interpreting the Qur'an in a manner consistent with the life and teachings of the Prophet Muhammad himself. There is an overlay of later culture in the Arabic text (reflected in the addition of vowel marks) that, in some ways, may have reflected the social mores at the beginning of the eighth century CE. Twenty-first-century scholars are not discarding the interpretations influenced by this addition but are re-examining and questioning the cultural developments that may be at odds with the life and personal witness of Muhammad himself.

This may be the place to consider more deeply what a renaissance in Muslim critical scholarship might mean in terms of an appreciative analysis of the Qur'an. For some, such a renaissance would involve a "rebirth" of the Qur'an, using modern critical techniques remarkably akin to a type of scriptural investigation that occurred during an era of textual compilation in the century following Muhammad's death. An impressive introduction to twentieth-century developments in this direction in Turkey is presented in the next chapter in relation to the Hadith. At this point, we will dare examine an illustration of the same with respect to the Qur'an itself.

The work of Laleh Bakhtiar and others has succeeded in producing progressive interpretations of the Qur'an as a basis for the Muslim resurgence in our time. This is based not on anything new, but on a more pure understanding of the original revelation to Muhammad as safeguarded by

Hafsah and as commented on by Muhammad in a trustworthy reassessment of his Hadith.

Laleh Bakhtiar was born in the United States of a Muslim father and a Christian mother. Her father returned to his native Iran to practice medicine while Bakhtiar was raised by her single-parenting mother. Her American mother was a Protestant, but for reasons of convenience, she had Bakhtiar educated in the Catholic system at a school near their home. Bakhtiar took First Communion at the age of eight, at her own volition, and was confirmed in church with her mother's blessing. When she was twenty-four years of age, Bakhtiar went to Iran to pursue graduate studies and reconnected with her father. She learned Persian, embarked on an intense study of Arabic literature, and in becoming an Arabic-language specialist also became a Muslim. The necessity of understanding the Qur'an in a Western progressive manner led her to begin her own meticulous translation, though she was convinced that there were no corruptions in the text as once offered to the world by Hafsah.

Laleh Bakhtiar is now a mature American Muslim community leader and a respected scholar of the first rank, practicing her faith in the Sufi tradition and avoiding both Sunni and Shiite labels. She is also a grandmother who has not worn the hijab since September 11, 2001.

Her acclaimed volume, *The Sublime Quran*, makes use of critical techniques to produce a translation that is reflective of her Western sensibilities, truest to the original text, and capturing something of the evocative power in oral presentation that is of the essence of the Qur'an. Published in 2007, followed in 2008 by a complete concordance, and with an Arabic version for 2009 (original consonantal version), *The Sublime Qur'an* is one of many fine examples of reformist scholarship and spirituality that is the basis of the Islamic renaissance in the twenty-first century. It is also available in recitation on DVD.

But it almost did not happen. The translation that Bakhtiar hoped to supplant had been the Wahhabi version widely circulated throughout the world through Saudi influence. This is a blatantly anti-Semitic and anti-Christian text in English that, for example, insists on translating *kufr* by the pejorative "infidel" in reference to many non-Muslims. Bakhtiar agrees with other scholars who suggest that "ungrateful" is equally as good a translation, and more in keeping with the tone of the verses in question. Many Christians and Jews in Muhammad's experience were indeed lackadaisical in their faith and appeared ungrateful to God, even while they were to be acknowledged by him as "People of the Book," not infidels.

At this point, Laleh Bakhtiar had spent two years honing the English translation of the first three chapters or surahs. Halfway through surah 4 she came to ayah (verse) 34 and felt stabbed by the thrust of something she had heard absentmindedly in Arabic many times. She had not recognized the extent of the threat toward women until researching the meaning of a certain word. As anyone paying close attention to the text might realize, this ayah instructs that a rebellious wife be first "admonished," then "left alone in bed," and finally "beaten," unless she changes her attitude, the last phrase being the currently common translation of the Arabic *daraba*.

As Bakhtiar told the *New York Times* in an interview quoted on her Web site, "I decided it either has to have a different meaning, or I can't keep translating. I couldn't believe that God would sanction harming another human being, except perhaps in war."

Careful research reveals that depending on how one arranges the vowels or on which vowels are actually added, *drb* in the original text can be understood and translated as "go away from" as well as "beat," "slap," "make an example of," "pet," "stroke," or "seduce." All these possibilities have been considered for various translations, and the Arabic worshiper does not necessarily hear "beat," except if that is the mindset that he or she brings to the hearing of the recitation. Linguists suggest that there are actually as many as twenty-five possible translations of the phrase, and "depart from" had already been used in at least one English translation.

Many Muslims today, not wishing to dishonor Islam, appear to be in denial regarding the reality of abuse against women in that culture, in much the same way that Iran's president, Mahmoud Ahmadinejad, at the United Nations, denied the presence of homosexuals in Iran. He appeared taken aback by the unexpected laughter and ridicule from most delegates, many of whom know of the widespread but clandestine gay culture in Iran. Likewise, incidents of abuse are possibly no more or any less numerous in Muslim households than is the actual situation in other cultural environments. However, physicians, police, and other witnesses frequently testify in court that a significant number of Muslim men justify violence against women by quoting the Qur'an, whether in Europe, America, or the Middle East.

The most egregious passage of the Qur'an in this regard is surah 4, ayah 34 (chapter 4, verse 34), as it is expressed in English in *The Sublime Qur'an*, where the original consonantal *drb* requires different vowel treatment to get away from *daraba* or "beat." Bakhtiar herself ignored the diacritical solution and used what is called "formal equivalence" to reveal the original meaning, and for both critical and religious reasons, it was important for her to address this issue in a truthful, scholarly manner.

In reference to "rebellious" wives, Bakhtiar, still uncomfortable with the traditional understanding *drb*, settled on, "Those whose resistance you fear, first admonish, then abandon them in their sleeping place, and finally go away from them." She translated thus based on the recorded behavior of Prophet Muhammad himself when faced with such dissension in his own household. In Western scholarship, making such an interpretive assumption would be a valid critical technique, given Mohammad's role in transmitting God's revelation and given his reputation for living out his understanding of it. It was not possible for Bakhtiar to dishonor either the Prophet or the Qur'an by a translation in which God would sanction even "gentle" slapping of a woman, as some authorities have described this practice, because of what that such divine sanctioning has led to and the mindset it represents in cultures all around the world.

Laleh Bakhtiar's understanding is to be encouraged, not merely in English translation, but as part of a social reorientation throughout the Muslim community, regardless of language and culture. Words do matter, and even the English translation "slap" betrays an attitude of male superiority and control increasingly unacceptable to Muslims—an attitude that in the heat of dispute could lead to actions more severe than slapping or beating. These and other observations are spelled out most helpfully in Bakhtiar's preface to *The Sublime Quran*, the first translation by an American woman ever. The translation recovers the original text as passed on by Hafsah with meanings crying out to be released by critical techniques. In its reliance on critical techniques, Bakhtiar's translation makes advances in Qur'anic interpretation that compare to advances made in biblical studies. In this instance, older Islamic techniques alone would not have solved the problem, but judging the issue by the *Sitz im Leben* of Muhammad, though a Western technique, would appear acceptable to all who hold the Prophet in appropriate high esteem.

Criticism is always the best guard against ideological or cultural interpretations of any text. In a postcritical era, it is clear that we still need critical techniques to help us understand what the Scriptures actually say before we move on to live out their implications. The jury is out around the world, but we can have confidence that the Scriptures will be set free from distortion and from skepticism about their authenticity, thanks in large measure to the forensic evidence.

The members of the jury are taking their role seriously and personally. I hope this modest attempt at illustrating the potential for experiencing and sharing in God's ongoing revelation will inspire keen minds and hearts, amateur and professional, Jewish, Christian and Muslim, to be part of this great unfolding miracle. William Blake once wrote that the whole universe is contained in a single grain of sand. Similarly, the Scripture contains a whole lifetime of intellectual and spiritual stimulation, as experienced by the author of J (perhaps David's daughter) and by the editor or redactor of the Pentateuch documents (likely Ezra); by the writer of Mark (quite likely Mark), and by the writer of the Q document (quite possibly the wife of St. James if not Mary Magdalene, the companion of Jesus); by Hafsah, Laleh Bakhtiar, and others, including current readers and students.

17

Reasonable Doubt

IN THE TWENTY-FIRST CENTURY an urgent necessity for the West to develop a more adequate knowledge and understanding of Islam has led to the sale of millions of copies of the Qur'an. It has been read by politicians, theologians, and other academics; by concerned citizens, clergy and people of faith; by Jews and Christians in particular. My own book, *Noah's Other Son: Bridging the Gap between the Bible and the Qur'an*, owes its success to this phenomenon, engendered by both anxiety about the world situation and hope for better relations among the members of "Abraham's dysfunctional family."

However, even academics and other friends who tell me they now read the whole Qur'an as often as once a year in a determination to "get it" cannot get it from the Qur'an alone. They frequently express frustration that for all their reading, they are unable to relate to Islam as practiced by Muslims they know and read about. Something is missing, and it took me a long time to realize what it is. The missing piece of the puzzle is available, even if more difficult to fathom than the Qur'an.

Most inquirers about Islam have heard of the Hadith, but few people have ever seen one, and fewer still realize their importance. The Hadith (the singular and plural forms of this word are the same) are not quite Scripture, and part of the reason Muslims do not think to introduce them to their friends is that they wish to draw our attention first to the Qur'an, the Scripture revealed to them by God. But while the Qur'an helps us understand what Muslims believe, it is the Hadith that explain how Muslims live. Moreover, since neither Jews nor Christians have anything quite like the Hadith outside their Scriptures as context or contemporary commentary, comparisons of materials approximating the Hadith are not as easy as when we place the Qur'an alongside the Hebrew and Christian Scriptures.

It would be hard to imagine, but suppose Moses had personally re-vealed the whole Torah and then his followers had composed a commentary about everything they ever saw him do or heard him say over the next twenty-three years. Would Jews in particular treasure such a compendium? It may be equally impossible to conceive, but imagine that Jesus had told the stories of the New Testament, and then, after he died many years later, a thousand details about his personal life and casual conversations were written up by all the people he had ever talked with over many years. Would Christians be interested in his opinions on everything under the sun, and in his personal habits as they related to his teachings?

Possibly the Jewish and Christian communities would not have designated such commentaries by the followers of Moses and the disciples of Jesus as Holy Scripture, at least not by the same definition of Scripture given to writings such as the Ten Commandments from Moses, the psalms by David, the parables of Jesus, or the Revelation of St. John—all considered to be directly inspired by God. But surely such biographical commentaries would be cherished in a very special way, and that is what we have regarding Muhammad in the Hadith. It is not Scripture, but it is sacred and cherished.

These illustrations may help to introduce the way Muslims value the Hadith, containing sayings and actions by the Prophet Muhammad. There is nothing like them in Christian tradition. Likewise in Judaism: Though over a thousand ancient commentators produced the Talmud, which has a look and feel akin to the Hadith, it gives the opinions of a variety of rabbis, none of whom had channeled the original Word from God as did, according to their followers, Moses, Jesus, and Muhammad.

The Qur'an was given to one person within a few years, written down, cherished, and safeguarded. For many years the Hadith, about the one who received it, were memorized and passed on orally. Then within a couple generations, while memory still functioned as to who quoted whom among the Companions of the Prophet, they were written down. There are about 160,000 such sayings, quotations, reminiscences, recollections, and observations about Muhammad: most about a sentence in length, some as long as a paragraph or two, all identified by the Companions (several thousand people), who had been with the Prophet for anything from a moment in time to many years under the same roof. It is widely believed that practically everything he ever said or did was recorded as a model for the lifestyle of Muslims. That this is largely unknown in the West is amazing, since it explains things from the roots of Sharia law, to personal hygiene, to relations between the sexes, to observance of festivals, to Muslim prayer life, to personal and communal sensitivities, to Muhammad's views and his actions respecting military and peacekeeping matters.

However, if Muslims have complete confidence in the text of the Qur'an, the same cannot be said of the Hadith, which exist in many volumes and have rankings as to the reliability of the various sayings and observations about the Prophet's life, depending on the number and reliability of people recorded as transmitters of his sayings and actions. This is another reason why some Muslims would be hesitant to share this material.

I had read many such Hadith in quotation, but never saw "a Hadith" in a bookstore, assuming it was a book. Muslim booksellers always mumbled about portions and commentaries, so in frustration, at an early stage of my research I e-mailed Laleh Bakhtiar, one of many helpful tutors who have helped me gain admission to this world of mystery and intrigue. I quote her articulate reply.

> In regard to the Hadith, the Sunnis follow 6 canonical works: Sahih al-Bukhari (9 volumes, Arabic-English); Sahih Muslim (4 volumes, English only); Sunan Abu Dawud (3 volumes, English only); Sunan Nisai (5 volumes, English-Arabic), Sunan Ibn Majah (5 volumes, English-Arabic) and Tirmidhi (5 volumes, English-Arabic). As you can see they are all extensive and more than I think you would need. There are 1 and 2 volume summaries but it is not clear which Hadith they chose to leave out.
>
> While there are 6 canonical collections which hold what are called the reliable Hadith, there are only about 5000 such reliable individual Hadith and many of them are repeated in the various books. Another 155,000 Hadith were not determined to be reliable by these 6 early scholars.
>
> The Shia also follow the Hadith in their own versions, which are all similar in nature but come from the books of the early Imams that were later put into book form at the same time as the Sunni canonical works.

I was none the wiser, but more appreciative of the conundrum we face. Later in the next chapter, I will give a small but dependable representative collection of Hadith for illustration and interest. We would be wise to recognize some other developments first, so that readers as naïve as I was until recently can have some rational basis on which to understand or at least appreciate this resource.

If the text of the Qur'an is secure, for all the reasons we have considered, the texts of the Hadith are currently going through a radical reassessment that may lead to major socioreligious reforms in significant parts of the Muslim world. This watershed development is well defined: grounded in Turkey; not much recognized in the West; gingerly anticipated by knowledgeable Muslims in Malaysia, Indonesia, North Africa, Egypt, Jordan, and the United Arab Emirates; scathingly condemned in conservative countries like Saudi Arabia and Iran.

This prospect is getting mixed reviews in Afghanistan and Pakistan, where reformers associated with the governing majorities are locked in a struggle with Taliban conservatives. Similar divisions on this matter are found in Palestine (Fatah versus Hamas) and Lebanon (Sunni partners of Christian government leaders versus Hezbollah). While they have made no statement yet, it would be clear where the ideologues of Al-Qaeda fit into this picture. (The ideologues of Al-Qaeda would be especially opposed to any reform of the Hadith.) So it will be increasingly important for Jews, Christians, and other observers to become respectfully conversant in the matter of possible reforms to the Hadith.

Facile comparisons between current Hadith reform movements and the Protestant Reformation of the sixteenth century are tempting but entirely inadequate and irksome to Muslims. My information comes from excited Turkish students and from religious leaders across America who have hosted me for purposes of dialogue, as well as from various media reports out of Turkey, including the BBC (Robert Piggott, Religious Affairs correspondent, BBC World News, 2/26/2008), and from worldwide syndications of McClatchy Newspapers (Dion Nissenbaum, Washington Bureau, 4/24/2008).

Various other programs and magazines have given the story passing mentions. But while this has not been front-page news in the West, a possible firestorm is approaching in the Muslim world. Or, while critics may abound, we may witness the most significant Muslim renaissance in several centuries as Islam flowers and flourishes in the publication of new resources like the one represented in this Turkish project. All who pray for the good of Islam might join in preparation for this positive development, due for release within one decade after September 11, 2001, when certain negative images of Islam became entrenched in the minds of so many.

In the context of Turkey's growing ties with Europe and its role as a bridge between West and East, the reform-minded government of Turkey's

Justice and Development Party (AKP) has financed and promoted the work of some eighty leading scholars from around the world for this project. Associated with the School of Religion at Ankara University and head-quartered in a stolid stone building next to Ankara's Central Mosque, the scholars have placed 160,000 sayings attributed to Muhammad (canonical and otherwise) into a computer system. Scholars have separated them by subject and have assigned teams to study the different subject areas. These teams analyze the sayings' authenticity and validity as well as the traditions surrounding transmission and interpretation.

The traditional Islamic method of critical analysis is called *ilm al-rijal*, the Science of Transmission, a well-authenticated method of ranking and evaluating this ancient material according to the validity of the reports and the reputation of the Companion-transmitters. This method is being combined with Western techniques of textual criticism in which contents are compared to deal with inconsistencies and conflicts. If something reportedly said by Muhammad in a Hadith is in clear contrast to the examples of his actions, this would result in a lowering of its rank, no matter how high the reputation of the Companion or transmitter. All scientifically valid methods are being rigorously employed in this exhaustive exercise: what many Muslims now chose to refer to as "forensic" procedures related to these sacred and highly influential materials.

Turkish authorities and their assembled scholars are between the proverbial rock and hard place, since up to this point powerful Turkish secularists refuse to accept the notion that Islam can be re-formed or modernized to apply to modern life; and fundamentalists, including Turkey's large conservative Shia population, object to the very attempt. In laying its plans well, however, the authorities have given graduate theological training to 450 women, have appointed them to positions as senior imams, or *vaizes*, and have given them the task of presenting and even championing the program at the community level throughout the country, with support from their male counterparts in "mainstream Islam" in Turkey.

18

Testimony

THE SLIMMED-DOWN, FIVE-VOLUME REVISED Hadith will be published initially in Turkish, Arabic (to make it available to Muslims worldwide), and in Russian (for fifty million Russian-speaking Muslims of Turkic origin in central Asia). Obviously this is an internal Muslim matter, not designed for English-speaking critics or for friends in the West, but its impact among Westernized Muslim communities in Europe and North America is expected to be immense.

This development, while featured in news reports because of Turkey's growing relationship with Europe and the West, is perhaps only the most visible of a number of such reforms in the Muslim world. We must understand that in this context, the concept of "re-form" refers to a return to original principles, whenever cultural or other practices and principles have deviated from true or pure Islam.

To draw some comparisons, the Hebrew Scriptures permit parents to sell their daughters into slavery, they enjoin believers to stone those who work on the Sabbath, and they condemn eating shellfish and engaging in homosexual activity equally as "abominations." But postmodern Jews today neither apply the letter of these Scriptures nor abandon the spirit that may account for their appearance in their early culture before being twisted or made harsh in developing law and practice. The reforms among most Jews today are inevitable and essential.

St. Paul writes that in Christ there is neither male nor female (Gal 3:28), leading many critics to assume that when Paul appears to forbid female leadership in worship, someone quickly amended the text to reflect a more conservative or even regressive position in the congregation to which the teaching was addressed. (For a review of such deviations from the true or original Christian message in the New Testament, see Bart D. Ehrman,

Misquoting Jesus, 183–86.) Most churches have reformed on this point, while Southern Baptists still resist the leadership of women and the Roman Catholic Church has yet to ordain them in spite of female leadership in religious orders and undeniable focus on women from the Virgin Mary to Mother Teresa. Promoting women's leadership is one order of business being addressed in the Muslim community—not merely in Turkey, though the Hadith project may be the signal for which many have been waiting.

A simple example of the proposed revisions, applying the original meaning and purpose of the Prophet, is in the matter of oral hygiene. It appears that Muhammad recommended that a follower brush his teeth with a certain durable twig, a practice adopted by some of Muhammad's more rigid followers today. In this case, the Prophet was obviously promoting the best oral hygiene he knew, however, rather than taking an antimodernist position against toothbrushes. How this will be dealt with in the Hadith revisions is not yet clear, but some attempt will be made to present the meaning and purpose of the Prophet's words. That simple illustration will be magnified in more complex issues.

It is clear that Muhammad had a far more supportive relationship with women than has appeared in Islamic culture since his lifetime, and it is expected that this will be reflected in revisions to the Hadith. An example of a saying that supports women but that has later been used to limit them is the Muslim restriction on females traveling long distances alone, based on Muhammad's concern for their safety in a violent environment. When balanced by a neglected Hadith in which the Prophet longs for the day when women can travel freely over long distances, it is clear what the Prophet's goal is. The new teaching may reflect new interpretation in ways that will increase the freedom of women in public. There is a responsibility for public safety, particularly for women who are more physically vulnerable than men, on the part of Muslim governments, some of whom choose to deliberately misinterpret the Hadith to suit their conservative bias.

On the surface, this appears much like restrictions on women behind Southern Baptist pulpits or Roman Catholic altars—restrictions purportedly based on Scripture, including in passages possibly needing review and clarification, or even revision with respect to cultural biases that no longer obtain.

A re-examination and reform of Hadiths on female genital mutilation may correct popular misconceptions linking this horrific custom to Islam. Despite low-ranking Hadith references acknowledging it, this practice of pre-Islamic cultures originated in Africa about two thousand years ago and was imported into Islam from African Christian, Falashan (Ethiopian Jewish), and animistic cultures at a time now believed to have been long after the Prophet's lifetime. The practice of female genital mutilation developed in a culturally restrictive era when female sexual pleasure was feared as a threat to marital faithfulness. It is still practiced among non-Muslims as well as Muslims in certain countries, though it is completely unknown in most Asian Muslim nations today.

The dubious sayings attributed to the Prophet in this regard may well be superseded by his other sayings, of which there are many, in support of female sexual expression. Among the canonical Hadith, there is only one saying in *Abu Dawud* that mentions genital mutilation, and there it is identified as a weak Hadith. Combining this tradition of the Science of Transmission with the Western practice of critical comparisons, the fact that the Qur'an actually promotes the concept of a wife being given pleasure during sexual intercourse might almost certainly suggest that reformed Hadith will forbid anything that is contrary to the Qur'an, such as the mutilation of genitalia, which reduces or eliminates a woman's pleasure during the act. By this same forensic approach, other horrific non-Islamic practices such as honor killings may then be forbidden in Muslim communities on the basis of a correct understanding of the Qur'an and the example of the Prophet as found in the Hadith. Reforms based on reinterpreting important texts are obviously preferable to reforms adopted uncomfortably or inappropriately in the name of modernity or Western mores.

Al-Qaeda is not the first extremist group to attempt to hijack Islam for its own purposes, but in Turkey and elsewhere a more correct understanding of Hadith is being actively promoted as a high priority. Hadith texts on war, homosexuality, marriage practices, and every aspect of life are under careful scrutiny, and no one yet knows how some of these matters will be treated. Nervousness and anticipation are among the many emotions awaiting release of this landmark work, even while Western media commentators are still wont to complain, "Where are the voices of moderation in Islam?" We may be about to find out.

The role and contribution of women are indeed at the forefront of many of these developments, led by both women and men. Through much of its history, women have been among the foremost teachers and interpreters of the Hadith, a practice that lasted until the sixteenth century CE when a decline in many academic pursuits took place across the Islamic world. Mohammad Akram Nadwi, a Sunni *Alim*, or religious scholar, at the Oxford Center for Islamic Studies in Britain has documented the tradition of female teachers of the Hadith in a forty-volume biographical dictionary, which is currently seeking a publisher. Through previously published biographies, classical texts, Madrassa chronicles, and letters between scholars, he has identified eight thousand female teachers of the Hadith, whose stories are being retold: female jurists, female scholars, female librarians, all who taught and functioned freely with male as well as female students and clients in previous centuries.

This information has always been available. But it has been largely ignored, beginning with the knowledge that just as Hafsah had a leading role in the production, preservation, and propagation of the Qur'an, another of the Prophet's wives, Ayisha, had a similar role in the establishment of the Hadith. Indeed, while neither Hafsah nor Ayisha had status in the Muslim community approaching that of Muhammad's first wife, Khadijah, and of his eldest daughter, Fatimah, during Muhammad's lifetime, they were not alone among the several wives and daughters who evinced influence as what he called the "People of the House" in the early Muslim community.

Many thousand Hadith are related by the more than one thousand female Companions of the Prophet. Some two thousand Hadith are ascribed to Ayisha alone and among the more highly regarded canonical Hadith, there are over one thousand Hadith written by and ascribed to some 150 women. The most accessible source in this regard is the *Encyclopedia of Muhammad's Women Companions, and the Traditions They Related*, by Shaykh Muhammad Hisham Kabbani and Laleh Bakhtiar.

To give a sense and feel for the Hadith as a whole, the individual Hadiths that I will quote are all from this source, partly because, on critical grounds, Hadith by women are considered among the most reliable. They survived and were included not because of attribution to men of influence or power, but because of reputation and merit. As the Qur'an is the collection of "recitations," the Hadith is the collection of sayings and activities that have been "related," the word used to introduce each one, along with the identity of the person making the recollection or quoting it.

Of the 1022 Hadith in my possession by women, about half are by Ayisha, the youngest wife of Muhammad, who survived well into the era when Hadith were written down in the various collections. Those quoted are not intended to illustrate anything in particular, and indeed, Hadith frequently appear almost pedantic and sometimes seem to contradict each other. They may be examined "forensically" in a more thorough and robust fashion than can the words of the Qur'an because even strict Muslims do not view them as the "very words" of Allah in the same way that they view the words of the Qur'an. Even now, as throughout history, Hadith frequently include ancient footnotes of authorities who challenge their points. The page numbers in parentheses refer to the collection by Kabbani and Bakhtiar.

To give the reader a flavor of some of the Hadith writings, a few randomly selected, but interesting and perhaps telling verses are presented below:

> Ayisha related: *Verses of the Qur'an referring to stoning to death and to breast feeding of adults were written on a paper and placed under her bed. When the Prophet died, they were busy with the funeral service, and their pet goat accidentally ate the paper* (55).
>
> Umm Salama related: *In the lifetime of the Prophet, the women got up when they finished the prescribed prayers. The messenger and the men would stay in their places as long as God willed. When the Messenger got up, the men would then get up* (121).
>
> Hafsah related: *God's Messenger said, "It is not sinful for a pilgrim to kill five kinds of animals: the crow, the hawk, the mouse, the scorpion and the rabid dog"* (146).
>
> Ayisha related: *God's Messenger was asked about an intoxicating drink made from honey. He said, "Every drink that causes intoxication is forbidden"* (175).
>
> Ayisha related: *God's Messenger said, "The best of condiments is vinegar"* (176).
>
> Umm Salama related: *The Messenger said, "One whose husband has died must not wear garments dyed with saffron or red clay or bejeweled garments. She must not apply henna or collyrium"* (183).
>
> Asma Bint Yazid related: *The sleeve of the shirt of God's Messenger came to his wrist* (185).
>
> Maymuna related: *The Prophet was asked regarding ghee in which a mouse had fallen. He said, "Take out the mouse and throw away the ghee around it and use the rest."* (194)
>
> Fatimah related: *They used to slaughter horse and eat it during the lifetime of God's Messenger* (213).
>
> Ayisha related: *The Prophet did not marry any virgin except herself* (222).

It is increasingly recognized that many of the women in Muhammad's life were literate, and that those closely related to him were particularly well educated. Little was made of this fact in a society in which surviving and sometimes making war were more valued than making documents. This was possibly regarded as women's work, though as has been attested, only some of what the women of the house wrote was of their own composition. The bulk of their writing available to us at this point may have been limited to their faithful recording of the great sayings and revelations, poetic and otherwise, by the seemingly wise and respected leading men around them: prophets, leaders, even kings and caliphs. We can start by recognizing what we have.

As noted previously, this template fits well the royal households of David and Solomon from the Hebrew Scriptures and the leading households of the early church in Jerusalem and elsewhere among those nurtured in the ancient environment of today's Middle East. This should lead to a reassessment of the female role in the production, protection, and propagation of Scripture across the region and throughout Abraham, Sarah, and Hagar's family.

While it has been mainly Sunni students of Turkish origin who have kept me up to date on these matters in my travels, I have also been invited to address students who belong to the Shia student organization known as the Thaqalayn Muslim Association.

Hadith are important to them too, including the Hadith that gives them their name. The *Hadith al-Thaqalayn* refers to what the Shia regard as "the two weighty things," namely, the *Qur'an* (Recitation) and the *Ahl al Bayt* (People of the House), the family of Muhammad, who have particularly high standing among Shia.

As we know, since his three sons all died in infancy, the great stock Muhammad placed in his family's leadership role in the community all devolved upon his four daughters, especially Fatimah, after the death of his trusted first wife, Khadijah. Next in importance among the People of the House were Muhammad's several wives, with influence not particularly limited to Hafsah, Ayisha, and Umm Salamah, though they are of greater interest here for their leading roles in the production of Scripture and sacred texts.

Muhammad had twelve wives after the death of Khadijah, all but one being widows of his leading Companions, living then under the protection of the community leader and serving in his household. That made them more like "partners" in the modern sense than like mere sex objects, as our stereotypical perspectives of Islamic culture and the of ancient roots of Judeo-Christian "Old Testament" culture would have us believe.

Indeed, we are here provided with insight that adds to developing understandings of the influence that women (companions in the entourage) had in the times of David and Solomon and so many others. Despite an ultimately patriarchal and exclusivist filter, the writings associated with Solomon, in particular, are especially noted as having been influenced by his association with, and great respect for, the feminine wisdom of his very spiritual—in many cases multinational—women companions. These points are key to the appreciation of the Muslim template for the production of Scripture, and the application of that template to the Judeo-Christian contexts.

In Islam, and in the related ancient cultures of today's Middle East, great wisdom and important contributions were derived from women who played vital roles as companions or as wives, despite being "veiled" or protected in aristocratic courts. The husbands of Muhammad's daughters and the fathers of his wives also played important roles in transmitting the Scripture and sacred text. These women were in effect the most central People of the House—revered by Muslims ancient and modern, not as highly as the Qur'an itself, but in a significant manner.

The Shia have preserved most of the documentary evidence to this effect. And while exalting women has not been a priority of the leading Shia government (the one currently ruling in Iran), the *Hadith al-Thaqalayn* bears witness to the ultimate importance of the *Ahl al-Bayt*, the People of the House. Except for Muhammad, only Mary, the person most mentioned in the Qur'an, has a higher standing in Islam, if we are to judge only by the Qur'an and the Hadith. The roles of Muhammad's first wife, Khadijah, and of their daughter, Fatimah, and the contributions of his later wives, Hafsah and Ayisha, may be not very different from contributions of women in David's household and from contributions of women in the early church.

19

Summation

THE DOCUMENTARY EVIDENCE WE sought to establish about the origins and textual integrity of the Scriptures is now on public record. We have also reviewed circumstantial evidence about nonessentials of interest and have presented some tantalizing conjectures about what the future may hold in both critical and postcritical dimensions of scriptural studies.

General readers and students keen to study and contribute further should now get down to work as they finish reading this book. There are three new forensic tools at their disposal, and instead of just reading about them, they can and should use them to become intimately familiar and almost expert with the texts of the Scriptures from the family of Abraham, Sarah, and Hagar.

Participants in this activity are encouraged to download the "Diagram of Sources of the Pentateuch" from BrianArthurBrown.com, and if their printers cannot handle 11-by-17-inch paper, they should send the image by e-mail or take it by disk to their neighborhood photocopy shop where they have equipment to run off color copies on paper of that size or larger. The next step would be to purchase a set of highlight markers and get out working Bibles, ones with thick paper pages, not the usual thin paper. Individuals should use the whole chart to decide which puzzles are the most intriguing and transfer the colors to the pages of the Bible by highlighter.

Those who choose Deuteronomy 34 may derive a feeling for how Ezra and his team included something from each of the sources, a colorful experience of the Israelite heritage. Those who really want to develop an appreciation for the intricate efforts of the Levitical priests who painstakingly combined J and E to reunite the people through Scripture, should try to highlight in their Bibles either the flood story in Genesis 7 or the story of Joseph in Genesis 37. The rest is child's play. Of course, this diagram can also be displayed on large screen television in the classroom setting, or downloaded for use in PowerPoint.

Every serious student should next acquire a copy of the classic chart, "A Diagram of Synoptic Relationships," by Allan Barr. The chart from T. & T. Clark in New York or London is expensive, at about a hundred dollars including taxes, but it should endure. Mine came on durable paper that has lasted fifty years. Besides, offsetting this expense, one gets both the "Diagram of the Sources of the Pentateuch" and the "Diagram of the Revelations of Allah in the Holy Qur'an" from BrianArthurBrown.com free of charge.

Then in their working Bibles readers might highlight Q in light blue and, with word processors, attempt to reassemble the original document onscreen (professionally edited texts are also available that might be used for comparison at the conclusion of this exercise). Q can then be read aloud slowly and deliberately to decide whether it "feels" like it came from an early woman leader in the Christian movement such as the wife of Jesus's brother James, or even from her and other women in his household and under his protection. Those who cannot acquire a copy of the Barr diagram may use the smaller facsimile found on BrianArthurBrown.com (even though the text on this smaller version of the diagram is hard to read) and then may highlight the Q verses in their Bibles before assembling the original Q in an integrated document onscreen.

These several hands-on forensic exercises will give readers a feel for the Bible that they have perhaps never experienced before.

Finally, participants in these exercises are invited to download an 11-by-17–inch copy of the "Diagram of the Revelations of Allah in the Holy Qur'an" in connection with the next chapter. In this instance, the paper size available on most home printers (8½ by 11 inches) also works quite well because the amount of material is less, and large chapter sizes on the smaller diagram are adequate. Then using either *The Sublime Quran*, the respected traditional version of the Holy Qur'an, by Yusuf Ali, or almost any standard version, such as those by Pickthall, Asad, or Malik, both general readers and students are ready for an exercise with material that will be less familiar to them unless they come from a Muslim background.

Individuals or groups may simply read through the Qur'an, watching for any verses of seven categories of materials that are perhaps not entirely unique to the Qur'an, in that they were revealed to Jews, Christians, and others in other times and places, or first recorded in another form. Those verses or portions of chapters should be marked on the chart with highlighters in the appropriate colors, creating a diagram similar to my diagram of the Pentateuch and to Barr's diagram of the Synoptic Gospels.

Where this exercise is being undertaken in university settings, a minimum number of colorings may be required to illustrate that seminarians or other students of religion have done an acceptable amount of work and have grasped the subject. Most will want a higher score and will not be able to restrain themselves from coloring many of the more familiar Jewish and Christian connections, both canonical and noncanonical. For example, those familiar with noncanonical Christian material will instantly recognize the story of the boy Jesus making clay pigeons and as a sign of his Messianic power blessing them so they could fly. This story is found in both the gnostic Gospel of Thomas and the Qur'an. An equally obvious connection for Muslims and Christians is the Muslim teaching that in the mêlée of chaotic activities on Good Friday, it was actually Judas who got crucified mistakenly by the authorities. This story is found also in the gnostic Gospel of Barnabas (not to be confused with the older Epistle of Barnabas, somewhat more highly regarded by the early Christian orthodox establishment and nearly included in the New Testament).

One does not need to be a seminarian to undertake these exercises and to profit from them. General readers who belong to congregational book clubs studying this text may regard themselves as "members of the jury" reviewing the evidence together. Some parts of the exercises may be done by individual members during their reading at home. On a table in the congregational library, they might share in the coloring of the chart by each contributing what they have discovered.

In the course of research and verification, I have been deeply impressed by the women who are leading scholars in these fields, practically dominating many important disciplines, from textual analysis through archaeological studies in scriptural context to literary and cultural research in parallel and related fields. Phyllis Trible, who lives in retirement in the shadow of Riverside Church in New York City, knows as much about the interpretation of the texts of all three religions in every age as anyone I have ever learned from previously—and I refer to both depth and detail in her knowledge. Sadly, she and other women scholars of the Christian community are able to produce the least amount of actual evidence for the role of women in scriptural formation. Those working in the Jewish and Muslim traditions can produce more evidence. The lack of evidence for the role of women in Christian scriptural formation could be due to scholars' benign neglect of the subject, to the accommodation of the gospel to then current cultural circumstances, or even to a not-too-subtle campaign to destroy the evidence. Jesus was possibly as progressive toward women as was Muhammad. But whereas the Muslim community soon became as regressive toward women as the early Christian church had been, the Muslim documentary evidence tells a much more complete story about the role of women.

Christian women, as well as male scholars who share their quest, sometimes appear to be quite frustrated that neither textual criticism nor archeological evidence have yet proven the roles that figures from Mary Magdalene to the legendary "Pope Joan" may have played in the life of early Christianity, its theology, and its scriptural writings.

For that matter, it is impossible to prove unequivocally even the activities undertaken by many of the male figures of Scripture and early Christianity. The difference is that there is so much more that has been ascribed to or written about these male figures, resulting in less impetus to find these absolute proofs.

The problem is, however, that conservative patriarchal forms of religion are less and less meaningful for many today who live in societies where, literally and metaphorically, the "veils" that have covered women's faces, expressions, and highest hopes and aspirations for humanity are perhaps finally being lifted away (proudly worn modest hijabs or fashionable scarves not withstanding).

Christianity is not entirely without evidence of techniques to fully "unveil" the contribution made by women throughout history. An example of this is a first-century Christian teaching document called the Didache, which shows how active women might have been in early Christian history and in ideological or literary pursuits, but further ancient sources were perhaps suppressed as the church became regressive in this regard. Indeed the Didache itself was lost until brought to light by Greek Orthodox Church leaders in 1873. Christians may experience continuing frustration in this quest unless and until they adopt an overall basis for any hypothesis regarding the role of women in Scripture production. The proposed template from Islam is such a model, supported by strong circumstantial and some documentary evidence of Scripture production by women in leading Muslim households.

Additional research to support this model comes from the Jewish side of the family. Carol Meyers of Duke University is especially well informed on language and gender in the Bible and on the life of women in ancient

Israel, as perhaps the world's leading authority on household life in biblical times. Given that Meyers is an archaeologist, the media have consulted her regularly for programming specials as diverse as the movie *The Prince of Egypt*, from Dreamworks, and various segments of the A&E Television's *Mysteries of the Bible* and *Biography* series. Her guidance for me, and her presentations at the launch conference, center on the daily activities of women in ancient Israelite households, including on their daughters' education and on their own opportunities for literary pursuits.

Ellen Frankel, the author of *The Five Books of Miriam*, even has documentary evidence (yet unpublished) showing how an unidentified medieval scribe interrupted a priority transmission to "feed the baby," leaving little doubt as to which gender that scribe belonged. But, again, if limited to the Israelite or Judean circles, investigation of such material about the gender of transmitters or copyists would be inconclusive. It is as we take all the evidence from the whole family that we will find the evidence for a template that applies to Christians, Jews, and Muslims alike. To the surprise of not a few Jews and Christians, however, it is the Muslim side of the family that possesses the clearest evidence for the influence of women in the transmission of Scripture.

Laleh Bakhtiar, the American female translator of *The Sublime Quran*, and Raheel Raza, the Canadian author and a female liturgist of Islam, may never rival the standing of Khadijah and Fatimah, or even of Hafsah and Ayisha, but they, along with the female *vaizes* of Turkey and others, are confident as they begin to recover the well-documented role of women in scriptural work in Islam, though many such women face the challenge of a cultural hangover of misogyny in many parts of contemporary Muslim society. They deserve the support of Jewish and Christian sisters and brothers in their shared endeavors, despite the continuing intransigence of certain Christian, Jewish, and Muslim denominations or groups.

The point here is neither to repeat the respect and gratitude I feel for these women expressed previously in the Acknowledgments, nor to suggest that male scholars are necessarily faltering, but to draw a parallel between the current situation and that which may have prevailed in centuries long gone by. This time, in a coordinated approach, and with a mutually acceptable starting point with the Muslim template, genuine progress may be made "on the record."

Eva Schwartzentruber, for many years my professional colleague in ministry, was previewing an early draft of some of these chapters when she sent me the following e-mail:

> I find it very interesting that it is women scholars that you depend on for the research you talk about in Part Three of your book. Will North American men not feel threatened by this when you all get to the launch conference? Maybe in some ways North America is more of a patriarchal society than the East which we accuse of being so. I am beginning to think that perhaps there is more real equality among the sexes at least among educated Muslims, even though, or perhaps because of, their understanding of differing roles. They don't seem to feel threatened by each other. Why is this not so in a large part of western culture? Women (I realize not all, but in a general way) have lost their status and have to claw and climb their way up some mythological ladder in politics, business, even church. Have women sold their birthright in some way or allowed it to been taken away from them by a scheming younger brother?

Before I could react, Eva had received the following e-mail from my daughter, Indira Sinton, a poet, theologian, and leadership and organizational development consultant, regarding a related discussion they were having. All this should be read in the context of the discussion about female authorship, which has been under consideration in seven of the twenty-two chapters of this book. Of course I include their comments with permission, but it is obvious that they were writing for each other and for me, rather than for publication.

> In my study of Islamic culture in Sub-Saharan Africa at the University of Toronto, we reviewed the lives of noble women in those cultures who were very literate and had influence ideologically and even in terms of governance, albeit remaining protected in the household. This is in contrast to the image of Islamic women always having existed as a second class—though they do now in fundamentalist or more brutal Islamic cultures, where might/ testosterone rules.
>
> One can see the need for protection in such cultures. If not physically attacked/raped . . . women are verbally attacked/raped by males who just don't have their brutish aggressive and sex hormones under control. In spite of all this, women have had wonderful independent and strong roles throughout history, sadly often behind the scenes/veils—protected or cautious or not having the same need to obtain official credit for their roles, perhaps because they can be sure of their children as their legacy. (Men can never

be 100% sure). Also, to some degree, women are simply not as physically/brutally strong—and history gets written by the victors and about the victors, those with the biggest clubs.

There is a basic instinctual need for the male to feel superior, and so women are often not acknowledged—or they know that if they seek acknowledgment it will be a problem for them. Jane Goodall's studies with gorillas in Africa showed this same behavior in the apes. The female gorillas actually had to sort of bow in deference to the Alpha male before she then moves into a role which is in every way his equal and in many ways assumes the main leadership role, so long as he is acknowledged.

There are many roles that women have held which by far exceed the typical "secretary" role Dad is picturing for the women in Muhammad's household. Nursing and teaching roles which were traditional women's roles were very vital and involved skills that often and in many ways exceed those of the male administrator or even doctor, though rarely acknowledged.

And women are present in all kinds of professional roles today. The majority of people entering protestant and Anglican ministry are now women, I believe. Roman Catholics have always had a great female quasi clergy in the convents—so devoted to spiritual leadership, teaching, community health and wellness and social justice.

There are many, many women doctors, lawyers and managers. My husband Judson has had more women as his managers than men at IBM and in the twenty-first century, I have personally worked with as many female managers and senior manager/directors as male ones in various large Canadian organizations. In such companies men and women are equally represented in management and professional roles (except maybe engineering and aggressive sales type roles). Senior Executive offices are still more populated by men largely because it tends to be highly assertive/aggressive and very career oriented people that want to go to that level, and also many women still do take time off or at least step back from the intensity of their careers while their children are young.

What I do notice, and I've heard other women speak of, including a woman who was the CEO of Lotus which is part of IBM . . . her name escapes me at the moment—ah isn't it always so . . . "women without names"), is that women do bring different strengths to managerial and professional roles. They do tend to be nurturers or enablers rather than "controllers." But THAT is actually the preferred leadership style in the knowledge/intellectual workforce settings of today. Women don't yell as loudly and will go unnoticed by some, but they are usually the better leaders in the current environment. Women enable men, children, other women, whole organizations and even nations.

It occurred to me that while the evidence is mounting concerning the role of women as authors and producers of Scripture, the reasons we might like to know about this are also interesting. Beyond the desire to push back against unwarranted restrictions on women, which are disabling to them and to society more broadly, there is the sense that a proper acknowledgment of women's roles in Scripture transmission may enhance our understanding of the texts in our minds and our feel for the material in our hearts.

If this is how Allah, the Divine, the Holy Spirit, works, men may have their appreciation enhanced, and women may be inspired and enabled to do more. It does now appear that women had an outstanding role in writing and producing Scripture, so we should continue to amass the evidence as something the ancients were unwilling or unable to do. This accomplishment may be among the hallmarks of the faith and of the Abrahamic faith family's experience together in the twenty-first century: one of the first fruits of the family reunion made possible by sharing our scriptural heritage.

Following the launch conference for this book, readers may visit a summary report and more succinct description of the Muslim template of Scripture production in Islam, as posted at BrianArthurBrown.com, for further discussion—especially among readers not present at the conference. It is my personal hope that a new awareness of what I call "the Muslim Template for Female Scripture Production" will lend credibility to arguments (made earlier in this book) for the female authorship of J and Q. Without the foundational principle that the Muslim Template provides, these assertions may not move beyond their present status as inflated postulations.

In any event, while *Forensic Scriptures* may be valued for the diagrams that accompany it and for elevating the Documentary Hypothesis of the last century to the status of the documentary evidence in the twenty-first century, it is my hope and prayer that "The Muslim Template of Female Scripture Production" may become a concept that goes forward and makes a significant contribution to progress in understanding the production and transmission of Scripture among Jews, Christians, and Muslims. Perhaps this introductory summary of the concept will embolden readers, whether scholars, students, or general readers, to move further in its adoption and use. At a minimum, let us establish the maxim for Scriptures: "If it is anonymous, it may be assumed that the writer is a woman."

20

Sequestered

A T THIS POINT, WE do not have an adequate forensic diagram to illustrate to the jury revelations prior to the Qur'an, but one is under construction, as seen on the two-page spread at the conclusion of this chapter. Readers, as members of the jury, are invited to work with the forensic scientists of Scripture to complete this task. As downloaded and experienced as part of the last chapter, the "Diagram of the Sources of the Pentateuch" has five columns, one each representing Genesis, Exodus, Leviticus, Numbers, and Deuteronomy, with separate colors for the verses derived from J, E, D, and P, like to the one on the front cover. On the back cover, the inset photo, the "Diagram of Synoptic Relationships," has basically three columns: one each for Matthew, Mark, and Luke, with four colors representing Mark, Q, material unique to Matthew, and material unique to Luke—verified by hands-on experience of members of the jury.

Also on the back cover, the sample section of the "Diagram of the Revelation of Allah in the Holy Qur'an" consists of two columns, one for the recitations given to Muhammad in Mecca and the other for inspirations at Medina, all in black and white so far. As far as possible, readers may complete the full prototype of this diagram in the text by color-coding for seven categories the above references and other background material as described in the legend on the diagram. Alternatively, as indicated earlier, fresh working copies of the "Diagram of the Revelation of Allah in the Holy Qur'an" can be downloaded from BrianArthurBrown.com free of charge.

Several distinct areas of previous sacred inspiration, or "revelation," may be of interest for investigation by Christians, Jews, and others hoping to learn from the Qur'an and working with Muslim counterparts. Some social and religious traditions contained in the Qur'an are simply condemned there as pagan and idolatrous; others are placed under new Islamic discipline, but they all remain of interest to the student—whether Muslim, Christian, Jewish, or other.

While sequestered, the jury may find it helpful to briefly summarize part 3 of this book and to review the cross-examination of Hafsah.

The *textus receptus* for the Qur'an has come down in orderly fashion to the Muslim world. The original Qur'an is believed to have been authored by God (surah 6:19) and is described as being written on a tablet kept in heaven (surah 85:21–22). It was brought down, as tradition tells us, by the angel Gabriel, to the prophet's ear and heart. Muhammad was chosen as God's messenger, having been prepared by his mother tongue and his life experience to receive the message and present it to the world. The revelations previous to the Qur'an, as witnessed by it, are interesting and revealing when seen through the lens of the Qur'an. Analyzing them need not be seen as a challenge to Islamic orthodoxy but rather as a means of shedding light upon faith, with the poetry of the revelations to Muslims coming from the Divine in accordance with their traditional understanding.

It is widely accepted that the revelations so perfectly preserved in the Qur'an, though easily memorized, were written down with the help of one scribe or another, at first by family members and then by Muhammad's secretary, Zaid, in later years. According to tradition, the serial additions were added to a collection and reviewed in detail by Muhammad and the angel Gabriel once a year, and twice in the year before he died. Such pious traditions are not affirmed by the sacred text, but they are precious nonetheless at the folk level of popular devotion.

The recitations themselves were certainly highly cherished and no doubt prayerfully reviewed, and various compilations and collections were made by Muhammad's household and by others. There is manifest evidence, however, from trustworthy Islamic sources among the first generation of Muslims that when Muhammad died, there was no complete collection of his revelations in any official form. Written portions had been collected during his lifetime by various persons in his community, certain portions had been memorized by individuals and groups, and it appears that some portions had been used liturgically in the worship of the community.

The first official collection, or codex, was made by a caliph, Abu Bakr, Muhammad's first convert outside his own household and briefly his successor as the first caliph in the majority Sunni tradition of Islam. Another tradition contends that this collection was made at the suggestion of Muhammad's nephew, Ali, who would eventually become the fourth caliph, and leader of the Shia schism. In any event, secretary Zaid was employed in assembling the Qur'an, probably with the help of Hafsah and other People of the House who had done so much of the original transcription.

The finished product was entrusted to Umar, the second caliph, and ultimately by him to Hafsah, who was its custodian and the guardian of textual purity until its universal acceptance. Hafsah, the original "guardian of the text," was actually Muhammad's fourth wife and young widow. She was also the favorite daughter of that Companion Umar the Great, the caliph of Islam's expansion. In ensuring the preservation of the original text, Hafsah played a role that was both heroic and historic.

Several rival copies of the Qur'an appeared in various places, each with particular claims to legitimacy. The text in Hafsah's possession was not universally accepted until Uthman, the third caliph canonized this so-called "Medina Codex" and ordered that all other collections be destroyed. Hafsah's role in safeguarding and verifying the first copies of the text regarded as authentic by all was crucial.

Others were employed in producing official copies to be sent to the major Islamic centers, but they worked with the text that Hafsah had preserved faithfully against any external attempt to revise the text that had come from Medina, where it had been produced by the People of the House of the Prophet. Two of the copies made from the Medina Codex are still in existence, one at the Topkapi Museum in Istanbul, Turkey, and the other in a mosque in Tashkent, Uzbekistan. Such preservation is another dramatic difference between the manuscripts of Islam, in which genuine first generation copies appear to be available, and the textual provenance of Scriptures available in Jewish and Christian tradition, in which most manuscripts are hundreds of years old, having been copied and recopied many, many times since the autograph originals.

Differences and variations in other early written collections of the Qur'anic recitations had been perhaps significant enough to cause some concern. Fragments of these other versions still survive in quotations in early books and correspondence, and hints as to their meaning or significance have sometimes been controversial. For example, it is believed by some that one or more early versions of the Qur'an contained references to the stoning of women taken in adultery, and that unsuccessful attempts were made to include such references in the revelations of the Medina Codex in Hafsah's possession and care. She would have none of it, but the attempt illustrates how some other extraneous and even false material may have made its way into the Hadith a few years later, since it had no such guardian.

Hafsah was among the several widows married to Prophet Muhammad in the years following his long monogamous union with his first wife, Khadija. Hafsah was a special friend of other young wives like Ayisha and Umm Salamah, who shared her literary interests, and of Muhammad's daughters like Fatimah. It would seem possible and even probable that all or most of these women, both daughters and wives of Muhammad, had a role in producing the text and discussing its contents. Their testimonies are included in particularly well-attested portions of the Hadith—themselves another example of the primary female contribution.

From this context we recognize that Hafsah knew well that pseudo-revelations like the stoning of women were not part of the original Qur'anic collection and had no validity in reference to the actions or lifestyle of the Prophet himself. From this example, we can also recognize that attempts to import ugly reflections of pre-Islamic culture into the Qur'an were successfully resisted by its guardian. That some such inferences might have crept in later through different traditions of pronunciation of words and diacritical vowel marks is a matter under current investigation by Islamic scholars. Such studies are likely to bear more extensive fruit in re-examinations of Hadith.

As we shall see, such questions are considered in the twenty-first century by Muslim scholars using techniques as old as the first Islamic centuries and as recent as the application of forensic methods of textual criticism developed first by Christians and Jews in reference to biblical investigations. These critical methods were also employed in recent years in study of the Qur'an in reference to the *Satanic Verses* controversy, a topic addressed more fully in *Noah's Other Son*. The joining of ancient Muslim critical methods with what now are called "Western forensic methods" of scriptural analysis is a subject that we have recognized. Muslims' use of the terms "scriptural analysis" and "forensic methods" provided the title of this book.

Meanwhile, the final task at hand is for readers to contribute to the establishment of a tradition of diagramming the Qur'anic references to previous revelations and of distinguishing those revelations that may be unique, either by using the prototype on the last two pages of this chapter or by downloading and printing the same from the Web site: BrianArthurBrown .com.

To receive credit for an assignment, seminarians at the launch conference for this book on forensic scriptural analysis were required to show all seven colors on their submission, attempting to find at least two in each category, preferably differentiated as separate examples, not repetitions. Keen students and scholars will go much further, and I am hopeful that many will favor me with electronic copies of their work.

For consistency and comparison with fellow students and colleagues, I recommend that those working to complete this chart in color use the color code on its legend to identify materials previously revealed elsewhere in the same or in other formats.

HINTS FOR FINDING AND COLORING
THE DIAGRAM OF THE QUR'AN

PINK: Biblical material from the Hebrew Scriptures and even extra-Judaic materials should be easy for most readers to identify. These are not regarded as quotations but as either amplifications or corrections, so the material in the Qur'an is rarely identical to the material in the Hebrew Scriptures. Rather the Qur'anic material refers to what had been revealed previously.

BLUE: Likewise materials identifiable as New Testament references in the Qur'an are familiar to many as echoes or amplifications of the Christian Scriptures. But the Qur'anic materials similar to Nestorian or gnostic sources would often appear to Christian readers as corrections as well as amplifications of these more esoteric texts relating to Jesus.

GREEN: References to paradise employ a Zoroastrian concept from Persia. The Sabeans used the lunar calendar and borrowed from the followers of both John the Baptist and Mani, the syncretistic founder of Manichaeism, itself rooted in Zoroastrianism and Hinduism.

YELLOW: Babylonian polytheism is represented by any polytheism condemned in general terms.

PURPLE: Monotheism not identified in either Hebrew or Christian Scriptures would be references to Hanifs.

ORANGE: The idolatry of Arabia was condemned more specifically than polytheism in general, and practices of polygamy and slavery were adopted under new discipline.

WHITE: Material Unique to the Qur'an will occupy less than half the chart.

A DIAGRAM OF THE REVELATIONS
OF ALLAH IN THE HOLY QU'RAN

MECCA

#		#	
1	The Opening	40	The believer
6	The Flocks	41	They Were Explained Distinctly
		42	Consultation
7	The Elevated Places	43	The Ornaments
		44	The Smoke
		45	The Ones Who Kneel
10	Jonah	46	The Curving Sandhill
		50	Oaf
11	Hud	51	The Winnowing Winds
		52	The Mountain
12	Joseph	53	The Star
		54	The Moon
14	Abraham	56	The Inevitable
15	The Rocky Tract	67	The Dominion
16	The Bee	68	The Pen
		69	The Reality
17	The Journey by Night	70	The Stairways of Ascent
		71	Noah
18	The Cave	72	The Jinn
		73	The One Who is Wrapped
19	Mary	74	The One Who is Wrapped in a Cloak
20	Ta Ha	75	The Resurrection
		77	The Ones Who are Sent
21	The Prophets	78	The Tidings
		79	The Ones Who Tear Out
23	The Believers	80	He Frowned
		81	The Darkening
25	The Criterion	82	The Splitting Apart
26	The Poets	83	The Ones Who Give Short Measure
		84	The Splitting Open
		85	The Constellations
27	The Ant	86	The Night Visitor
28	The Story	87	The Lofty
29	The Spider	88	The Overwhelming Event
30	The Romans	89	The Dawn
31	Luqman	90	The Land
32	The Prostration	91	The Sun
34	Sheba	92	The Night
35	The Originator	93	The Fore Noon
36	Ya Sin	94	The Expansion
37	The Ones Standing in Ranks	95	The Fig
38	Sad	96	The Blood Clot
39	The Troops	97	The Night of Power

IN COLORS DEPICTING GOD'S REVELATIONS
IN OTHER TIMES AND PLACES

MEDINA

100	The Chargers		2	The Cow
101	The Disaster			
102	The Rivalry			
103	By Time		3	The Family of Imran
104	The Slanderer			
105	The Elephant			
106	The Quraysh		4	The Women
107	Small Kindnesses			
108	The Abundance		5	The Table Spread with Food
109	The Ungrateful			
111	The Flame		8	The Spoils of War
112	Sincere Expression		9	Repentance
113	Daybreak			
114	The Humanity		13	Thunder
			22	The Pilgrimage to Mecca

Chapter titles are from The Sublime Qu'ran, translated by Laleh Bakhtiar

SCALE Surahs (Chapters) of less than 100 ayahs (verses) are shown as 1/8 of an inch, those less than 200 ayahs occupy 1/4 of an inch, and those less than 300 ayahs are presented as 3/8 of an inch in horiztonal bands. Many surahs are divided into sections which may be colored differently

LOCATION Surahs revealed at Mecca represent approximately 2/3 of the Qu'ran, while those at Medina represent 1/3. Materials from these locations differ in themes. Muslim authorities are not all in agreement about assignment of individual surahs to these locations.

MUSLIM BELIEF Revelations by God in previous times and in other places are not regarded as sources for the Qu'ran in any respect. The Qu'ran is unique and complete within itself as revealed to Muhammad, but many of its truths had been revealed to other peoples of the world and preserved in various ways, appropriate for comparison and study.

24	The Light
33	The Confederates
47	Muhammad
48	The Victory
49	The Inner Apartments
55	The Merciful
57	Iron
58	She Who Disputes
59	The Banishment
60	She Who is Put to a Test
61	The Ranks
62	The Congregation
63	The Hypocrites
64	The Mutual Loss and Gain
65	Divorce
66	Forbidding
76	The Human Being
98	The Clear Portent
99	The Convulsion
110	The Help

LEGEND Assignment of colors:
Pink: Hebrew Scriptures & Judaism
Blue: NewTestament, Church & Sects
Green: Zoroastrian & Sabean Monotheism
Yellow: Babylonian Polytheism
Purple: Hanifism & Desert Monotheism
Orange: Arabian Idolatry & Superstition
White: Unique to the Holy Qur'an

21

Conviction

WHETHER WE UNDERSTAND GOD'S revelation as "given once for all time" or "ongoing" might depend on whether that revelation is regarded as the "words" of God, as Muslims regard the Qur'an, or as the Word of God received in the hearts of believers as the words of Scripture are read or recited, as is the view of most Christians respecting the Bible. While the Jewish position varies from the Orthodox position to the Reform, this is an important basic distinction between the Scriptures of many Christians and Jews on the one hand, and of most Muslims on the other, and it is a distinction that goes also to the heart of certain divisions within each of these religions.

Of course, individual Muslims constantly grow in their faith, even if the words of the Qur'an are regarded as a fixed presentation of the Word of God, and it must be acknowledged that certain Christians and Jews regard their Scriptures as fixed and inerrant. All branches of Abraham, Sarah, and Hagar's family cherish Scripture, but the ways in which we understand Scripture can either cement the differences or become an arena where we can recognize and appreciate the differences, and even learn from each other in ways that enhance everyone's appreciation of the particular Scriptures they regard as so precious.

Virtually all Muslims regard the words of the Qur'an as the very words of God in much the same way that fundamentalist and very conservative Christians and Jews regard the words of the Bible. The Christian church as a whole recognizes the words of the Bible as "containing" the Word of God, and the actual words of Scripture are cherished as uniquely precious, but most Christians and many Jews make an important distinction between the words and the Word.

Jews might say the Word became community, though I have yet to hear it expressed in exactly those terms. To most Christians, the Word became flesh in Jesus Christ. He dwelt among us and we beheld his glory. To Muslims, the Word became the Qur'an on earth, and its words display God's glory.

Putting it that way is the beginning of the new attempt to see one another's religion accurately and in the best possible light. To do this does not necessarily mean agreeing with one another, but it does open up the possibility of appreciating one another, perhaps of admiring one another, or at least of understanding one another. Our views of Scripture offer the first, easiest, and most productive ways in which we can do this, which makes this discussion so important in our quest for better relationships. So we conclude this study with a focus on two particular views of Scripture: a positive statement of the view of the Qur'an held almost universally among Muslims, and an orthodox presentation of the Judeo-Christian view of the Bible.

It is high time for Christians and Jews to acknowledge that their traditional views of the Qur'an have been distorted by a deliberate attempt to discredit its purpose and its value. From Christian fundamentalists to a certain Jewish intelligentsia, the deliberate distortions of everything from the place of women in the Qur'an to the negative view of the Prophet himself have been dictated by prejudice and a self-serving bias. Some of that same unworthy spirit may be seen in the Muslim characterizations of Christians and Jews as failing to follow their own scriptural traditions, which Muslims regard as corrupt anyway, and without an accurate or proper interpretation of the *Taurat* and the *Injil*, as the Qur'an refers to the Jewish Torah and the Christian gospel. These judgments should be left to God, but meanwhile, bridging the gap between the Bible and the Qur'an requires goodwill on all sides.

We begin with a proper acknowledgment of the words of God as they are received by Muslims in the Qur'an. These words are not part of the canon of sacred Scripture for Christians and Jews, in much the same way that the Christian New Testament is not sacred Scripture for Jews. Muslims do recognize that the Bible, or "the Book" that God gave to Jews and Christians is sacred to them, and Christians and Jews may properly recognize that the Qur'an is indeed Scripture to Muslims, who are in the same extended religious family. This recognition should lead also to due respect for these writings. The normative tests of Scripture (authorization by the responsible parties, acceptance by the community, and self-authentication) are all met by the Qur'an. Moreover, if God can speak in a sunset or in a symphony, perhaps more to some people than to others, then God can certainly speak to a person meditating and praying in a cave retreat, through an angelic voice to his ear or heart.

It should not be difficult for any people of goodwill to humbly affirm with integrity and reverence that this happened to Muhammad in a way at least similar to the way it happened to Ezekiel in the valley of dry bones in the Old Testament, or to St. John, who wrote the New Testament book of Revelation after a similar experience in a cave on the island of Patmos in the Mediterranean. While the experiences were similar, there is no individual biblical writer who claims so complete a revelation as that given to Muhammad, and none for whom this phenomenon was repeated over such a long number of years. Indeed, as all Muslims know, it was a Christian who first authenticated the revelation to Muhammad as being from God, and Muhammad had two Jewish wives and many Jewish friends who made the same acknowledgment. Jews and Christians in the twenty-first century are called to reassess the historical prejudices they have developed in the intervening centuries.

Muhammad's first and totally unexpected experience of revelation took place in the Cave of Hira, near the summit of Jabal al-Noor, the Mountain of Light, where he liked to go on retreat after his caravan trips. Even as a teen, Muhammad had accompanied his uncle on such trips to Syria, and as an experienced young caravaner, he so impressed his forty-year-old employer, Khadijah, that she proposed marriage and made him the boss of caravans. More or less illiterate, but apparently adept at accounting, Muhammad was an acute observer of everything around him. He cultivated his customers and took in the sights and sounds of the world in caravan treks that went still further abroad. All this exposed the young idealist to the sins and turmoil of the world that were just as bad as the idolatry and debauchery in the corrupt Arabia in which he grew up.

Eventually, while meditating on this turmoil at a more mature stage of life, this religiously devout individual was agonizing over the state of the world in his favorite cave retreat when God gave him what some might call a divinely inspired poem. It was like a psalm that had a rhyme and a rhythm that were easily recited and remembered, something like the experience of a musician or a composer who receives an inspiration and does not know where it comes from.

Perhaps such things come from deep within the subconscious or collective unconscious rooted in the Divine. Perhaps that is where God speaks first, but when such divine inspiration comes to the surface, only an idiot imagines it came out of his own genius. In this case, it caused Muhammad to feel almost faint, and it came with the urge, or as an instruction from God, to "recite this" in response to the world situation and questions about the meaning of life. To Muslims, the evidence is manifest and overwhelming that it was God's own words that came to Muhammad.

The beauty and power of the Arabic rhyme and rhythm, direct from the Divine source, cannot be adequately translated, but its essence, in the paraphrase of *The Sublime Qur'an* and in other paraphrases, addresses the basic questions of where life came from and the problem of evil in the world, the matters over which Muhammad may have been agonizing. Traditionally presented as surah 96, or chapter 96, in the Qur'an, even this initial revelation makes direct reference to Scriptures that the Bestower (one of Islam's ninety-nine beautiful names for Allah) had already given by the pens of others, namely Christians and Jews.

THE BLOOD CLOT

In the name of God, The Merciful, The Compassionate
Recite in the name of your Lord who has created;
He has created the human being from a clot.
Recite: Your Lord is the Most gracious, Who taught by the pen,
Who taught the human being what he knew not.
Nay! Truly the human being is defiant
when he considers himself to be one who is self-sufficient.
Truly to your Lord is the returning.
Have you yourself considered one who prohibits a servant
when he invokes blessings?
Have you yourself considered if he was on guidance
or commanded Godfearingness?
Have you yourself considered if he denies and turns away?
Knows he not that God sees?
Nay! Truly if he refrains himself not,
We shall surely lay hold of him by the forelock,
A lying, inequitable forelock.
Have him call to his conclave;
We shall call the guards of hell.
Nay! Truly obey you him not,
But continue to prostrate yourself to God and be near to Him.
(*The Sublime Quran*)

The acknowledgment that life comes from the Creator (another of Islam's ninety-nine scriptural appellations for Allah), and that the Divine Word has been revealed by the pen in previous times both refer to things heavy on Muhammad's heart, and that people deny and resist at their peril. From the beginning, the details of the words or even the focus on conscious awareness of the message was not as important or as impressive as the undeniable sense that the diction, sound, rhythm, and emotive experience were from God. Easily recalled and recited in Arabic, these words carried meaning that would be pondered through the centuries, as it is in the modern world where the "blood clot" of human origins is regarded as the embryo. But the immediate effect was the felt assurance that God had given these words and had commanded that they be shared with others.

Muhammad went home, possibly mumbling his precious verse over and over, and he recited it to his dearly beloved Khadijah immediately upon his arrival. Her probable reaction was, "Where did you get that?" He told her, and she responded with something to the effect of, "Yes dear, you could not have made that up yourself. You know I love you, but you have no such way with words. Let's go to visit my cousin, Waraqah ibn Nawfal, and see what he thinks of this. He is a Christian and I'd like to know if he thinks your little poem should be recited in public." Their account of all this is actually contained in the Hadith.

The rest, as we say, is history. Waraqah was instantly impressed that this recitation was from the Most High and was like the oracular utterances given by the prophets revered by Jews and Christians. He pointed to Deuteronomy 18:18 in the Bible, where Moses prophesied the coming of an Arab prophet. A few others became convinced, and Muhammad had the experience of receiving words from God again and again. A religion was born, but not from some program of those who wanted to reform Arabia or the world. Reform was a by-product of the religion that itself was born in direct response to these revelations that were given by God to Muhammad to recite.

When those new to the Qur'an begin to read it today, they are frequently overwhelmed by the apocalyptic-sounding language. They need to be reminded that they have seen this kind of language before. Jews have seen this manner of expression in the book of Daniel, and Christians know of it from the book of Revelation. As a matter of fact, it is Gabriel who speaks to Daniel in the Hebrew Scriptures, and Revelation was the last book to be added to the Christian Bible—so it is perhaps helpful to realize that the Qur'an, which chronologically comes next after it in terms of Scripture writing in this family of religions, is written in the same style—even with references to the figure of the angel Gabriel.

Non-Muslim readers sometimes comment that the order of the surahs or chapters in the Qur'an makes no sense to them, since they are just organized by length with no progression or development of topics. The truth is that, again, we have seen this in the book of Psalms, where there is no unfolding order; but this fact does not stand out there, simply because people are used to it.

However, it is not in the reading that newcomers should be introduced to the Qur'an's beauty and peace or to the powerful effect of the Holy Qur'an. The Qur'an is first and foremost a revelation in the form of recitations, and the written version is actually secondary. With all due respect to the written text, the difference between the written text and the recited words is like day and night. The haunting, resonant tones of the Qur'an as recited are evocative as nothing else on earth in the opinion of believers, and that otherworldliness has been the experience of many openhearted observers as well.

Today non-Muslims of goodwill attempt to read the Qur'an, and many sincere Christian and Jewish scholars are attempting to do so on a regular basis, but they are missing something in that experience. God commanded that it be recited, and the written version is only there as an aid to memorizing. Chapter 1, or surah 1 in Arabic, can be read with the sense and feel of a psalm, and the narrative style of the story of Joseph in surah 12 is like most Bible stories; but those who would understand Islam need to hear the Qur'an, even without a working knowledge of the Arabic language.

The language of the Bible conveys some of that majesty and awe in parts of the original, in the Hebrew of the Old Testament, powerfully revived in the Jewish community in our time, and in the Greek of the New Testament. Certain translations also catch something of the sound of God's voice: the Latin Vulgate used for many centuries in Rome, the Old Slavonic in Russia, the Syriac text in India, and others, including the authorized King James Version in English.

For that matter, the Jacobite Church (Syrian Orthodox) in India has used an Aramaic liturgy from time immemorial because Aramaic was the language of Jesus, first used in a time when it was a living language across today's Middle and Far East. The teachings and sayings of Jesus in Aramaic are presented for children to learn in this elegant, symbolically and orally rich and resonant language with Hebrew and Arabic roots. Aramaic was the language spoken in Palestine and Judea in the first century and in terms of sound and experience, its recitation evokes a connection to the ancient—almost as if the very exact breath and vocalizations of the Divine can be heard and recited.

During the last fifty years, there have been more new translations of the Bible into English that in all previous centuries put together, and they have helped Christians to a better and more accurate intellectual understanding of the words. Yet still today, the parts that most English-speaking Christians can recite, such as the Lord's Prayer and the Twenty-third Psalm, are all from the King James Version. When we fill our churches at Christmas, we want to hear from Luke's gospel about the "baby wrapped in swaddling clothes and lying in a manger," not about a baby "bundled in strips of cloth and resting in a food trough," as one new version puts it.

The Qur'an, expressing what Muslims believe to be the very words of God in a language that is basically poetic in its essence, affects the believing hearer from beginning to end in a way similar to the impact of Aramaic liturgy or portions of the King James Bible. In some important ways, the content is secondary to the experience of closeness to the very breath or spirit of the Divine in reciting such sacred words through one's own chest cavity, or in hearing those words reverberate in one's ears and heart.

This is why most Muslims throughout the world learn at least enough Arabic to recite or listen to the sound of the Qur'an with reverence and some understanding. The danger in so emphasizing recitation of the Qur'an is that not enough emphasis is placed on its content, leading to the possibility of serious misunderstandings, heightened by certain corrupt Hadiths. This is at the heart of the Islamic renaissance in our time. The translations of the Qur'an into Turkish and Persian languages in use today, shocking as that may be to some and unacceptable to Arabic purists, have been produced by the best scholars, with all the care that went into the King James Version of the Bible, for example; but this is another of the hottest areas of contention within the worldwide Muslim Ummah (community).

The rest of Abraham, Sarah, and Hagar's family can hardly contribute to this sensitive debate, except to suggest that in their own ways, they too have had to face similar issues and have had to balance faith experience with the content and meaning of the texts. Translations that help us understand the content are not necessarily so sterile that believers miss the experience of a holy encounter with the God who speaks, but the inclusion of both rational and emotive elements, especially in translation, is a challenge for all members of this family with their presentations of Scripture.

Translations and techniques of scholarly analysis of Scripture have not destroyed the faith, but, on the contrary, have confirmed the meaning of the text so that we have moved beyond blind faith to faith with eyes wide open. Discoveries like the Dead Sea Scrolls and the Nag Hammadi library have authenticated the integrity of both the text and the work of the scholars that have labored over it through the centuries, and such experiences of thus authenticating the Islamic texts can be commended to Muslim cousins with confidence.

Understandably, the discovery of a possible manuscript of another version or collection of the Qur'an in Yemen in 1972 CE has struck terror in the hearts of some traditionalists; such reactions are just like the first Christian and Jewish reactions to the discovery of the Dead Sea Scrolls and the Nag Hammadi library. It was in a "paper grave" of manuscripts retired from use according to custom, and although very ancient, it appeared at first to conform to the Medina Codex. However, two German Christian scholars photographed it prior to the Yemeni authorities' placing restrictions on anyone's viewing it. The negatives of the photographs show clearly that the material is "palimpsest," that is, written on older parchments that have been washed. The image of the original earlier text is clearly visible in the negatives, and it is a version of the Qur'an that was supposed to have been destroyed—protests, explanations, and denials by traditionalists notwithstanding.

This cannot be, according to most Muslim traditionalists; but they all know there were many earlier versions of the Qur'an, resulting in the order for them to be destroyed. That one or more copies of an alternate version of the Qur'an somehow survived should not come as a shock or be seen as a plot to discredit the Qur'an. That a Qur'anic manuscript, possibly predating the exclusive promulgation of the Medina Codex, is kept now, inaccessible to scholars, in the House of Manuscripts in Sana'a, Yemen, testifies to an extreme defensiveness concerning this material. If the Qur'an is true, then there is nothing to fear from the shedding of more light upon its compilation.

There are rumors of the existence of at least one other such early copy, perhaps kept secret in North Africa; and still others may be found, but such research will only confirm the careful stewardship of Hafsah and the wisdom of Caliph Uthman. Any minor challenges to the *textus receptus* will verify the authenticity of the traditional understanding, and, where valid, the variants may help solve minor textual questions that have been discussed by Islamic scholars even many centuries ago. This is a very exciting time in Islamic scholarship, and again, on the experience of Jews and Christians, there is absolutely nothing to lose and much to gain from exploring alternate Qur'an manuscripts even if unauthorized.

Rhetorical criticism, new to Christians and Jews, is actually a well-established discipline in Islam, and its most widely recognized fruit is the result of comparisons between the voice heard in the Qur'an and the voice of Muhammad himself in the Hadith—the first considered to be revealed by Allah and the second conversational among people, but both articulated by the Prophet.

Critics may suggest that this approach, validating the traditional Muslim understanding of the Qur'an, is oblivious to suggestions that perhaps Muhammad composed it by copying and editing from the many sources available to him, or that it was composed over a century later by a variety of authors. The evidence for these unnecessary hypotheses is weak and perhaps too conveniently suited to the agendas of those who would discredit the Prophet and denigrate Islam. These theories are almost as unworthy as the intolerant suggestions common among Jews and Christians a century and more ago that Muhammad was epileptic and in seizure when he received the revelations, or that he was delusional.

Christians and Jews can accept the traditional understanding of the composition of the Qur'an as a matter of good faith, and for purposes of the dialogue and the sharing that is now taking place. There is nothing in the traditional understanding that should prohibit the sharing of Qur'anic scholarship within the rest of the Judeo-Christian-Islamic family and beyond, or anything that should inhibit the conversation that may lead to new insights about God's manner of revelation.

22

Appeal

WHILE MUSLIMS APPEAR EAGER to develop a new appreciation of the content of Scripture and other sacred writings, Jews and Christians may be ready to recover a greater sense of the oral expression and the aural impact of Scripture.

The Jewish community, in reviving Hebrew as the common language for the establishment of the state of Israel, perhaps inadvertently solved this conundrum for the religious element in that community. Biblical Hebrew, which had limited use for liturgical purposes in recent centuries, has become universal in synagogues around the world, and its revival in Jewish homes provides Judaism with an authentic aural experience akin to the voice of God in the recitation of the Qur'an. This remakes the whole Jewish community—including the State of Israel, but not limited to it—into a scriptural community-in-covenant. The Scripture itself acts as the glue that binds the people worldwide on a spiritual basis, every bit as much or more than the State of Israel does this on a political basis.

Like Christians in certain other traditions, English-speaking Christians once had more of that experience in the verbal reading and hearing of the King James Authorized Version of the Bible. It and others were revised in the twentieth century mainly because as the English language has evolved, specific word meanings have changed enough that significant misunderstandings have emerged. Additionally, advances in biblical scholarship had led to better understandings and interpretations of early ancient copies of the Scriptures.

Very important is the fact that scholarship also began to shed light on some rather unholy motivations that influenced the translation of the King James Version in a way that is now recognized as highly problematic. This included an agenda influenced by xenophobia (particularly by anti-

Semitism), the ill will of the king and others at this time toward women and women's spiritual experience, and a great and almost desperate desire to preserve the increasingly archaic and endangered feudal structures of worldly lordship and kingship.

Continental Christians in Europe also knew something akin to the evocative aural experience we are describing in the oratorios and cantatas that set the Bible to music in most of the significant compositions from the seventeenth until the nineteenth century. People who barely understand the words now perform and enjoy the Christian classics in Tokyo and Seoul because these works so enable the soul to soar.

This quality of enabling the soul into a place of sacred transcendence also appears in Christian architecture and art, from Gothic arches and spires to the color and symbolism of stained-glass windows and classic Christian artwork like the anonymously crafted icons of Eastern Orthodox churches, Michelangelo's *Pieta* at the Vatican, Salvador Dali's *Sacrament of the Last Supper*, or the Blessed Hildegard von Bingen's *Scivias* artwork of the medieval period.

There are well-known parallels in Judaism, and Islamic art (with its emphasis on abstract pattern and sacred geometry) is becoming more widely appreciated. But in many parts of the world, Christianity currently lacks effective experiential presentation of its spirituality or stories as compared with the aural power of the Hebrew Bible or the Muslim Qur'an.

Elders of my generation recall a time when the King James Version conveyed something of the *mysterium trememdum*, to use the term coined by Rudolph Otto. But, as already discussed, the fact that some of the messages are inappropriately conveyed in the King James Version has become problematic for many. To appreciate the power of words and to almost touch the supra-natural, our grandchildren must turn to Harry Potter—a joy to read, hear, and view onscreen (and perhaps reflective of many Christian values), but not a substitute for a grounding in more ancient Christian stories and imagery, as author J. K. Rowling knows from her own regular Sunday quest for that experience in the Church of Scotland.

The singing of sacred music by cantors in the Anglican tradition and the chanting of the Latin Mass have fulfilled the function of aurally evocative worship at various times in certain Christian communities. The ache for such experience today is such that the Roman Church sometimes appears almost ready to return to the Latin Mass, as increasingly permitted, if not encouraged, by Pope Benedict XVI. Both Catholic and Protestant churches are increasingly making use of sacred Christian Celtic folk music, which carries a sense of the "sacred space and sound" away from everyday existence; but even this has not filed the void left by the retreat of the Bible into a critical abyss. While the Jewish community has recaptured something of the Bible's central role in its successful revival of biblical Hebrew, for Christians the exploration of this dimension of spiritual experience may be the single most beneficial aspect of the new awareness of the beauty and power of the Qur'an.

Personal friends and colleagues have chided me as possibly the only United Church minister who believes that the Protestant Reformers made a mistake in jettisoning the Latin Mass. This is a humorous exaggeration on their part, though I have objected to the increasing trend of "dumbing down" both the liturgy and the Scriptures as we see in some current English translations of the Bible. We do need understanding of the words, and inclusive language is a response to where the Holy Spirit is leading the churches, but for something as important as the Bible, people can learn a few words that are even linguistically new to them, a beautiful language of worship and poetry. To those who say, "Nobody uses words like *thee* and *thou* any more," I sometimes retort, "No, except when singing national anthems, writing love poems, or in prayer."

Be that as it may, I believe the landmark English translation of the Bible for the twenty-first century is soon to be produced. It will capture something the emotive power of the Qur'an and biblical Hebrew, will maintain the critical advances of the last century in biblical scholarship, and will have the authorized or "consensus" feel of the King James–New Revised tradition. It will also be made accessible and accurate though clear and inclusive language, and will include the lyricism of recent evangelical attempts, but without trendy colloquialisms that have limited the shelf life of some translations. The Bible Translation and Utilization Committee of the National Council of Churches in the USA began work in this direction in early 2009. Meanwhile, "A Song of Faith," the new Statement of Faith of the United Church of Canada, has integrated all these elements, poetically lifting theology above dispute as almost a prequel to what English-speaking Christians need from their Bible.

At the same time, reviewing the recently discovered older versions of the Qur'an, and re-examining vowel-mark diacriticals, which were added to the text of the Qur'an at a later date, is the business of the Muslim community, along with work on the Hadith that is going on mainly in Turkey at present, and beginning also in other centers. Other members of the Judeo-Christian-Islamic family have an interest and a stake in this, because their recent "discovery" of the Qur'an will shed a lot of new light on the other Scriptures of this family—possibly more than either the Dead Sea Scrolls or the Nag Hammadi library. Just as those particular documents relating to the Bible were discovered by Muslims, so Christians and Jews can provide tools for the work of Islamic scholars now. At the same time, Christians and Jews are about to learn more about their own Bibles as Scripture.

An example, as mentioned, is the Riverside Church 2009 international conference in New York City on the topic "what the Qur'an reveals about the Bible." At such events, Christian and Jewish scholars, professors, students, and laypeople are to be exposed to information in the Qur'an that relates directly to biblical passages that have been puzzling for centuries. They are also exposed to the experience of hearing the Qur'an in services of interfaith worship—in this case, worship in a great architectural environment of the Spirit.

But to restate a key point, if we are to understand one another and assist one another, we need to recognize that the Qur'an is regarded as unique in its completeness, and it is authentic as Scripture in the context of Islam. It has been preserved without corruption of the original text, and it is available in an unedited and untranslated format that can be experienced in recitation that has remained unchanged for a millennium and a half. This is its essence (e.g., the essence of the Qur'an), and this need not be challenged in and of itself by other members of Abraham's family. They should appreciate and celebrate the Qur'an for what it is, and possibly learn some lessons from both its content and its aural power.

The Bible, on the other hand, is a different kind of Scripture, and I think Muslims are generally as misinformed about the Bible as Jews and Christians are misinformed about the Qur'an. For example, when Muslims assert that the Bible has contradictions within it and that its content is jumbled, they are correct; but they miss an important point. Unlike the Qur'an, viewed and presented as given by God at one time and place and through one medium, the Bible is accepted as a work in progress still today, in the life of the community for Jews and as the cradle of Christ for Christians.

A summary of what we have considered in that regard may also be in order. Before the invention of writing, stories like those of Abraham, Sarah, and Hagar were told around campfires by the elders and by women in the home and among neighbors for nearly a thousand years, and in differing versions depending to which tribe one belonged. If Indiana Jones ever does find the lost ark of the covenant with the Ten Commandments inside, they may be written in Egyptian hieroglyphics, because the period when Moses lived was hundreds of years before written Hebrew existed. Around the time of King David, things began to get written down, including his psalms and some older psalms (dating back to Seth, according to Islamic belief). Next to be written down was the J ("Yahwist" or "Jehovah") material, which we now recognize as about a third of Genesis and Exodus. Material and documents from sources known as E, D, and P all got edited into the national compendium we call the Pentateuch or Torah by about 400 BCE. This Torah got its finishing touches from Ezra, who may have been happy to describe it all as "the law of Moses."

The expanding collection of Holy Scriptures continued with proverbs of various sorts, followed by speeches and writings by the prophets, as well as other Hebrew writings. Then, with the destruction of Jerusalem by the Romans in 70 CE, the rabbis of Judea had a meeting at Jamnia and voted on an official Jewish list that eliminated some and included others.

It is Jewish and Christian belief that every step of this process was inspired by the Divine, from the first encounters between humanity and the Spirit of the Creator in the blessing of Creation, the "garden" of Eden, to the legends and histories of Noah, Abraham, Sarah, Hagar, Moses, Ruth and Naomi, and so many others.

Historical figures, storytellers, writers, compilers and editors, copyists and rabbinical councils that voted on which Scriptures were holy, in their devout opinion, were all influenced by the Divine in their lives and work.

The New Testament has a similar story, beginning with epistles from St. Paul to the first Christian congregations as they were getting organized, letters never intended to be part of a Bible. These were followed by gospels written as teaching aids for new members when the original apostles began to die off. A history of the missions called the Acts of the Apostles appeared, and some more letters by other leaders, which were cherished enough to be circulated. Eventually the Council of Laodicea voted on a list of Christian Scriptures that should be read aloud in churches. They decided to eliminate the gospels of Peter and Philip, the epistles of Mary and Barnabas; and after much debate later on, they included a dramatic writing being circulated like an underground newspaper from Rome: something called the Revelation, given by God to St. John in a trance during the persecution.

A few years later, St. Jerome translated the whole collection into Latin in a masterful piece of work that was used for a thousand years. In monasteries, monks worked in teams to make copies, sometimes correcting spelling errors and sometimes adding errors of their own, which took scholars of the church years of textual comparison to identify. The Holy Spirit was in all this, speaking in and through the faithful community.

The Creator gave Johann Gutenberg the inventive inspiration to construct the first printing press with movable type, a boon to all manner of communication and educational advances—not least to the speeding up of Bible production, his first project. The Bible was then translated again into European languages and eventually into practically all the languages of the world, honed and refined again and again as languages themselves changed. Bible societies provided Scriptures in hotel rooms, and Sunday schools taught the meaning to children. Parents sometimes give children a copy of the Bible as their first book, and each Christian reads it with the guidance of the Holy Spirit. We know it is a work in progress from the elders at ancient campfires to the child reading his or her first book today.

The Bible itself is a cave for each reader, and as Christians read the words with their own eyes and minds, they believe that the Holy Spirit gives them the divine Word in their hearts. Groups reading in Christian church settings ideally have the same perspective. In many churches, scriptural readings are followed with the phrase "Hear what the Spirit is saying to the church."

When Muslims point to places where the Bible appears jumbled, they should not be incredulous, because we should expect it to be jumbled at points where some of the editing is rough. In 1 Samuel 16, for example, as a young man David joins the royal household of Saul as counselor, musician, and therapist for the old king in his depression. Then in chapter 17, David appears as a young boy with a slingshot. When David kills Goliath, King Saul asks in amazement, "Who is this boy?" as if the two had never met. Much material has come together at this point, and even with the leading of God's Spirit, the editors had some difficulty making it smooth. That takes nothing from the meaning and invites believers to understand how God works with them also, as they endeavor to make sense of life by standing in this tradition of those meditating in the cave of Scripture.

There are a few Christians who regard the Bible in much the same way that Muslims view the Qur'an: without error and given by God as straight dictation, but they represent a minority of the overall Christian community. Most Christians study the words of Scripture as the cave in which they experience God's love in Jesus, who tells them, "Love one another in the way that I have loved you." The situation in Judaism is similar regarding each person's part in relating directly to God through a sense of scriptural community. This matter is not usually described in exactly this manner by Jews or Christians, but just as learning other languages makes people more articulate in their mother tongue, so this interfaith dialogue may now assist all the members of Abraham, Sarah, and Hagar's family to more fully understand and to better articulate their own faith.

The Qur'an is so powerful, so beautiful, so haunting, so evocative, and so resonant that those for whom it was revealed quite appropriately regard it as Holy Scripture and unmatched for its purpose in their midst. The Bible has something of that meaning and power, but it is a work in progress, not complete in itself until received by the believer and accepted in community. The Qur'an is to Muslims what the scriptural community is to Jews and what Jesus Christ is to Christians. In all three cases, the words of Scripture point to a revelation of the Divine. The Qur'an requires Muslims to generously appreciate other peoples of faith, and iterations of the Golden Rule within Christianity and Judaism implore people of these faiths to do the same.

For evangelizers and proselytizers among our readers, there is nothing here to forbid the sharing of our family treasures with one another—whether the treasure is the importance of the holy community, God's love for the world expressed in Christ, or the majesty of God's Word presented in the words of Scripture. How sharing among the Abrahamic faiths will play out acceptably in the twenty-first century is yet to be seen.

Does appreciating community require one to become Jewish? Does recognizing God's love of the world in Christ Jesus require one to join the church? Does "islaming" or surrendering to God require one to become a Muslim? These questions are nuanced to imply a negative answer, and as Amir Hussain said in the foreword, "The heart of interfaith dialogue is . . . not that we seek to convert each other, but that we help each other to find what is meaningful in our own traditions of faith."

I am a Christian, with every intention and expectation that I shall remain in my church my whole life. But can I learn to cherish community more, and can I more completely surrender all to God? I think so. Jewish students may be especially loyal to their community. But can any growth in appreciation of the Jewish progeny, Jesus, take place without threatening that community, and might they surrender anything precious to gain peace with neighbors of another community? Many appear ready, willing, and able to do so. Can Muslims learn to live in pluralistic societies, respecting the broader community, and is there any way that other views of their beloved Jesus might result in a more complete understanding of what God has revealed to them? That broadening to pluralism at least is a hope of many progressive Muslims today who face the challenge of entering the mainstreams of European and North American life. These are awkward and difficult questions, and the jury is still out reviewing the verdict.

Who knows which publisher will have the courage to publish the first edition of Judeo-Christian-Islamic sacred texts in one volume? It would be a publishing sensation, but if presented with care, it need not offend the purists unduly. No one need feel that any one testament is supreme because it is first or central or final; on the other hand, no one need feel that any one testament is denigrated because of its placement. Christians believe the First Testament is Scripture for Jews and for themselves. Jews believe that only the First Testament is Scripture but might concede that the New Testament and the Qur'an are scriptural for others in the family of Abraham, Sarah, and Hagar. Muslims believe the Qur'an is the complete Scripture for them, the third testament within this family, already acknowledging that the Word of God was revealed to both Jews and Christians, as well as to others.

The dysfunctional family of Abraham, Sarah, and Hagar has unfinished business with the rest of the world, and with other people who have Holy Scriptures of their own. But for now, as a token of respect and with a degree of mutuality, might we begin with a common compendium of our own: the Hebrew Scriptures, the Christian Scriptures, and the Muslim Scriptures, in a book of world monotheism? Such a book of sacred wisdom might contain three distinct parts for use in certain interfaith gatherings and for study purposes, or might make a statement on our coffee tables at the office or at home. This is not to suggest that we should have a new, expanded Bible with the kind of blending that happened in the Torah long ago. Rather, Jews, Christians, and Muslims should have available something like a study Bible that includes, instead of maps and a concordance, the full text of the Qur'an. Muslims already have editions of the Qur'an in which commentaries, including very extensive quotations from the Bible, are more voluminous than the Islamic holy writ itself. Indeed, in the most famous English translation by A. Yusuf Ali, non-Qur'anic material is more than ten times the text of the Qur'an, about evenly divided between commentary on Jewish, Muslim, and Christian Scriptures.

Direct linkages between the texts already exist, more in the sequence of the texts themselves than in such things as the appearance of the angel Gabriel in all three. Jews may not have always appreciated that the Christian Scriptures begin with the Gospel according to Matthew, which has the unique characteristic of connecting with the Hebrew Scriptures to provide proof texts for the Christian understanding that Jesus is the Messiah. Christians may not have previously realized that the book of Revelation is written in the same apocalyptic style as the Qur'an. This final book in the New Testament was the last book to be accepted into the Christian canon of Scripture and almost acts as a prologue to the Qur'an with its focus on the end of days, the Last Judgment, and life in paradise.

Such a publication of the three holy texts in one volume, sensitively produced, might become a powerful symbol of rapprochement in a day and age seeking such a signal from believers representing those currently engaged in violence in many parts of the world. The addition of three diagrams featured in this book might help present the modern compendium as more of a study edition than as a devotional book. I am willing to contribute mine, and I hope to have some completed diagrams of the Qur'an sent to me so that I might recommend them for inclusion in such a publication.

Jews are used to seeing Bibles that contain the New Testament and even to using them on public occasions. If Christians can use Hebrew Scriptures routinely, and since Muslims already recognize the Scriptures of the People of the Book, then only those uncertain about the ultimate validity of their own Scriptures could object to seeing them together in certain circumstances. Family reunions are often strained affairs, but the family scrapbook and the photo album are ties that bind in a similar way, and we are hoping to promote more reunions of the family of Abraham, Sarah, and Hagar in these days.

The biblical Torah is where Jews today enter into the burning-bush experience with Moses, without which there can be no freeing of slaves and no crossing of the Red Sea. It is where Jews today share the mountaintop experience on Sinai, without which there could be no communal covenant to guide the people through the wilderness of life, and no Promised Land. The New Testament is where Christians kneel at the manger, sit at Jesus's feet to hear his stories, stand at the foot of the cross and stare in amazement at a stone rolled away from the tomb. The Holy Qur'an is where Muslims hear God's voice speaking directly to them in a clear echo resounding through the recitation of the sacred text.

Whether lovingly fondling or massaging the words of Scripture through study, or exalting in the audible experience of the Word of God in worship and recitation, Jews , Christians, and Muslims find in their Scriptures what is necessary for the fullness of life. Jews, Christians, and Muslims may remain confident, each in their own traditions, but now we begin to get a glimpse of the ways in which God blesses the others in our family.

Epilogue

WITNESS PROTECTION

Behind the Veil

She stands
in line beside you
at a coffee shop
or street news stand
or drug store check out.

Who is this woman
in her hijab
or veil?

From what far off place
does she come—
Jordan, Morocco,
Egypt, Oman?

And the veil?
What does it signify—
restriction, modesty, nobility, faith?

You've often noticed her reading
newspapers—
English, French, Arabic.

She shakes or nods her head,
clutching the news sometimes,
or holding it lightly in her hands.

You have seen her on the train
carrying her laptop
or working busily on it
writing—
reports perhaps
or correspondence.

You watch her,
from a distance.

She reminds you of the women
in Bible stories you learned as a child.
Is she—
the "Samaritan woman" at the well,
"a woman from a certain town,"
"a woman" with no name?

Is she all of those women?

Have you always known her—
and never recognized her?

She does
have a name.

Her name
is Mary.

You've seen her featured
a thousand times—
in her flowing shawl or stole-like cloak,
arms outstretched,
eyes opened serenely—
determined.

She is there
in the Pieta sculpture of a Madonna and Son,
in the stained glass image of an Abbess or Sister,
in the dark oil painting of a woman evangelist
who stands
outside a tomb.

She is there even in
orthodox icons
of solemn women saints.

Her name
is also Priscilla—
colleague of Saint Paul,
theologian and teacher,
composer of scripture.

And her name is Khadijah—
who chose for her husband
a young man called Muhammad
so soon a great prophet,
though he did not read or write.

She was the writer.

Her name is also Hafsah,
first keeper and preserver
of the sacred Qur'an.

Men came eventually
with copies of the text
calling for the stoning
of a faithless woman.

She revealed a text
which made no reference to this.
Some would have stoned her for that—
yet she survived.

This woman before you,
so draped in veils,
has other names too—
more ancient yet.

She is Tamar,
Ill-treated daughter-in-law of Judah.

She is another Tamar also,
descendant of the first,
a daughter of
King David.

Desired by a prince with a lustful love
that soon violates,
then hates,
and tries to forget
and obliterate—
this woman might have lost her life.

Yet,
like her for whom she is named—
this woman recovered.

Tamar and her sisters
achieved so much
in lives not chronicled
as the lives of kings
or powerful men of state.

Yet, did you ever ask the question—
who were the chroniclers?

Like their mothers and their mothers' mothers,
passing on legend through oral tradition
at bedside
or hearthside
or campfire setting,
what stories did these women tell—
claiming not much personal glory?

From whence did the Scriptures come,
so many
with unnamed authors?

Who were the unnamed?

Who is this woman
in her hijab or veil,
whom you see everyday
in your neighbourhood?

She is all of these women.

She is every woman.

She is before Sarah and Hagar.

She is before Adam
and also with Adam—
and of Adam.

She is Eve.

Do you wish to know her?
to announce her name?

Perhaps the moment has arrived
to connect with her—
and unveil,
not a stranger,
but a partner.

Who is she, you ask?

Who do you say that she is?

Appendix

THE FORENSIC SCRIPTURES CONFERENCE

THREE-DAY THEOLOGICAL CONSULTATION **What the Qur'an Reveals about the Bible**, hosted by The Riverside Church in New York City, May 15–17, 2009, co-sponsored by Auburn Multi-faith Center, New York Theological Seminary, St. Andrew's Theological College in Trinidad, Snow-Star Institute in Canada, The Jewish Publication Society, The Rumi Forum, New York Faith & Justice, Hofstra University, Graymoor Ecumenical & Interfaith Institute and Cascade Books, in a retrospective on *Noah's Other Son* and to launch *Forensic Scriptures* by Brian Arthur Brown, a book and manuscript used in recent Riverside study classes.

Friday Evening Introductory Session—Isha'a Prayers, Social Encounter, Discussion:

6:00 pm Canadian Muslim womanist Raheel Raza leads Muslim Isha'a prayers in a mixed-gender, interfaith context after suitable preparation and guidance for guests by Amir Hussain.

7:00 pm Late registrations, finger foods and beverages, several authors signing books, and complimentary copies of Cascade Books' *Forensic Scriptures* by Brian Arthur Brown.

7:30 pm Welcome address by Rabbi Justus Baird: "Jews and Christians have interfaced dynamically on Scripture for centuries and now a new dynamic in the scriptural family of Abraham, Sarah and Hagar extends the Judeo-Christian paradigm in reference to Islam."

7:45 pm Conference organizers polled each other internally to identify three of the world's leading scholar-theologians who might be the first to address issues raised in *Noah's Other Son* and *Forensic Scriptures*. Tying Walter Brueggemann, who is unable to attend on these dates, was **Max Stackhouse** of Princeton Theological Seminary, editor of the four-volume

God and Globalization, author of the final volume, *Globalization and Grace*, and current president of the American Theological Society. **Mahmoud Ayoub** was considered by our Muslim scholars as "hands down" the *éminence grise* of Islam, in North America at least. He has taught at San Diego State University, University of Toronto, McGill University, Temple University, and is currently at Hartford Theological Seminary. Among his recent books is an Orbis Books bestseller, *A Muslim View of Christianity*. It happened that both Stackhouse and Ayoub had already signed on for this conference. The organizers were of the view that America's leading feminist scholar might be found among our renowned Jewish presenters at the conference, but those scholars chose to defer to the world famous doyen of feminist textual investigation and rhetorical criticism, **Phyllis Trible**, of Wake Forest and Union Theological seminaries, who had also indeed planned to be at this conference.

These three leading scholar-theologians will be onstage together during the first evening, in conversation with the new senior minister of the Riverside Church, Rev. Dr. **Brad Braxton**, on the topic, "If the world cannot find peace until the religions achieve peace, what role could greater appreciation of each other's Scripture play in this process?" This conversation may link scriptural aspects of two dominant forces in the globalization of world cultures: new appreciation of women in Scripture and the rise of Islam in the West.

8:30 pm Roundtable moderated by Brian Arthur Brown with Joy Abdul-Mohan, Chris Bullock, Henry Carrigan, Eleazar Fernandez, David Galston, Lisa Harper, K. C. Hanson, Daisy Khan, James Loughran, Lucinda Mosher, Indira Sinton, Ali Yurtsever and evening host Eugene Melino, Riverside's *Study Guide* author for *Noah's Other Son* in paperback.

9:15–9:30 pm Professor Kurt Anders Richardson presents a brief address to prime our Saturday symposia with reviews of the books *Noah's Other Son* and *Forensic Scriptures*.

Saturday Afternoon Symposium I: 1:00–2:30pm (Amplifying the book *Noah's Other Son*)
Qur'an and Hadith as the "New" Dead Sea Scrolls and the "New" Nag Hammadi Library
This symposium is hosted by Riverside minister Rev. Robert Coleman and moderated by Brian Arthur Brown, with the panel of Mahmoud Ayoub,

Amir Hussain, Hussein Rashid, and Kurt Anders Richardson in discussion with James Christie, Elias Mallon, Judith Plaskow, and Max Stackhouse. This conference is not a dialogue of mutual sharing, of which there have been many, but a program designed to allow leading Jewish and Christian scholars to pose searching questions to respected Muslim colleagues. Like the Dead Sea Scrolls and the Nag Hammadi library over the last fifty years, in future years the Muslim Scriptures may yield valuable information about the Bible. From the Qur'an we may now receive answers to biblical conundrums, and from the Hadith we learn ancient lore of what we now call the Middle East, including material omitted from and illuminating the biblical texts.

From the Qur'an and the Hadith we learn of Mary's parents and her priestly vocation under sponsorship by her uncle, Zechariah; details about the Bible's mysterious Sabeans; Noah's fourth son, who drowned in the flood; the names of women unnamed in the Bible like Pharaoh's daughter, Potiphar's wife, and the Queen of Sheba. We get another view of the Gospel of Thomas and gnostic writings of interest in secular literature and the media, including what heterodox pictures of Jesus as the Messiah may have once looked like.

In this symposium we will also revisit the practice of scriptural memorization and recitation, long discarded by many Christians and Jews as "mindless repetition without meaning." We will also consider Muslim experience with the power of words. Jewish Shabbat liturgy will be offered in a mixed-gender, interfaith context by Rabbis Julie Roth and Justus Baird, with Cantor Eric Meyers.

Saturday Afternoon Symposium II: 3–4:30 pm (Amplifying the book *Forensic Scriptures*)
Islamic Texts Respectfully Examined by Creative Employment of Critical Methods hosted by Dr. Arnold Thomas of Riverside Church, moderated by Brian Arthur Brown, with a panel of Mahmoud Ayoub, Laleh Bakhtiar, Amir Hussain, and Hussein Rashid in discussion with Adam Gregerman, Judith Hauptman, Rod Hutton, and Fred Weidmann. Just as the Documentary Hypothesis ascribes multiple sources to the Torah without questioning the divine origins of the revelations to the writers per se, these symposia raise no question about the angel Gabriel's presentations to Muhammad as being from Allah—who, in the Muslim view, quoted stories God had given to Jews, Christians, Zoroastrians, and Haniffs, recorded faithfully or in garbled versions.

The Qur'an may be seen as a template of scriptural production from the last major culture to spring from the ancient culture of today's Middle East in which reliable information about scriptural development has never disappeared from view. To illustrate the model, Muslims believe Muhammad was illiterate. Many chapters or surahs of the Qur'an may have been written down by the women of his household, led by Hafsah, who was entrusted with preservation of the Qur'an and transmission of it to the world. The Hadith presents conversations of the Prophet as recorded by his Companions, both male and female, prominently including another wife, Ayisha. Recognition that such materials may have been penned by women does not rely on secondary sources or conjecture. Islamic primary sources, under rigorous re-evaluation by Islamic scholars today, may have the potential to reveal whole new paradigms that can now also be applied to the Biblical text.

Saturday Evening Symposium III: 7:30–9:00 pm (Further amplifying *Forensic Scriptures*)

Muslim and Other Women as Purveyors and Transmitters of Abrahamic Scripture Riverside Church's Desirée Baxter hosts this panel moderated by Brian Arthur Brown: Lelah Bakhtiar, Ellen Frankel, Carol Meyers and Phyllis Trible on rhetorical criticism, Joy Abdul-Mohan, Lucinda Mosher, Raheel Raza, and Indira Sinton, with a reflection by Adam Gregerman.

Women have been household scribes in tent complexes and palaces of socioreligious potentates in what is today called the Middle East. If the tent complex of Muhammad is a recorded example, why not consider the palace of King David or the Jerusalem home of St. James? Queen Noor, an American wife of King Hussein of Jordan, recently wrote this way for the Hashemite monarchy, and this female role can be observed in tents of Bedouin leaders. Women in leadership faced situations similar to women in compounds of illiterate Afghan warlord-parliamentarians, who, in irony they scarcely recognize, depend on educated wives, both foreign and Afghani, for computer literacy. Skeptics suggest there is no biblical evidence for this female role, but the powerful influence of educated foreign wives in courts of Solomon, Ahab, and others is well documented. Influences of aristocratic Jewish women might not be much less, even if anonymous in the biblical culture. This throws a whole new light on assumptions about certain writers of Scripture who have hitherto been judged by norms relating to Western women, whereas we are still learning of the roles of biblical and Muslim women. Even if psalms were composed by King David, there is not a scrap of evidence that he personally wrote any of them down.

Likewise, Proverbs "from the lips of Solomon" may be from the pens of his wives and sisters, like one who could have written the Book of J. Similarly, the Book of Ruth comes from the royal household's family memory of David's great grandparents, Chronicles corrects the records of Samuel and Kings to the liking of David's "household," and both Ecclesiastes and Song of Songs might be reviewed to consider who did the actual writing. Pushing this envelope to norms attested by the Qur'an, we might find that if the New Testament "Q" came from a scribe in the household of St. James, it was probably by his wife, and the Epistle to the Hebrews may well have come from Priscilla in the household of a wealthy businessman, Aquila. We should look for similar patterns in anything in the Scriptures that is anonymous, even Job, with the prominence given to his daughters, or Esther, the story of well-connected women in high places. Twentieth-century scholarship established that biblical peasant women had stories, songs, and prayers. We may be able to now recognize anonymous literature coming from a class of educated aristocratic women.

Sunday Morning Final Plenary: 9:00–10:30 am (Consideration of where to from here)
Scriptures of the Family of Abraham, Sarah, and Hagar Coffee followed by a roundtable on public uses of shared Scripture, hosted by Riverside Church's Susan Switzer, moderated by Brian Arthur Brown, with publishers Ellen Frankel, K. C. Hanson, Laleh Bakhtiar, and Henry Carrigan, Professors Christie, Hutton, Irvin and Weidmann, and public interest interlocutors Ali Yurtsever, Lisa Harper, David Galston, Daisy Khan and Chris Bullock.

Sunday Morning Public Session: 10:45 am–12:00 pm (Led by New York Theological Seminary President Dale T. Irvin)
Christian Worship Service One thousand Muslim and Jewish guests at Riverside Church, Cantor Eric Meyers, Muezzin Sheikh Ahmed Dewidar, and Leo Thorne, representing the American Baptist Church, hosted by Brad Braxton with Brian Arthur Brown preaching. The official book launch of *Forensic Scriptures* at 12:30 pm follows the worship service in the hall.

Forty Presenters, Responders, and Lead Participants in this Conference

Joy Abdul-Mohan, Principal of St. Andrew's Theological College (Presbyterian) Trinidad

Mahmoud Ayoub, Islamic interfaith specialist and author, Hartford Theological Seminary

Justus Baird, Director of the Center for Multifaith Education, Auburn (Presbyterian) Theological Seminary

Laleh Bakhtiar, Acclaimed translator of *The Sublime Qur'an* and works about *The Hadith*

Desirée Baxter, Member of the Riverside Church and Faith and Justice representative

Brad Braxton, Interfaith scholar and Senior Minister of the Riverside Church, host congregation

Chris Bullock, Baptist pastor; NAACP, civil rights, justice, prison-reform, and interfaith activist

Henry Carrigan, Assistant Director and Senior Editor at Northwestern University Press

James Christie, Dean of Theology, University of Winnipeg, United Church of Canada

Robert Coleman, Minister for Mission and Social Justice at the Riverside Church

Sheikh Ahmed Dewidar, Imam of ISMM Surat al Qaf Surat al Muminun Surat al Zumr

David Galston, Brock University chaplain and a Director of the SnowStar Institute of Canada

Adam Gregerman, Jewish Scholar in Residence, Institute for Christian & Jewish Studies

Lisa Sharon Harper, Executive Director, New York Faith and Justice and author

Judith Hauptman, Jewish Theological Seminary; author of *Rereading the Mishnah: A New Approach to Ancient Jewish Texts*

Amir Hussain, Author of *Oil and Water*; Interfaith Professor, Loyola Marymount University

Rod Hutton, Professor of Old Testament / Islamic Studies, Trinity Lutheran Seminary, Columbus, Ohio

Dale Irvin, Professor of World Religions; President, New York Theological Seminary; Riverside Church member

Eleazar Fernandez, United Theological Seminary of the Twin Cities; United Church of Christ representative

Ellen Frankel, Author, CEO, and Editor-in-Chief of the Jewish Publication Society

Daisy Khan, Executive Director, American Society for Muslim Advancement

James Loughran, Director, the Graymoor Ecumenical and Interfaith Institute

Elias Mallon, Catholic ecumenist and Franciscan interfaith educator, scholar, and author

Carol Meyers, Duke University; archaeologist and biblical consultant on household life

Eric Meyers, Duke University; archaeologist and synagogue Cantor.

Lucinda Mosher, Interfaith consultant, author of *Belonging* and *Faith in the Neighborhood*

Judith Plaskow, Feminist theologian, Past President of the American Academy of Religion

Raheel Raza, Author of *Their Jihad—Not My Jihad!* Director for Interfaith Affairs of the SnowStar Institute

Hussein Rashid, Hofstra University; founder of islamicate.com

Kurt Anders Richardson, Abrahamic Scripture specialist at the University of Toronto and Qom

Julie Roth, Executive Director of the Center for Jewish Life / Hillel at Princeton University

Indira Sinton, Canadian Poet and Leadership & Organizational Development Consultant

Max Stackhouse, President, American Theological Society; author of *Globalization and Grace*

Susan Switzer, New York Theological Seminary; Riverside Church member

Arnold Thomas, Minister of Education, the Riverside Church

Leo Thorne, Associate General Secretary, American Baptist Church; Riverside Church member

Phyllis Trible, Wake Forest & Union Theological seminaries, Past President of the Society of Biblical Literature

Fred Weidmann, Auburn Theological Seminary, formerly Riverside
Church staff member

Ali Yurtsever, Professor, researcher, and President of the Rumi Forum,
Washington DC

Bibliography

PRECEDENTS

In respect to this emphasis on the primacy of the actual texts of Scripture, two editions of the Qur'an in English are listed in this bibliography because of specific references. Students and readers my refer to whichever versions of the Bible they find helpful since no particular versions of Christian or Hebrew Scriptures are referenced, except for copyright acknowledgments following the title page. Most standard encyclopedias, including *The New Catholic Encyclopedia*, *Encyclopedia Judaica*, and *The Encyclopedia of Islam* may also be considered with relative confidence with respect to many matters considered in this book, in addition to the following more specialized works. The relationship between the texts of Scripture and the many commentaries about them, and works on the religions related to them, as referenced in this bibliography, are summed up appropriately by Walter Brueggemann.

> Obedient communities of faith (Christian, Jewish, Muslim) are the proper venue for scripture interpretation, even though we may be well informed by the critical study offered by the academy. . . . In my opinion, the best read of biblical text is a *direct, hands-on exploration of the internal rhetoric* of the particular text. For a very long time during the days of hegemony of historical criticism, very much critical study did not read the biblical texts, but only read *about* biblical texts or, in an even more remote way, read primarily about historical contexts that were taken as the lead clue to the intent of the text itself. The methodological "turn" in scripture study toward rhetorical criticism that viewed texts as arenas of interpretation contestation, turned attention to the text itself. That in turn has become a primary preoccupation of current scripture reading, in the academy as in church . . .

Bibliography

Thus much of my teaching has been to empower students to have enough courage and imagination to go at a text, and to be surprised by the text in a way that allows a genuine "revealing" not known ahead of time. One can learn a great deal by close attentiveness to the text, and that is the way the text has characteristically been read in the church. But that does not mean that one should be intellectually thin and rely exclusively on one's own judgments and impressions. As the work of historical criticism has always assumed, attention to a wider horizon of data will protect from a thin ideological reading that only echoes back one's prejudices and interests.

—Brueggemann, *A Pathway of Interpretation* (12, 118–19)

Ali, Yusuf Abdullah. *The Holy Quran: Text, Translation and Commentary*. 3rd ed. Beirut: Dar Al Arabia, 1968.

Armstrong, Karen. *The Bible: A Biography*. Books That Changed the World. New York: Atlantic Monthly Press, 2007.

Ayoub, Mahmoud. *A Muslim View of Christianity: Essays on Dialogue*. Maryknoll, NY: Orbis, 2007.

Bakhtiar, Laleh, translator. *The Sublime Qur'an*. Chicago: Kazi, 2007.

Barr, Allan. *A Diagram of Synoptic Relationships*. With an Introduction by James Barr. 2nd ed. Edinburgh: T. & T. Clark, 1995.

Bloom, Harold, and David Rosenberg. *The Book of J*. New York: Grove, 1990.

Bonvillain, Nancy. *Language, Culture and Communication: The Meaning of Messages*. 5th ed. Upper Saddle River, NJ: Prentice Hall, 2008.

Brown, Brian Arthur. *Noah's Other Son: Bridging the Gap between the Bible and the Qur'an*. New York: Continuum, 2007.

Brueggemann, Walter. *The Bible Makes Sense*. Rev. ed. with a new Introduction. Louisville: Westminster John Knox, 2003.

———. *Cadences of Home: Preaching among Exiles*. Louisville: Westminster John Knox, 1997.

———. *A Pathway of Interpretation: The Old Testament for Pastors and Students*. Eugene, OR: Cascade Books, 2009.

———. *Praying the Psalms: Engaging Scripture and the Life of the Spirit*. 2nd ed. Eugene, OR: Cascade Books, 2007.

Campbell, Edward F. *Ruth*. Anchor Bible 7. Garden City, NY: Doubleday, 1975.

Conteh, Prince Sorie. *Traditionalists, Muslims, and Christians in Africa: Interreligious Encounters and Dialogue*. Amherst, NY: Cambria Press. 2009.

Crook, Jay R. *The New Testament, An Islamic Perspective: Early Christianity and the Assault of Hellenism, Being a Comparison of the Stories of the Prophets and Other Personages from the Quranic Commentary by Abu Bakr ʿAtiq Nishaburi Surabadi with Those in the New Testament, the Apocrypha, Pseudepigrapha, and Other Relevant Writings of the Classical and Early Christian World*. Chicago: Kazi, 2005.

Bibliography

——. *The Old Testament, An Islamic Perspective: Being a Comparison of the Stories of the Prophets and Other Personages from the Quranic Commentary by Abu Bakr ʿAtiq Nishaburi Surabadi with Those in the New Testament, the Apocrypha, Pseudepigrapha, and Other Relevant Writings of the Ancient World*. 2 vols. Chicago: Kazi, 2005.

Ehrman, Bart D. *Misquoting Jesus: The Story behind Who Changed the Bible and Why*. New York: HarperSanFrancisco, 2005.

Frankel, Ellen. *The Five Books of Miriam: A Woman's Commentary on the Torah*. New York: Putnam 1996.

Friedman, Richard Elliott. *The Bible with Sources Revealed: A New View into the Five Books of Moses*. New York: HarperSanFrancisco, 2003.

——. *Who Wrote the Bible?* New York: HarperSanFrancisco, 1997.

Holmes, Janet. *An Introduction to Sociolinguistics*. 3rd ed. Learning about Language. New York: Longman, 2008.

Hussain, Amir. *Oil and Water: Two Faiths, One God*. Kelowna, BC: CopperHouse, 2006.

Kabbani, Muhammad Hisham, and Laleh Bakhtiar. *Encyclopedia of Muhammad's Women Companions and the Traditions They Related*. Chicago: Kazi, 1998.

Kamionkowski, S. Tamar. *Gender Reversal and Cosmic Chaos: A Study on the Book of Ezekiel*. Journal for the Study of the Old Testament. Supplement Series 368. London: Sheffield Academic, 2003.

Kloppenborg, John S. *Q: The Earliest Gospel*. Louisville: Westminster John Knox, 2008.

LaCocque, André. *Romance, She Wrote! A Hermeneutical Essay on Songs of Songs*. 1998. Reprinted, Eugene, OR: Wipf & Stock, 2006.

——. *Ruth*. Translated by K. C. Hanson. Continental Commentaries. Minneapolis: Fortress, 2004.

McAuliffe, Jane. "Reading the Qurʾan with Fidelity and Freedom." *Journal of the American Academy of Religion* 73 (2005) 615–35.

Meyers, Carol L. *Discovering Eve: Ancient Israelite Women in Context*. New York: Oxford University Press, 1988.

——. *Households and Holiness: The Religious Culture of Israelite Women*. Facets. Minneapolis: Fortress, 2005.

——, editor. *Women in Scripture: A Dictionary of Named and Unnamed Women in the Hebrew Bible, the Apocryphal/Deuterocanonical Books and the New Testament*. Boston: Houghton Mifflin, 2001.

Mosher, Lucinda. *Belonging*. Faith in the Neighborhood 1. New York: Seabury, 2005.

Nicholson, Ernest. *The Pentateuch in the Twentieth Century: The Legacy of Julius Wellhausen*. Oxford: Clarendon, 1998.

Raza, Raheel. *Their Jihad—Not My Jihad! A Muslim Canadian Woman Speaks Out*. Ingersoll, ON: Basileia, 2005.

Robinson, James M., Paul Hoffmann, and John S. Kloppenborg, editors. *The Critical Edition of Q*. Hermeneia Supplements. Minneapolis: Fortress, 2000.

Stackhouse, Max L. *Globalization and Grace*. God and Globalization 4. London: Continuum, 2007.

Streeter, B. H. *The Four Gospels: A Study of Origins, Treating of the Manuscript Tradition, Sources, Authorship, & Dates*. London: Macmillan, 1924.

Swimme, Brian, and Thomas Berry. *The Universe Story: From the Primordial Flaring Forth to the Ecozoic Era—A Celebration of the Unfolding of the Cosmos*. San Francisco: HarperSanFrancisco, 1992.

Bibliography

Trible, Phyllis, and Letty M. Russell, editors. *Hagar, Sarah and Their Children: Jewish, Christian, and Muslim Perspectives*. Louisville: Westminster John Knox, 2006.

United Church of Canada. "A Song of Faith." Toronto: United Church of Canada, 2007. Online: http://www.united-church.ca/beliefs/statements/songfaith/.

————. *We Cannot Keep from Singing: Images from "A Song of Faith," A Statement of Faith of the United Church of Canada*. Illustrated by Joy Cosby. Toronto: United Church of Canada, 2007.